I0809993

Historic MOVIE THEATERS *of* DOWNTOWN CLEVELAND

Historic MOVIE THEATERS *of* DOWNTOWN CLEVELAND

ALAN F. DUTKA

THE History PRESS

Published by The History Press
Charleston, SC
www.historypress.net

First published 2016

Manufactured in the United States

ISBN 978.1.46713.646.4

Library of Congress Control Number: 2016931803

Notice: The information in this book is true and complete to the best of our knowledge. It is offered without guarantee on the part of the author or The History Press. The author and The History Press disclaim all liability in connection with the use of this book.

CONTENTS

FOREWORD

The camera obscura (dark room), known by the Greek philosopher Aristotle, was literally a large room with a hole on one side that projected light onto the opposite wall to create an image. Centuries later, Leonardo DaVinci used it to help him gain perspective for drawing purposes. The camera obscura was the ancient ancestor of the photograph.

When Joseph Niepce took the first photograph in 1826 on a pewter plate covered in chemicals (exposure time eight hours) and Louis Daguerre demonstrated the daguerreotype process in 1839, preserving an image on a copper plate (exposure time twenty minutes), they introduced a new technology and art form never before seen; it changed the world forever.

But as remarkable as photographs were, nothing captured the imagination and thrilled people more than the invention of motion pictures, or movies, as they're called today. Movies have influenced and fascinated people from the beginning to the present day. Dreams and illusions, factual history and fantasy, all projected at twenty-four frames per second. In many cases, movies are a reflection of the society and culture. As one British author put it, "My mother took me to the silent movies in a spirit of ostentatious condescension and told me they're nothing like real life and I must not believe them. And she was wrong. Because everyone who comes from England to America and goes back says one thing first: It's more like the movies than you'd ever dream."

On a large scale, during the 1930s and 1940s (often referred to as the golden age of Hollywood), movies provided relief and entertainment to a depression- and war-weary nation.

On a smaller scale, there are stories of people who were inspired by a movie and went on to fame and fortune. Charlie Chaplin performed comedy in English music halls until he saw his first "flicker," decided to perform comedy on film and became the top silent film comedian of all time, now considered an icon of comedy. Walt Disney was an artist illustrating ads until he started doing ads for films. He switched to making movies, and the rest is history. Liberace started out as a classical piano player. Then he saw the movie *A Song to Remember* about the life of Chopin. He completely changed his style, adopting the elaborate costumes and candelabra that he saw in the movie, and became world famous as "Mr. Showmanship." In 1955, a very young Paul McCartney and John Lennon saw the film *Rock Around the Clock* and were so excited about this new rock-and-roll music that eventually they formed their own group, the Quarrymen (later the Beatles). Many young girls were inspired to study ballet after seeing the 1948 British film *The Red Shoes*, and many high school boys decided to study law after seeing Gregory Peck as the lawyer Atticus Finch in *To Kill a Mockingbird*. The 1985 film *The Breakfast Club* spoke for a whole generation as no other medium could.

These examples and many others illustrate the powerful effect movies can have on people. This, of course, happened in cities across the country. One of those cities was Cleveland. As a longtime researcher of Cleveland history, the movie theaters of Cleveland have always interested me.

Now, with the latest book by Alan Dutka, we, the readers, are treated to a very thorough, well-researched and detailed history of the movie theaters of Cleveland. Alan's skill at digging to the very bottom gives us information of all kinds we can't really find anywhere else. On top of that, he tells the most fascinating, unusual stories about some of the owners, managers, actors and theatergoers, which give the most important part of any history: the human element. When you read one of Alan's books, you learn about not only the subject of the book but also many other related subjects. He lets you into a time long ago and far away, and when you finish his book, you are a better-educated person. So let's all read and enjoy *Historic Movie Theaters of Downtown Cleveland.*

DAVID HORAN
Historian

PREFACE

Three months shy of my fourth birthday, I first entered a movie theater—not a neighborhood film house but, rather, the downtown Allen Theater. My father took me to see a reissue of *Pinocchio*, and the outing created a family crisis. Entering near the middle of the movie, we stayed through the cartoons, news and previews to pick up what we had missed. When I realized Pinocchio's adventures would keep returning to the screen, I asked if I could see the film a second time—and then a third time. When we returned home, seven hours after our departure, my panicked mother had just started to telephone the police. In today's world, I'm sure it is hard to imagine that just seven years later, my friends and I would attend downtown theaters by ourselves, without any parental supervision.

Working as an usher at the age of sixteen, I watched movies for free and earned money at the same time. Without a doubt, July 17, 1959, marked the highlight of my three-year stint in downtown Cleveland's theaters. Among many other duties, I often worked as a doorman at the Stillman Theater. Cary Grant, promoting his yet-to-be-released film *North by Northwest*, stopped at the Stillman on a publicity tour. Two hours prior to Grant's scheduled appearance, I sat virtually alone at the theater door with little reason to expect anything but dullness for at least the next hour. But soon I noticed a distinguished-looking gentleman entering the Stillman from the adjoining Statler Hotel. As he walked up the long lobby, I realized that in just a few seconds I would meet a legendary film star. Grant explained that he wanted to talk with the theater manager to discuss a few logistical issues prior to his appearance. When I told him I constituted the only employee in the theater at the time, he looked straight into my somewhat terrified seventeen-year-old eyes and, with a big smile, asked, "Well, would you mind if I chatted with you for a few minutes?"

Even in the 1960s, as the downtown movie palaces rapidly declined, I still journeyed into the heart of the city to see many films at the Palace, State, Ohio, Allen and Hippodrome Theaters. Motivated only partly by nostalgia, I recognized that you would always get a good seat at the nearly abandoned downtown theaters, even for the biggest blockbusters. And parking never proved to be a problem because I knew plenty of relatively safe free parking spots.

A few generations later, I now live downtown, no more than a three-minute walk from the Allen Theater where I witnessed my first movie. Although I often attend the beautifully restored Playhouse Square theaters, I have only managed one seven-hour outing since *Pinocchio*—viewing both parts of *Angels in America* at the Palace in 1995. I hope you enjoy reminiscing with me, or learning for the first time, about Cleveland's downtown movie theaters.

ACKNOWLEDGEMENTS

CLEVELAND PUBLIC LIBRARY
Bill Chase (Special Collections)
Jean Collins (Literature)
Amy Dawson (Literature)
Nicholas Durda (Photographs)
Thomas Edwards (History)
Pamela J. Eyerdam (Fine Arts and Special Collections)
Patrice Hamiter (Photographs)
Ann Marie Wieland (Archives)

CLEVELAND STATE UNIVERSITY
William C. Barrow (Special Collections)
Lynn M. Duchez Bycko (Special Collections)

THE HISTORY PRESS
Anna Burrous
Dotti Campbell
Aaron Clark
Karmen Q. Cook
Cameron Haines
Hilary Parrish

INDIVIDUALS
David Dutka
Priscilla Dutka
Diane Ghorbanzadeh
David Horan

INTRODUCTION

In the summer of 1896, many amazed Clevelanders caught their first glimpses of motion pictures at the Saengerfest Hall (located on the west side of East Fifty-fifth Street where it intersects with Scovill Avenue). The hall integrated Thomas Edison's Vitascope pictures into its vaudeville shows and orchestra concerts. The *Plain Dealer* described Edison's latest technological marvel in glowing terms:

> *In the center of the stage is a high picture frame, enclosed by a white cloth. When the hall is darkened, there appears upon the screen exact reproductions of living, breathing beings, of life size, lifelike and full of action. It is wonderful, this simulation of human beings in action—famous actors, actresses and people of the day as they appear before audiences.*

Throughout the summer, the hall's patrons thrilled to images of ocean waves at Manhattan Beach, vaudeville dancers, beach bathers, trotting races, boxing matches and hundreds of other very short films. Reserved seats for the combined vaudeville and movie shows cost thirty-five cents; general admission tickets sold for twenty-five and fifteen cents.

Despite their initial astonishment, audiences soon grew weary of movies that lacked actors or plots and flickered, flashed and jumped in an annoying manner across cloth or canvas screens. By the end of 1896, the Lyceum Theater, located on Public Square, had installed a Biograph, a projector developed by the American Mutoscope Company (soon renamed the

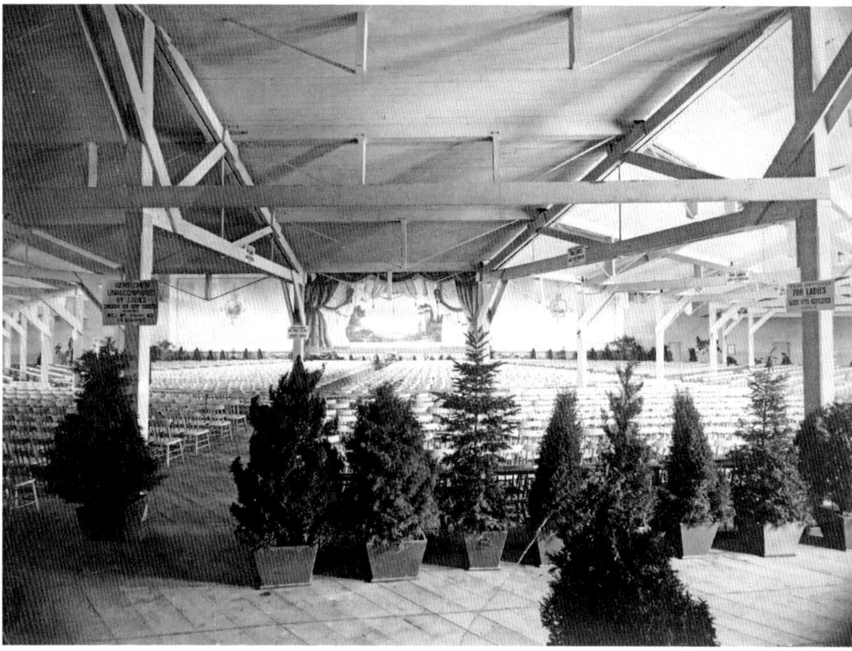

The twelve-thousand-seat Saengerfest Hall introduced Clevelanders to movies projected on a screen. *Courtesy of Cleveland Public Library, Photograph Collection.*

Biograph Company). Sparse attendance caused the *Plain Dealer* to lament, "The Biograph is a wonderful mechanical creation. It did not draw half as well as it should, which is a surprising thing, for the city these days is for novelties." The following year, the newspaper described an improved Biograph as "an invention more startling than the Vitascope."

In the movie industry's earliest years, the Biograph Company released more than three thousand short films, each less than two minutes in length. But film companies soon realized that their growing collection of commonplace scenes would not sustain the initial growth of their new entertainment wonder.

In 1897, under the glare of specially placed electric lights in Carson City, Nevada, cameramen filmed all fourteen rounds of Bob Fitzsimmons's world boxing championship victory over Jim Corbett. These films, shown in Cleveland at the Lyceum Theater, provided sports fans with superb entertainment and the first scientific device to scrutinize the accuracy of referee calls. That same year, the Star Theater (a burlesque house on Euclid Avenue) installed Cinematographe, a Biograph rival, and drew its biggest crowds to witness films of President McKinley's inauguration.

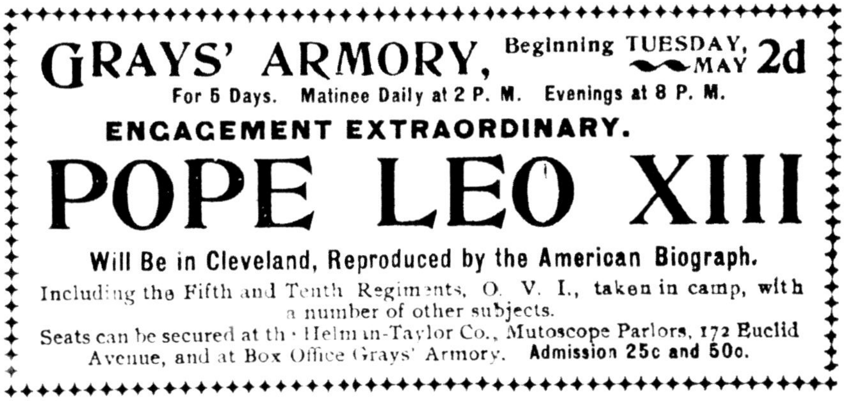

Grays' Armory displayed the first images ever filmed of a pope in the Vatican. *Courtesy of the* Plain Dealer.

Clevelanders also enjoyed watching early movies in a few nontraditional venues. Euclid Beach introduced motion pictures in 1898. The following year, Grays' Armory presented a sensational attraction: images of Pope Leo XIII in the Vatican. But the most unique setting for movies may have been Rafferty's Monkey House. In 1905, Cleveland residents could devour liquor and beer in 2,475 saloons within the city. To gain a competitive advantage, Rafferty's (a drinking establishment on the east side of Ontario Street just north of Huron Road) introduced free Saturday night movies.

In addition to the films, Ed J. Rafferty's customers marveled at the commotion caused by a trio of monkeys wandering through the saloon and several raccoons walking freely across the sawdust-covered floor. Confined to cages, three-legged chickens resided near the bar. An ape named Kye intimidated more than a few customers while an ill-tempered bear, acquired from Luna Park because of his poor disposition, appeared menacing even to the saloon's most inebriated customers. Prizefighters, moonlighting as bartenders, often battled one another between serving drinks. Rafferty also owned a "kangaroo cat" whose out-of-proportion legs forced it to walk in a hopping motion. The feline resided at the Stag Hotel on West Sixth Street, another of Rafferty's rather out-of-the-ordinary establishments.

Meanwhile, the movie industry continued to grow. By the turn of the twentieth century, vaudeville theaters had added short films as novelties to augment their traditional live performances. In the new century's first decade, nickelodeons offered very crude versions of the grand movie palaces that would arise in the 1920s.

Chapter 1

VAUDEVILLE EMBRACES THE MOVIES

The inclusion of films in vaudeville bookings helped popularize movies and, in the process, hasten the demise of vaudeville. In downtown Cleveland, the Empire, Lyric and Prospect Theaters ranked among the most important in nurturing the allure of movies.

In 1900, the city's first large playhouse dedicated strictly to vaudeville debuted on Huron Road. Attracting Cleveland's wealthiest and most prominent citizens, the 1,400-seat Empire Theater featured twenty-four exclusive boxes decorated with green draperies and white-enameled chairs, a beautiful complement to the ivory and gold proscenium arch. Demand for opening-night tickets justified a special auction that commanded premium prices.

From the initial performance, either short Biograph or Edison Kinetoscope films enhanced the vaudeville programs. In 1901, customers packed the Empire to view "the first authentic movie" of Queen Victoria's funeral. Yet live performances remained the major attraction. A few weeks after the theater's debut, the *Plain Dealer* predicted an obscure escape artist "will certainly not be unknown on his next visit, as before the week is out his mystifications will become town talk." The newspaper correctly anticipated the rise of Harry Houdini. Two years later, juggler W.C. Fields added a few new tricks to his routine prior to emerging as an entertainment legend.

In 1904, the Empire abruptly abandoned vaudeville, choosing not to compete with the powerful Keith organization that had purchased the nearby Prospect Theater. The Empire struggled to mold a new niche in

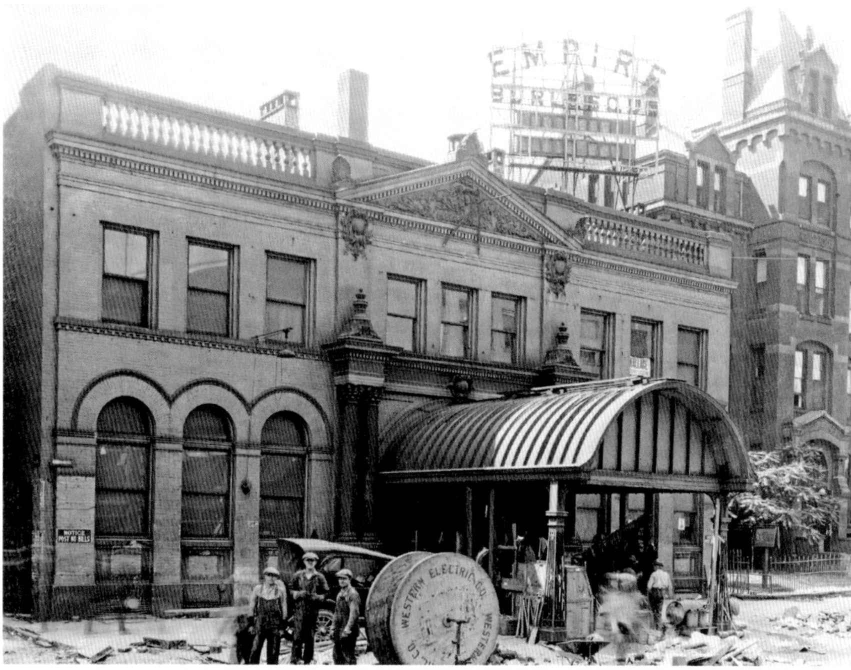

The Empire Theater exhibited movies to supplement its vaudeville acts. *Courtesy of Cleveland Public Library, Photograph Collection.*

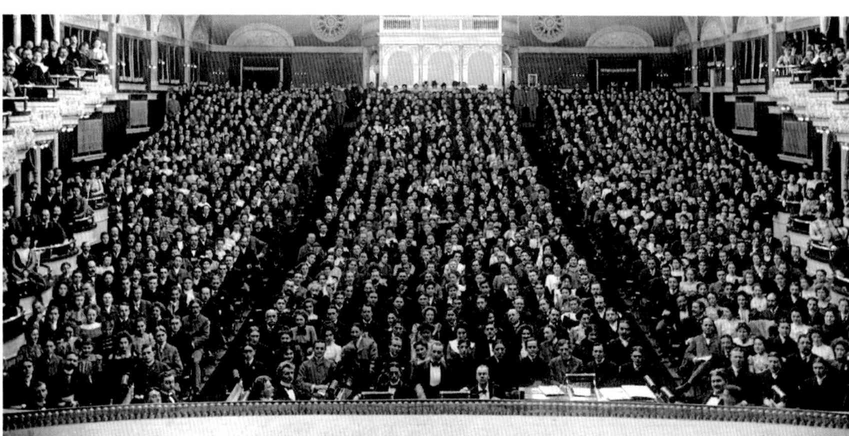

Taken on March 7, 1900, with a revolutionary "electric flash," this photograph of the Empire Theater's audience hung framed in the theater's lobby by the end of the performance. *Courtesy of Cleveland Public Library, Photograph Collection.*

Cleveland's entertainment market. It reopened as the winter home of the Garden Theater Opera Company (which performed in an outdoor theater on Euclid Avenue), but the experiment lasted only seven weeks. William Farnum, star of the stage version of *Ben-Hur*, created a stock company to finish the season. Farnum assumed the male starring role in productions of *Romeo and Juliet*, *The Three Musketeers*, *Camille*, *Spartacus* and many other classics. Within ten years of his short Empire Theater undertaking, Farnum reigned as one of Hollywood's highest paid actors, earning $10,000 per week. He continued in movies until a year before his death in 1953.

Following a summer break, the Empire launched the 1905 fall season as a burlesque house and added a five-hundred-seat balcony. Here, the young monologist Will Rogers worked on perfecting his art. Wrestling matches soon developed into a strong box-office attraction while movies remained as part of the burlesque programs.

Although never quite achieving star status, Lillian Graham and Ethel Conrad composed one of the Empire's most unique acts. In 1912, Lillian (with Ethel serving as an accomplice) shot, but did not kill, millionaire New York hotel owner W.E.D. Stokes. The wealthy executive had arrived at Lillian's apartment to pay her blackmail and to retrieve letters that he had written to her. Later facing an attempted murder trial, Lillian mysteriously disappeared while free on bail. Discovered in a Poughkeepsie hotel using an assumed name, she claimed someone had kidnapped her, but she could not supply any specific information because her mind had gone blank.

During the trial, the defense proved that her apartment had been ransacked prior to the shooting, while the majority of Stokes's letters had been stolen after the incident. A jury acquitted both Lillian and Ethel. Capitalizing on their previous showgirl experience, the duo (calling themselves "the shooting show girls") developed *The Girls Who Dared* musical production, which consisted mainly of the singing of a few songs. Religious groups lobbied unsuccessfully to prevent the showgirls' Cleveland appearance, but booing from the audience caused the performers to leave town in the middle of the booking.

In 1914, an unknown Ed Wynn appeared in a chorus just prior to his rise to fame in the *Ziegfeld Follies*. The Empire continued the burlesque and wrestling format until its closing in 1922.

Originally intending to operate a German playhouse, the Lyric Theater owners launched their new venue in 1904 in a remodeled German Lutheran church situated on East Ninth Street at Bolivar Avenue. Even prior to the theater's debut, stockholders had decided against the German concept and attempted to sell or lease the pristine 1,150-seat theater highlighted by an "art nouveau" interior with six large chandeliers hanging from the ceiling.

Following a brief lease by a stock company, two Detroit capitalists conceived of a concept so unique that they applied to patent their idea. The duo planned to initiate grueling four-a-day vaudeville performances that also included movies. Intending to rename the playhouse the Merchant's Theater of the United States, their innovative idea consisted of selling all the tickets to local businesses to give away as sales promotions. Theater patrons would never purchase a ticket; in fact, no theater box office would even exist. Never successfully implementing the scheme, the Detroiters sold the Lyric to another vaudeville owner who initiated "high class vaudeville, ideal for ladies and children."

The theater presented three performances per day (which included both vaudeville acts and movies) that cost ten or twenty cents. Making good on the promise to appeal to children, the theater manager scheduled numerous animal acts—dogs, horses, lions, bears and elephants. The combination of low ticket prices and family appeal seemed ideal. Yet, in 1906, a bondholder purchased the Lyric at a foreclosure sale.

A new management team retained the vaudeville acts and improved the movie format by introducing "cameragraph," promoted as the latest innovation in motion pictures. A nursery in the basement, filled with toys and dolls and staffed by two nurses, accommodated young children. But in 1908, the Lyric abruptly shut down without even notifying incoming performers of the closing.

In 1909, the Grand Theater (the reopened and renamed former Lyric) debuted with excitement not confined to the stage. In the Grand's first two months, a gunman flashed a loaded revolver in the theater lobby following an argument with a ticket seller; a fireman rescued a puppy from an abusive boy but suffered a concussion when a theater electrician hit him over the head as he attempted to smuggle the dog into the theater; and police arrested the theater's manager for employing children under the age of fourteen. On the stage, the vaudeville and movie format continued. Movies of Pittsburgh defeating Detroit in the World Series topped the year's film attractions.

In 1911, clarinet virtuoso Philip Spitalny, who would later play an important part in the early success of the Allen Theater, made one of his first stage appearances at the Grand. Beginning in 1912, the Grand exhibited movies all day on Sundays. During the showing of the five-reel epic *The Battle of Gettysburg*, the Empire employed singers and instrumentalists to accompany the film. In 1916, films of ex-president Roosevelt's trip through the African jungles drew large crowds. By 1919, the vaudeville-movie format still continued, but feature-length movies had become the major attraction as famous actors (including Douglas Fairbanks) and directors (such as D.W. Griffith) attracted large audiences.

Following its closing in 1921, the Grand reopened the next year as the New Empire burlesque house to replace the razed Empire on Huron Road. The theater garnered its best attendance from boxing and wrestling matches. In 1925, an unusual match pitting heavyweight versus lightweight contestants did not involve grapplers or pugilists; customers instead enjoyed a battle composed of different-sized shimmy dancers. Adhering to a policy of "smoke if you like," the *Plain Dealer* characterized the New Empire as a "smoke-filled auditorium fit only for a rowdy element." In 1928, the second incarnation of the Empire closed.

The Prospect Theater debuted in 1904 with the mission of presenting "high-class plays at a low scale of prices." The grand opening developed into a social affair with many of Cleveland's upper crust attending a performance presented by a stock company. The format lasted a mere seventeen weeks until the Keith organization purchased the theater and turned it into a vaudeville house with accompanying Biograph movies. Films of the 1906 San Francisco earthquake generated especially large audiences. Harry Houdini returned to downtown Cleveland to baffle Prospect Theater audiences. Boxing and wrestling matches also drew large crowds.

In 1908, when the B.F. Keith chain purchased the downtown Hippodrome Theater, the organization converted the Prospect into a short-lived playhouse specializing in movies. Travelogues and short comedies composed the greatest portion of the seventy-minute shows where tickets sold for five and ten cents. The Keith organization added vocalists to accompany the films, advertising the innovation as "Keith's singing-living-selected pictures."

The Keith chain made a practice of suppressing its competition. In 1909, rumors persisted of the opening of a "small time" vaudeville theater on Euclid Avenue near Public Square. Although noted for operating "first-class" vaudeville houses, Keith nevertheless met the new threat by converting the Prospect into a "small-time" vaudeville venue with movies shown between live acts and all day on Sunday. A local theater critic described the offerings as "acts of less than headline caliber but of good quality." Audiences enjoyed performances by mostly obscure singers,

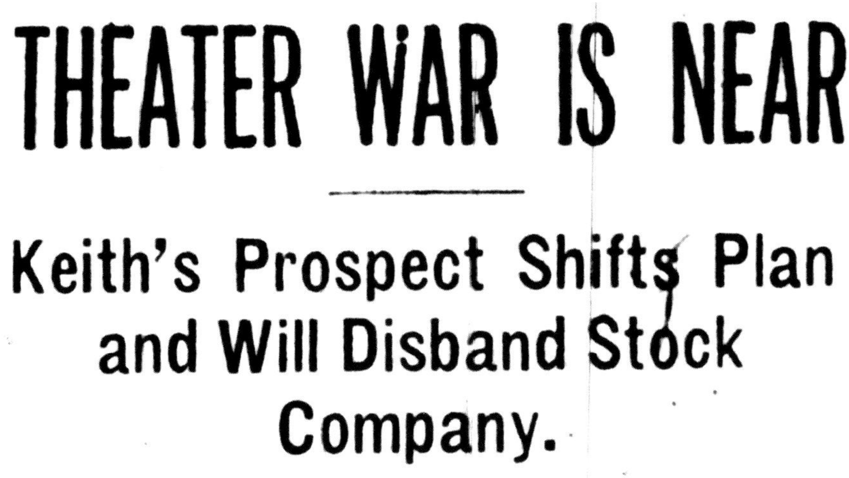

THEATER WAR IS NEAR

Keith's Prospect Shifts Plan and Will Disband Stock Company.

The Keith organization turned the Prospect Theater into a vaudeville house to suppress a potential rival. *Courtesy of the* Plain Dealer.

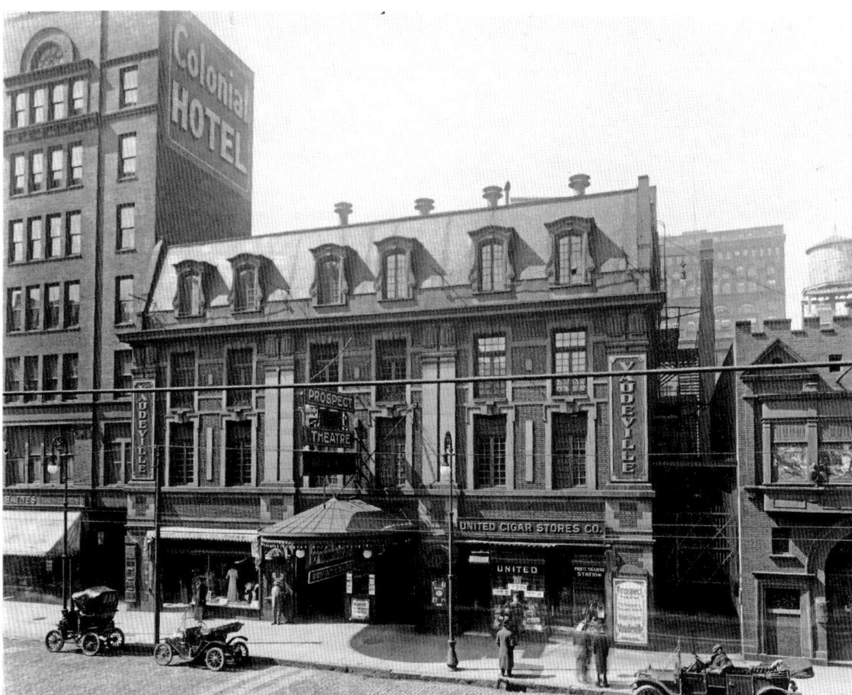

The novelty of movies added extra appeal to the live entertainment at the Prospect Theater, shown here in its vaudeville period. *Courtesy of Cleveland Public Library, Photograph Collection.*

dancers and comedians along with trained cockatoos, gymnastic dogs and mechanical horses. Yet Prospect patrons did witness future star Will Rogers rope a horse on the theater stage. Keith even offered a novelty in its exhibition of movies. A "Daylight Motion Picture" apparatus allowed films to be shown with remarkable clarity in the well-lighted theater. The novel experiment became known as "daylight motion views."

By 1911, with the threat of a competitive theater crushed, live dramas evolved as the theater's main attraction, with movies relegated to Saturdays and Sundays. But in 1917, the Prospect played an entire summer of feature-length movies and developed into a movie-only theater just before its closing in 1923. For more than three-quarters of a century, Clevelanders believed the playhouse had been totally demolished for commercial development. Yet in the first decade of the twenty-first century, construction workers peeled off lawyers of false fronts to expose the ceiling and a wall of the old theater.

While the Empire, Lyric and Prospect Theaters all closed in the 1920s, a few second-generation vaudeville venues, including the Hippodrome and Palace, transformed themselves into magnificent movie theaters.

Chapter 2

THE NICKELODEON ERA

In 1894, New Yorkers excitedly embraced the latest entertainment innovation, the Kinetoscope parlor. Placed inside attractive oak cabinets, Thomas Edison's movie machines created an image of movement by using spools to revolve film. A coin dropped into a slot triggered an electric light to shine on the film. The machine projected the lighted image onto the end of the cabinet. Curious customers watched dancers, animals, boxing matches and other sights that emphasized motion, viewed through a peephole just large enough for the eye. The film show continued for about one minute, and the novelty of watching movies from machines survived for a mere six months.

Edison and his competitors correctly presumed customers would enjoy viewing movies projected onto large screens rather than watching films from a peephole. Since Edison considered movies no more than a quickly passing novelty, he balked at spending the small amount of money needed to adequately protect his movie machine and projection equipment through patents. As a result, the technology to project images onto screens progressed rapidly, as did the era of the nickelodeon.

Nickelodeons debuted in downtown Cleveland during the first decade of the twentieth century. The term "nickelodeon," combining the five-cent admission price with the Greek word signifying an enclosed theater, denoted an early theater designed exclusively for movies. The nickelodeons did not employ coin-operated machines and, in fact, led to the machines' obsolescence except in risqué settings.

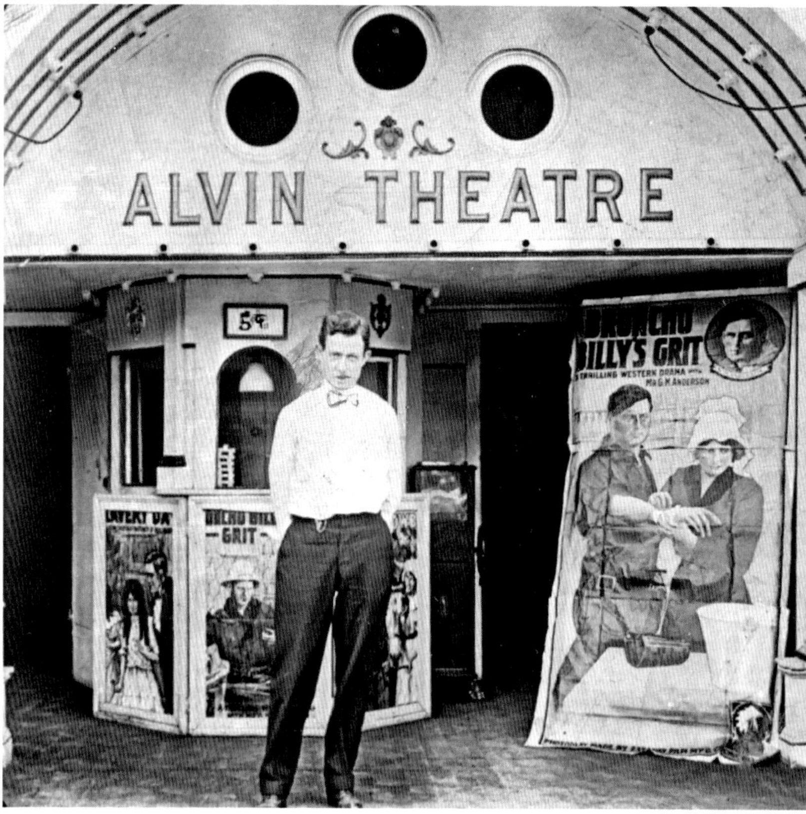

One of Cleveland's first nickelodeons, the Alvin (shown here in 1913) survived as a movie theater into the late 1920s. *Courtesy of Special Collections, Michael Schwartz Library, Cleveland State University.*

Nickelodeons exhibited single-reel movies on screens (or sometimes bedsheets) that hung on back walls; added attractions incorporated lectures, slides and music played on phonographs. A singer, using hand-colored slides depicting a song's lyrics, often plugged the latest popular melodies while the projectionist changed movie reels. A piano player usually provided accompaniment for the movies while audience members ate peanuts, tossing the shells on the floor. These primitive movie theaters all seemed to share one common characteristic: incredibly uncomfortable wooden seats, sometimes constructed from sawed-off telephone poles with planks nailed to the poles to create the backs of the chairs.

Three of Cleveland's earliest nickelodeons evolved in a converted store on the corner of Superior Avenue and West Third Street, in the fifty-seat

Alvin Theater on Ontario Street opposite the Sheriff Street Market and in the American Theater on Superior Avenue across from the current Federal Reserve Bank.

Alvin Theater patrons desiring a musical accompaniment to their film viewing reached through a hole in the theater's wall and placed a nickel in an old Wurlitzer piano located in a next-door saloon. The music easily

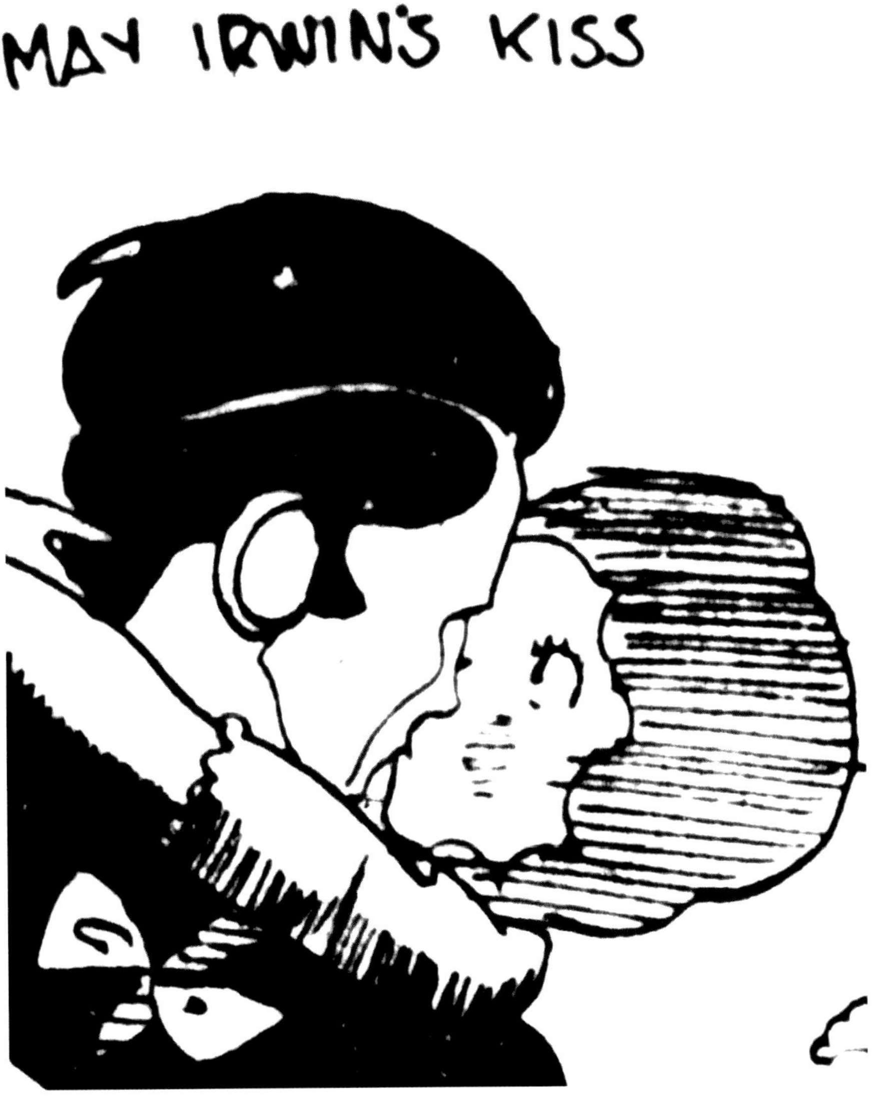

Stage actors May Irwin and John C. Rice participated in the film industry's first close-up kiss. *Courtesy of the* Plain Dealer.

traversed the flimsy wall separating the beer parlor and theater. The Alvin's owner eventually rented the saloon, knocked down the wall and greatly expanded the theater that continued into 1926 as a silent movie theater.

Samuel Bullock paid $325 per month rent when he opened his American nickelodeon. A projectionist used one hand to crank the "movie machine" while he rewound the previous reel with his other hand. The projection booth, constructed from tin to achieve fireproofing protection, hung suspended from the ceiling by a metal strap.

During its first weeks of operation, few people showed any interest in the new theater. Bullock even paid women to enter his showplace in the hope that their presence would add a sense of respectability to the business. Rather than a film, a phonograph record of President McKinley's Buffalo speech, delivered just before his assassination, turned into the earliest audience favorite. Films of the tragic 1908 Collinwood school fire did phenomenal business until Cleveland authorities halted the showings in the belief that the theater should not profit from the dreadful disaster. Bullock then hired a narrator and exhibited the films in nearby cities.

Also in 1908, the American presented *Ingomar the Barbarian*, a very early D.W. Griffith movie, and advertised talking films. In 1911, the American provided coverage of the Mexican revolution by combining films and lectures.

Initial films purporting to tell actual stories (especially Edwin S. Porter's *The Life of an American Fireman*, *Rube and Mandy at Coney Island* and *The Great Train Robbery*) first appeared at the Empire and Prospect vaudeville houses and at the American nickelodeon. Usually including a "chase scene," these early movies won back bored audiences by exploiting the "motion" in motion pictures. The first close-up kiss in movie history created excitement as May Irwin and John C. Rice pressed their lips together in a scene, lasting less than twenty seconds, filmed from their stage success *The Widow Jones*.

The nickelodeon era ended in 1914 as admission prices escalated to a dime. A new generation of larger theaters replaced most of the antiquated storefront movie houses.

Chapter 3

SECOND-GENERATION MOVIE THEATERS

Offering comfortable seats and movies running longer than two minutes, the Bijou Dream Theater, situated next to the Opera House on Euclid Avenue near East Fourth Street, could be considered Cleveland's initial "second-generation" movie theater. Debuting in 1906 and existing for less than twenty years, the Bijou Dream's wide variety of films included *The Life of Christ*, early Charlie Chaplin movies, World Series highlights and bloomer-clad female employees of the William Taylor & Sons department store playing baseball on the roof of the store's Euclid Avenue building.

In 1907, the Wonderland Theater opened on East Ninth Street on the ground floor of the Ellington Apartments. The theater's interior originally simulated a railroad car; a ticket taker, dressed as a conductor, greeted the theater's excited patrons. Fastened-down seats on rockers, along with the sounds of whistles, bells and hissing steam, provided even more realism as audiences delighted in viewing a passing landscape filmed from an actual train's back platform. In 1911, the realism of *Witch of the Everglades* proved fatal to a male customer. The sight of an Indian massacre caused his heart to fail; he died in his Wonderland seat.

Fred Kohler, Cleveland's police chief, did not share the public's enthusiasm for this new form of entertainment. In 1907, Kohler concluded, "Pictures are either indecent or of a character detrimental to youthful morals in their views of robberies, safe cracking and train holdups" and promised to "stamp out all that is obnoxious in the picture shows." Although the police chief's views may seem very puritanical today, many of the films did contain vulgar,

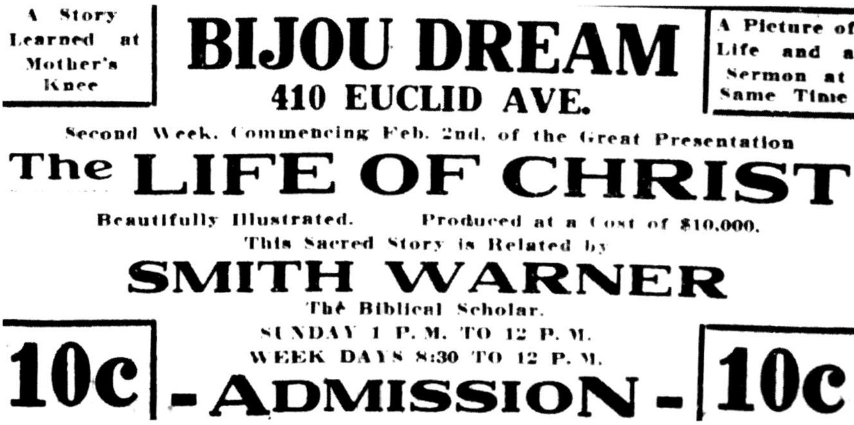

In 1907, the Bijou Dream Theater's exhibition of *The Life of Christ* most likely marked the first instance of a movie playing for more than one week in a Cleveland theater. *Courtesy of the* Plain Dealer.

offensive, immoral and indecent content, especially judged by Victorian standards. Kohler and Cleveland mayor Tom L. Johnson also combined to stage an unsuccessful campaign to ban movies from Sunday showings.

Euclid Avenue added another movie theater when the Avenue, located three doors east of the Opera House, debuted in 1910. The Avenue promised "live-size motion pictures" for ten cents. Initial films included wild animals being lassoed in Africa and Charlie Chaplin movies. The theater operated into 1925 without any particular distinction other than a tragic incident in 1921. When patron Arthur Price and a woman sitting near him engaged in a loud argument, usher Joe Saunders escorted Price out of the theater, warning him not to return. Price then initiated an ill-conceived fight with Saunders outside the theater on Euclid Avenue. Using only his fists, Saunders killed Price.

The year 1917 marked the beginning of the thirteen-year history of East Ninth Street's Gaiety Theater. Amid a seemingly never-ending dose of William S. Hart westerns, the theater carved out a special niche by presenting dramas concerned with "social" themes. The search for a syphilis cure composed the subject matter of *The Spreading Evil*, while *Are You Fit to Marry?* examined heredity and physical causes of mental defects and argued for national eugenic laws (as did another Gaiety film, *Temptation: The Eternal Combat*). *Are You Legally Married?* dramatized court battles created by conflicts among state laws regarding divorce and remarriage. *Open Your Eyes* exposed "the terrible consequences of ignorance and recklessness" in

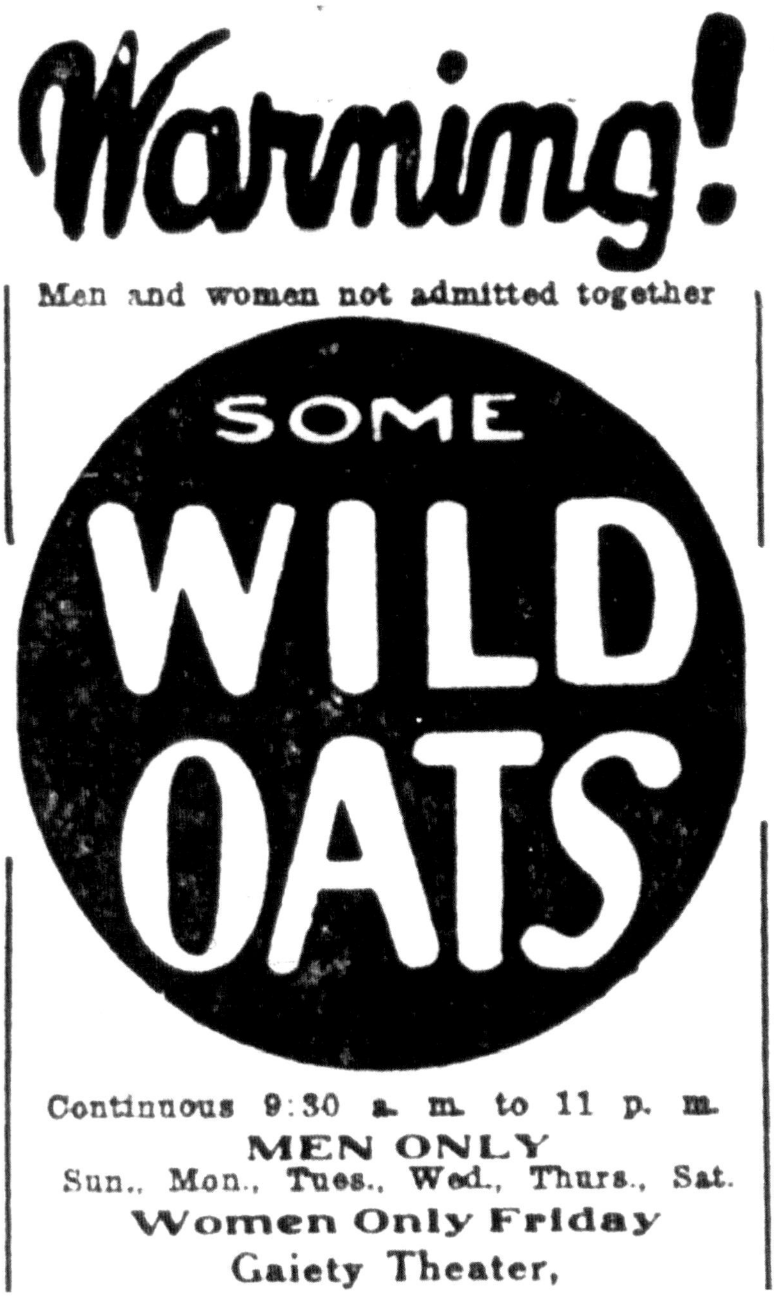

The Gaiety Theater exhibited sensational movies exploring "social themes," such as *Some Wild Oats*, where male and female customers could not view the films together. *Courtesy of the* Plain Dealer.

sexual activity, and *Society's Open Shame* scrutinized sexual problems and social diseases. Advertisements for the six-week run of *Fit to Win* promised "vice stripped of all its glamour in order to point out the dangers of the social evil." Meanwhile, *The World Aflame* sensationalized the battles of labor and Bolshevism.

Crowds justified a five-week run of *Some Wild Oats* even though the film had played earlier two-week runs at the downtown Miles and Grand Theaters. In this film, a doctor advised a young country bumpkin about venereal disease prior to the boy's big-city fling before entering the navy. During the runs of *Fit to Win* and *Some Wild Oats*, ladies could enter the theater only during Thursday matinees when the Gaiety banned men from viewing the films. The opening of the Playhouse Square theaters rendered the Gaiety increasingly irrelevant. The theater, still exhibiting silent movies, closed in 1930.

In 1920, the tiny four-hundred-seat Terminal Theater debuted just west of Public Square, opposite the Hotel Cleveland. During the Depression, the showplace remained in operation by successively converting itself into a foreign movie house, burlesque theater and combined cabaret and nightclub. Prior to its 1937 closing, the Terminal played second-run double-features. Possibly the Terminal's most interesting historical event occurred in 1930 when an usherette filed suit against the theater's projectionist for creating a permanent scar when he bit her on the neck.

Briefly reopened as the City Theater, a foreign movie house, the old Terminal emphasized Hungarian movies. Popular Hungarian film stars and directors even visited the theater during their United States tours. Six thousand people packed the small theater during the opening weekend of the three-week run of *Professor Mamlock*, a Russian drama. Before permanently closing in 1939, a six-week run of a French version of *Mayerling* established itself as the theater's longest-running film.

The three-hundred-seat Princess Theater, situated in the Williamson Building at Public Square, debuted in 1907. Four years later, the Princess exhibited the movie *Almost a White Slave*; the film's central theme involved a naïve country girl's entry into white slavery while visiting London. A committee of city officials and clergymen deemed the film objectionable and banned its showing. Cleveland's leaders desired to keep movie theaters free from all movies depicting crime.

In 1912, Mayor Newton D. Baker launched another campaign against movie theaters showing films of murders, holdups and other crimes. The mayor instructed Police Chief Kohler to "close every place that violates the order. This is not the time to worry about technicalities. We will look after any legal questions that may arise. Act at once." Police arrested the proprietors of the Princess and nearby Mall Theaters, confiscating their films and advertising posters to hold as evidence. The theaters successfully sued to recover the films and dismiss the cases.

In 1919, the Princess gained distinction as Cleveland's first all-night movie theater. Although the little showplace closed during the Depression, it briefly reopened as the Labor Stage, where local unions produced plays dealing with workers' issues.

In 1914, the second-run Reel Theater opened on East Ninth Street between Euclid and Prospect Avenues. Charging admissions of five and ten cents, management described the Reel as "the most beautiful small picture theatre in the world."

George W. Ryder, manager of the Reel, had been one of America's pioneering moving picture showmen. In the very early days of movies, Ryder transported a "motion picture machine" from town to town to display films of boxing matches. He charged ten cents to view a single round or fifty cents to observe six rounds.

The relatively new Fotoplayer may have been the theater's biggest attraction. Using a player piano as its base, the device incorporated pipe organs and sound effects to enhance the viewing of silent movies. Advertising described the Fotoplayer in glowing terms:

> *The all but human orchestra—The instrument that plays with the pictures and brings out their every detail in music. Worth the price of admission to hear this wonderful instrument alone. It is without doubt the only exact reproduction of an orchestra, combining the music of pipe organ, piano, reed organ, drums, traps, violin, flute, clarinet and many other musical instruments—playing every kind of music and producing every desired effect. This is an exact counterpart of instruments installed in most prominent theatres throughout the United States charging two dollars admission.*

By the end of World War I, the rapidly growing popularity of movies had rendered the tiny Reel Theater obsolete; it closed in 1919. Cleveland Trust used the former Reel space for its mailroom operations. By this time, movies had become firmly entrenched in large vaudeville houses, such as the Hippodrome, and in newly built and larger movie theaters, including the Standard and Strand.

Chapter 4

ROAD-SHOW PRESENTATIONS

As movies evolved from one-minute travelogues into full-fledged spectacles, the city's classiest "legitimate" playhouses (rather than movie theaters) often exhibited the most prestigious films. The engagements typically included an overture, intermission, reserved seating, advanced prices and a long waiting time prior to a popular-priced presentation in other downtown or neighborhood theaters. The staging of these movies (known as road-show engagements) mimicked those of theatrical attractions rather than motion pictures. The films of legendary producer/director D.W. Griffith inspired many of the early road-show exhibitions shown at the Euclid Avenue Opera House and Colonial Theater.

Audiences of the Euclid Avenue Opera House, located on the southeast corner of Euclid Avenue and East Fourth Street, thrilled to viewing enormous stage productions, spectacular shows (such as the *Ziegfeld Follies*) and the nation's best operatic and Shakespearean companies. In 1913, the Opera House presented its first movie, a filmed version of Sarah Bernhardt in *Oedipus Rex*. A few years later, the playhouse booked First World War films shot on location, many presented in color. About this time, the Opera House also exhibited conventional feature-length movies during the summer months.

In 1917, the Opera House hosted the Ohio premiere of one of the most sensational movies ever made, but only after fifty million people throughout the world had already seen the film. Although D.W. Griffith's *The Birth of a Nation* had debuted in 1915, Ohio censors, fearing race hatred and rioting,

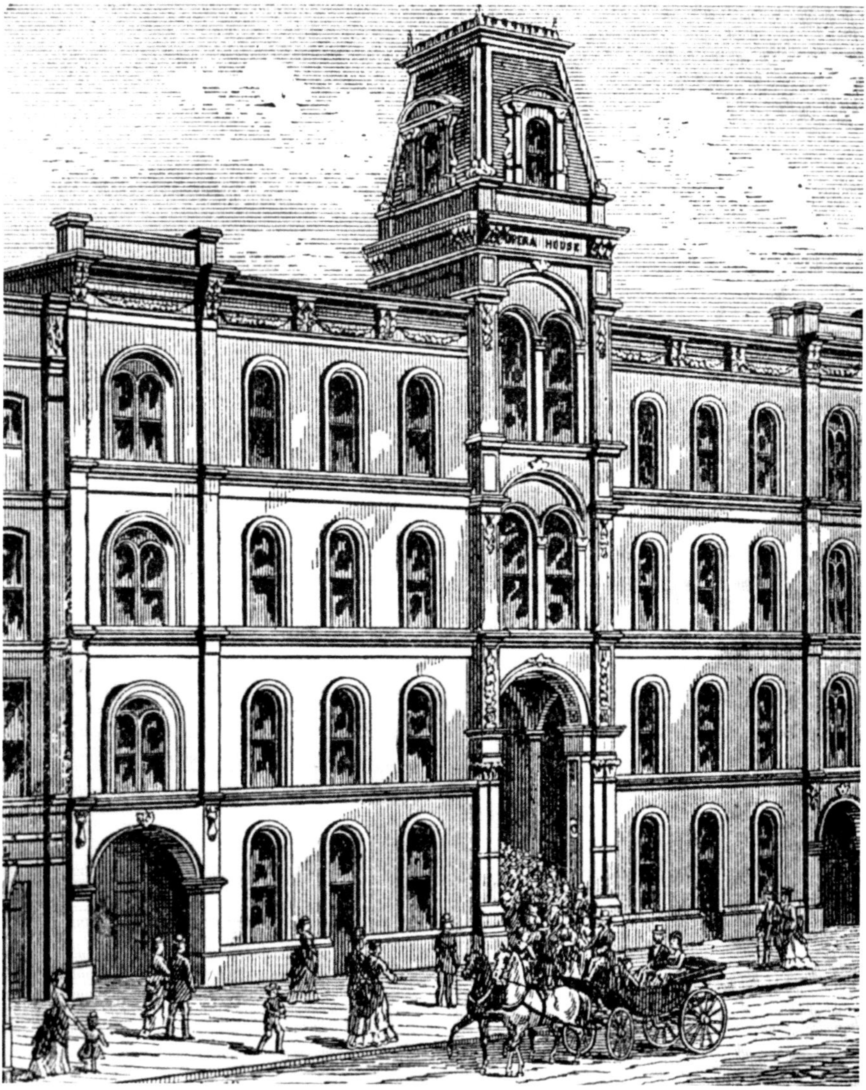

The Euclid Avenue Opera House, one of Cleveland's finest theaters in the late nineteenth century, actually faced East Fourth Street. *Courtesy of Cleveland Public Library, Photograph Collection.*

withheld their approval to show the film. The Ohio Supreme Court upheld the banning, even though Ohio stood alone among the states in prohibiting the movie's exhibition. Two years later, the court finally consented, but Cleveland mayor Harry L. Davis urged the city law director to thwart the Opera House engagement. Davis promised, "I'll do all in my power to

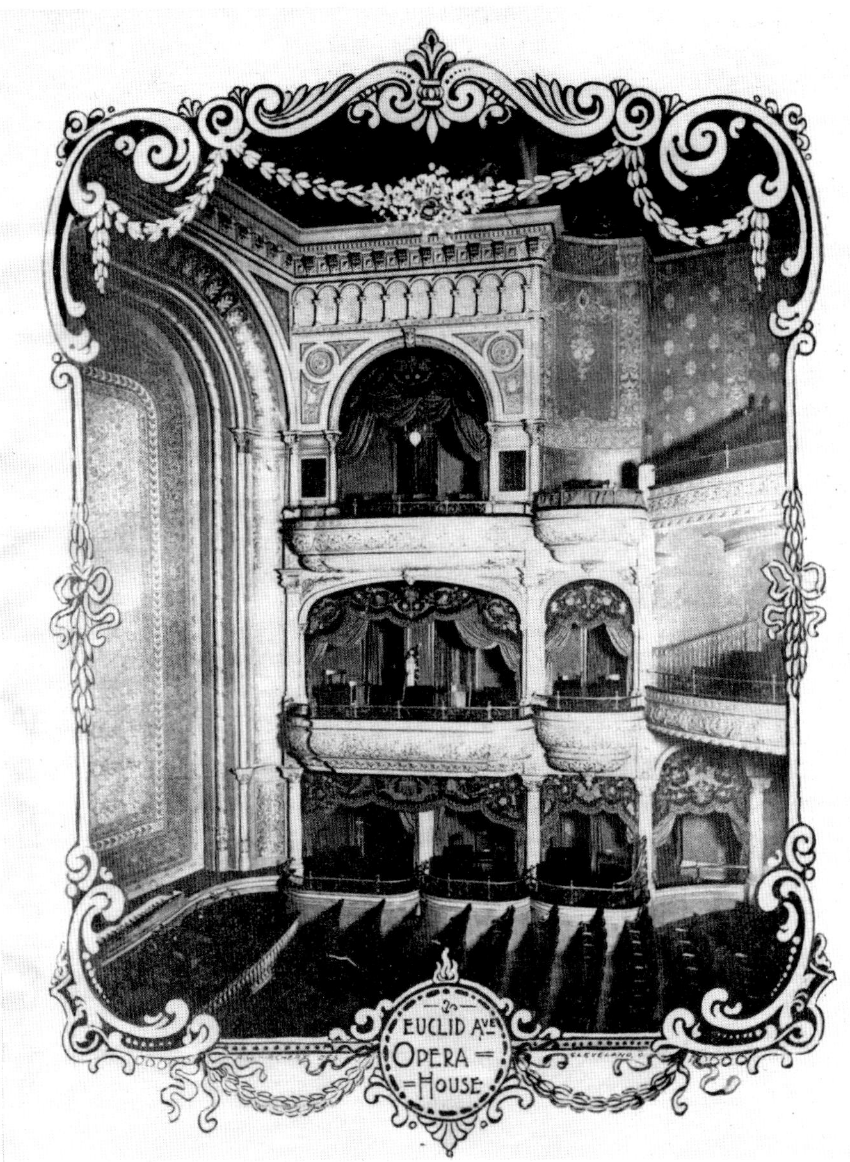

Constructed in 1875, the Euclid Avenue Opera House remained a leading theater until the opening of the Playhouse Square showplaces. *Courtesy of Cleveland Public Library, Photograph Collection.*

prevent *The Birth of a Nation* from being shown in Cleveland." But the public prevailed, and the Opera House hosted an eight-week reserved seat, road-show engagement of the controversial drama set during the Civil War and

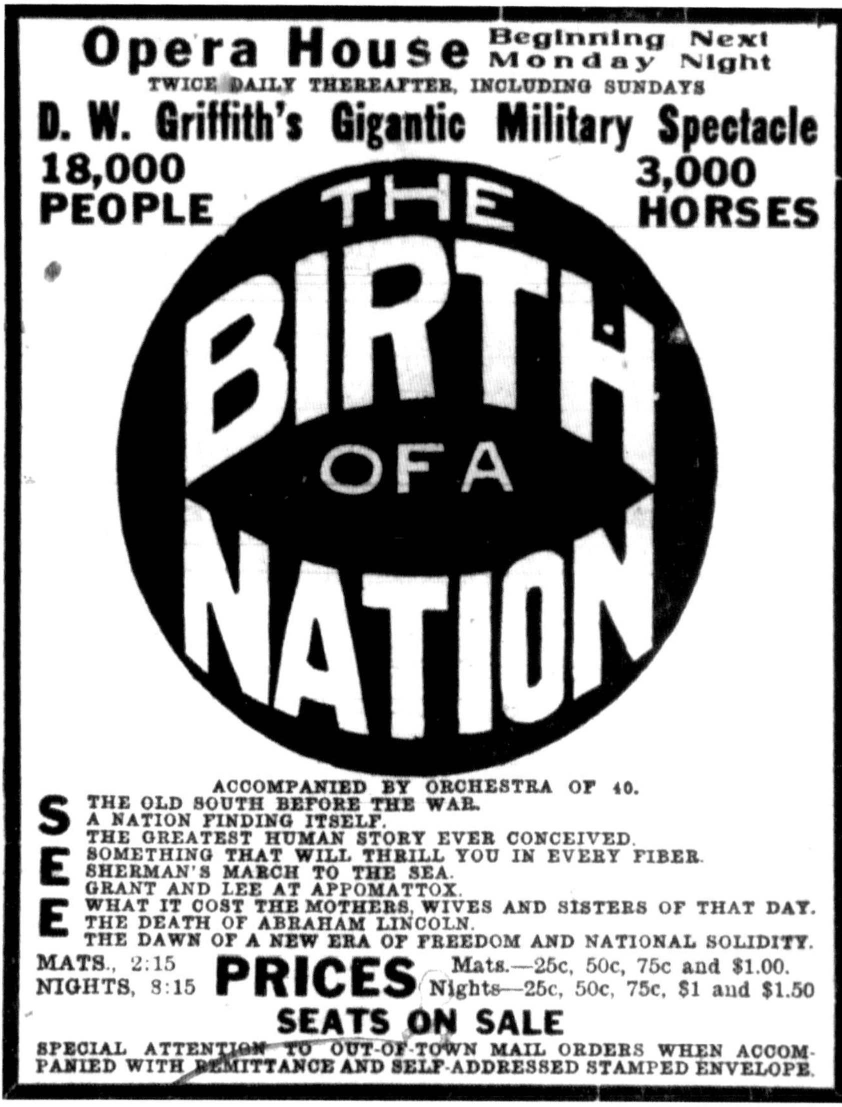

Banned in Ohio by censors for two years, *The Birth of a Nation* finally made its Cleveland debut at the Euclid Avenue Opera House. *Courtesy of the* Plain Dealer.

Reconstruction. More than fifteen months following its closing at the Opera House, the film reemerged at the downtown Orpheum Theater in its first popular-priced showing in Cleveland.

Following *The Birth of a Nation*, the Opera House showcased *Intolerance*, D.W. Griffith's next film, as another road-show presentation. The three-

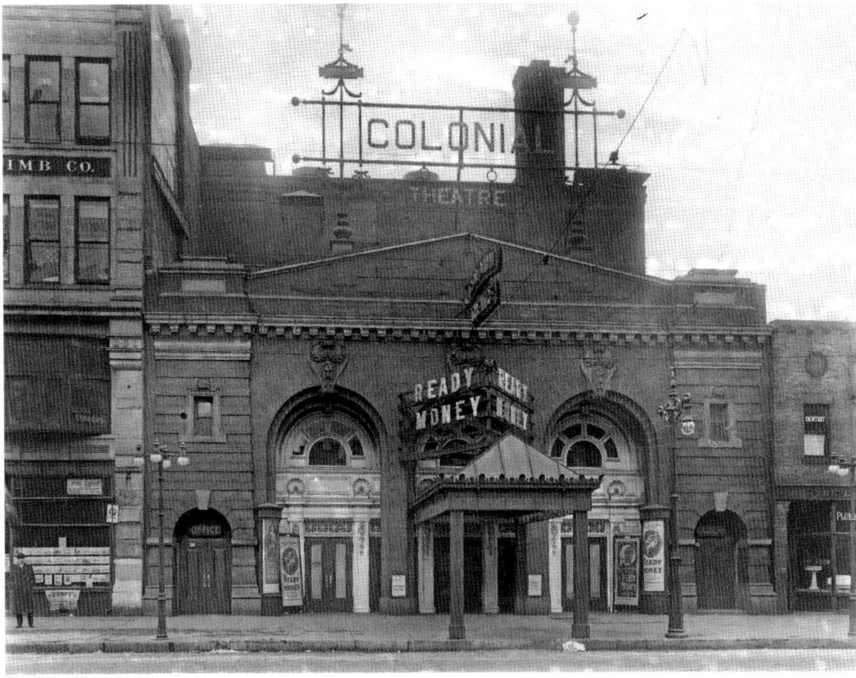

Usually hosting vaudeville or stage productions, the Colonial Theater also booked some of the early movies presented as "road shows." *Courtesy of Cleveland Public Library, Photograph Collection.*

and-a-half-hour spectacular interwove four separate stories of intolerance: one in ancient Babylon, another in Judea at the time of Christ, a third in France during the reign of Charles IX and the last a contemporary melodrama. Publicity emphasized the epic nature of the production, which employed 125,000 people, seven thousand horses, 1,200 chariots and 500 beautiful, bewitching Babylonian dancing girls.

In 1918, Theda Bara in *Cleopatra* merited an Opera House road-show engagement. As an added inducement to purchase tickets, the Opera House advertised that no other Cleveland theater would exhibit the film for twelve months.

In 1921, the Opera House booked *Way Down East*, another D.W. Griffith film, for a ten-week engagement, the longest run in the theater's history. Griffith and Lillian Gish, one of the film's stars, appeared in person to commemorate the 100th showing of the movie in Cleveland.

In 1903, the 1,472-seat Colonial Theater, originally a "high class" vaudeville house, debuted on a Superior Avenue site now occupied by the newer Federal Reserve Building. On opening night, Ida Fuller entertained audiences with a fire dance, while mimic Henry Lee offered impersonations of William Shakespeare, Teddy Roosevelt and Pope Leo XIII. Future vaudeville superstar Nora Bayes commanded only seventh billing that evening. Through the years, Al Jolson, Fred Astaire, Ethel Waters and Sophie Tucker all performed on the Colonial stage.

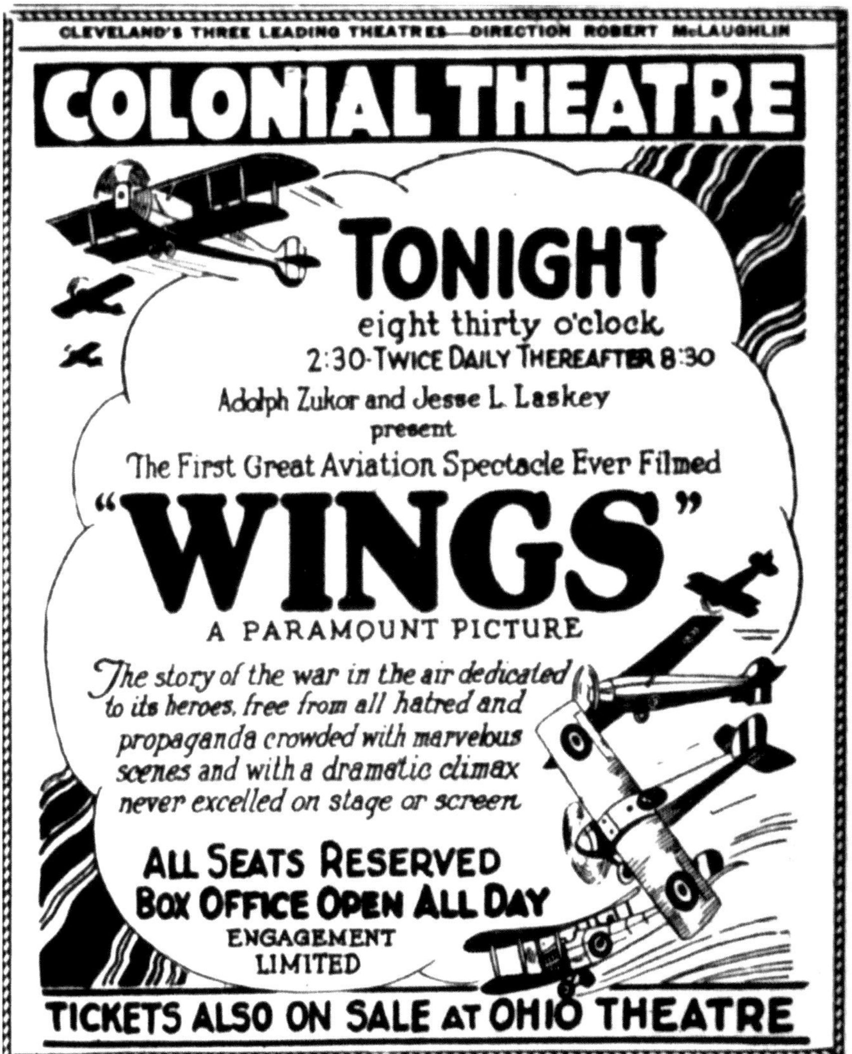

The Colonial Theater's thirteen-week engagement of *Wings* established a new length-of-run record for motion pictures at a Cleveland theater. *Courtesy of the* Plain Dealer.

Kinetograph, a primitive motion picture process, turned into a novelty act in the Colonial's vaudeville programs. In 1912, a colorized Kinemacolor movie documented ceremonies in India honoring King George and Queen Mary. That same year, a four-week engagement of "new movies" consisted of views of Germany in a travelogue format, a trip in a balloon, the birth and growth of plants and the burial of the USS *Maine* battleship. Other film offerings during the period included *Traffic in Souls*, a white slavery exposé, and *The Life of Our Savior*, a French movie narrated by different local ministers at performances during the Easter season. The combination of thirteen episodes of *The Adventures of Kathlyn* (the first "cliffhanger" serial) produced a successful two-part movie.

In 1918, D.W. Griffith's acclaimed war drama *Hearts of the World* ran for four weeks as a road-show presentation with flags of the Allied nations draped over the box seats. The film, produced at a cost of more than $1 million, commanded admission prices ranging from $0.25 to $1.50. After completing its road-show run, the first popular-priced engagement began seven months later at the Grand Theater on East Ninth Street.

The Colonial continued its showcasing of first-run movies with Theda Bara in *Salome* (1918), the Italian import *Theodora* (1921) and an all-amateur cast in *The Miracle*, a Passion play (1925). In 1928, the five-week run of *Simba*, a film documenting a real-life African jungle adventure, incorporated music and a narration presented in a sound process called Dulcetone.

By the late 1920s, the newer Ohio and Hanna Theaters booked virtually all the road-show movies. In 1928, because of scheduling difficulties at these theaters, the Colonial exhibited a thirteen-week, reserved-seat engagement of *Wings*, the first movie to win the Best Picture Academy Award. Four years later, wreckers demolished the Colonial. For the next two generations, road-show presentations continued in Cleveland's downtown theaters (especially at the Ohio and Palace), as well as in a few neighborhood film houses. During the 1960s, every downtown first-run theater booked at least one road-show engagement.

Chapter 5

THE HIPPODROME THEATER

On December 30, 1907, ushers dressed in khaki and usherettes wearing blue uniforms and red roses in their hair greeted the Hippodrome Theater's opening audience. The size of the 3,592-seat theater challenged Clevelanders' imaginations; the 1,500-seat balcony itself surpassed the capacity of most of the city's theaters.

A thirty-two-foot-wide lobby extended between Euclid and Prospect Avenues to anchor box offices and entrances on both streets. Rose, ivory and gold composed the Hippodrome's main color scheme while decorations in the Louis XV style pervaded the theater's interior. Outside, touring shows used the alley now known as East Eighth Street to unload and load scenery and costumes.

Patrons entering the Hippodrome directly from automobiles and dressed in touring clothes (goggles, caps, veils, gloves and dusters) sat in "automobile seats" on the sides of the theater, where they enjoyed shows "without the embarrassment of being on exhibit to the audience."

A gigantic 13,528-square-foot stage, divided into four sections, exceeded the size of every theater stage in the United States except the New York Hippodrome. Each section could be independently raised to the height of a four-story building (while still remaining in full view of the audience) or lowered into the theater's basement. A 435,000-gallon water tank, built beneath one portion of the stage, provided an ideal setting for divers, animal acts and daredevil motorcyclists to soar through the air from an elevated runway into the immense water container.

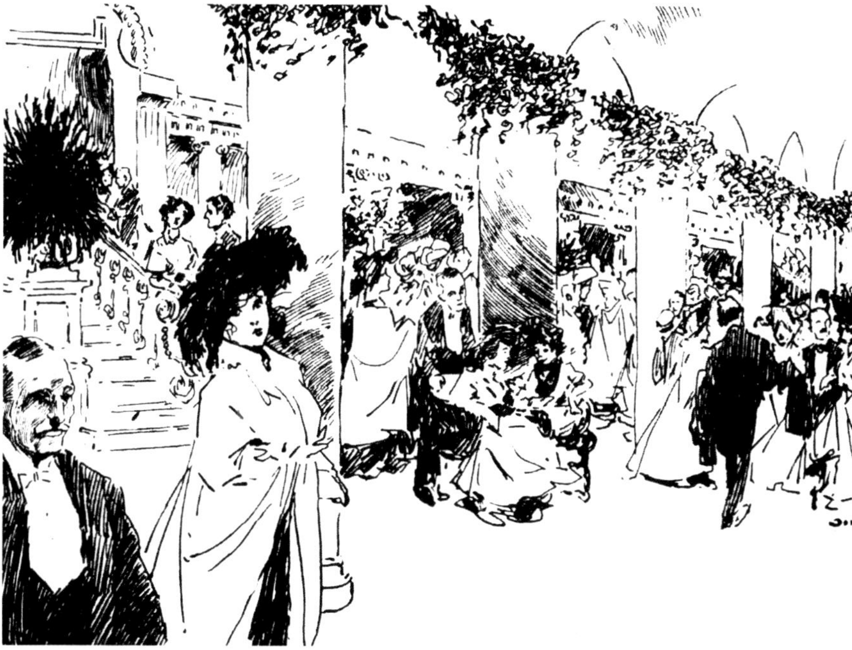

On opening night, Cleveland's fashionable society members gathered to inaugurate the stunning Hippodrome Theater. *Courtesy of the* Plain Dealer.

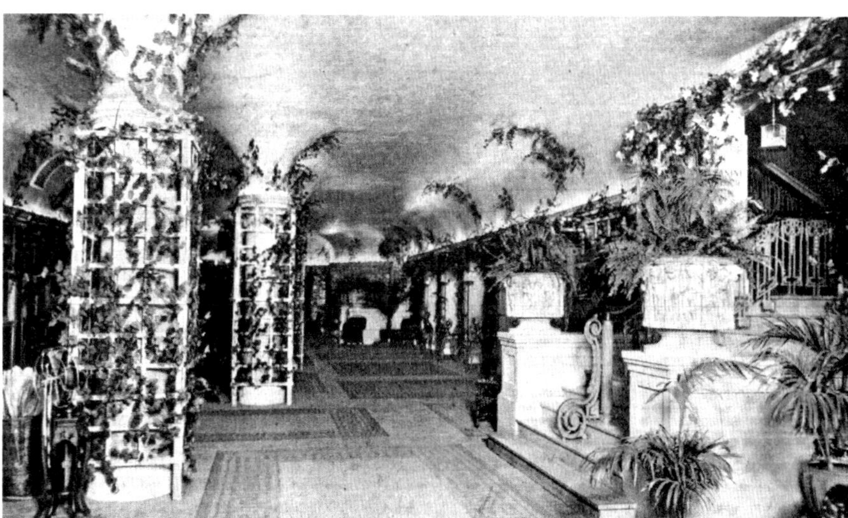

The Hippodrome's beautiful lobby stretched the entire distance between two major downtown streets, Euclid and Prospect Avenues. *Courtesy of the author.*

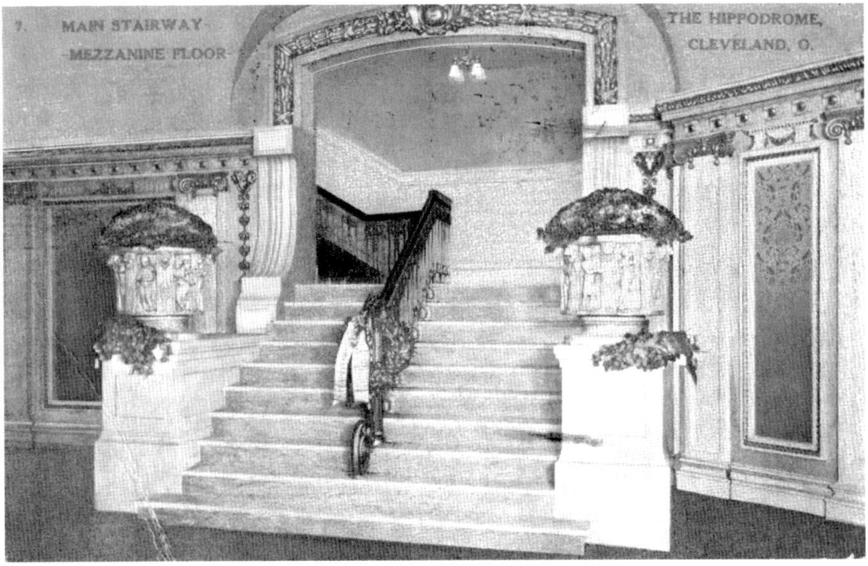

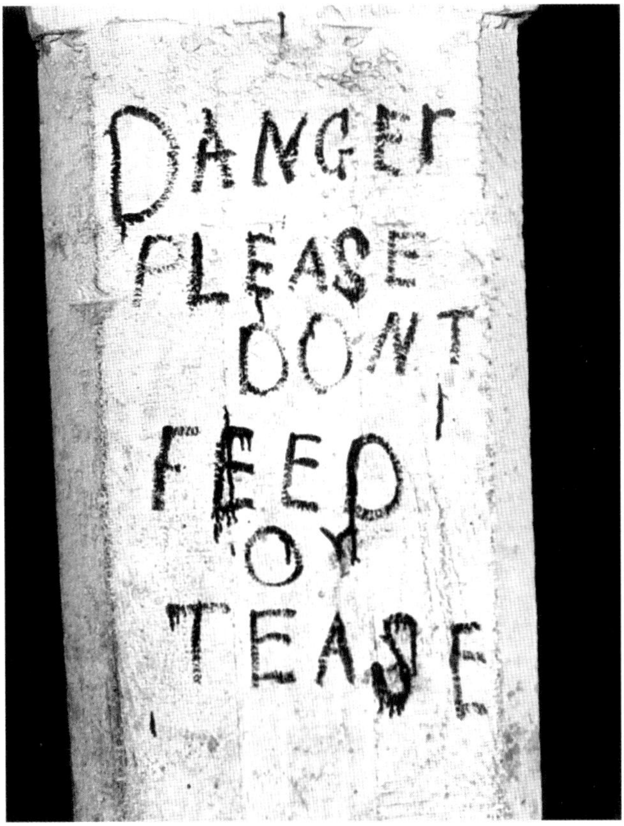

Above: Theatergoers entered the mezzanine and balcony from a marble staircase situated in the ground-floor lobby. *Courtesy of the author.*

Right: Far below the Hippodrome's exquisite lobby and auditorium, makeshift signs warned against teasing or feeding animals confined to their "stables" when not performing. *Courtesy of Special Collections, Michael Schwartz Library, Cleveland State University.*

Actors, dancers and ballerinas rehearsed in either of two special rooms above the theater's forty-four-foot proscenium arch. Forty-two dressing rooms on six floors afforded accommodations for performers. Major stars laid their claims to the lower floors, with rooms providing comfortable couches, tables and chairs. Secondary performers climbed flights of stairs to rooms on higher levels outfitted with only utilitarian accommodations. Every dressing room came equipped with an iron used not only to remove wrinkles from costumes but also to fry eggs for quick consumption between performances. A set of "stables" housing animal acts sat below the stage in the basement.

During the initial program, customers paid twenty, fifty or seventy cents to witness horses diving into the huge water tank, elephants dancing on the stage and cats partaking in spirited competitive races. Horses pulling coaches dashed up a makeshift hill while farm wagons and hunters on horseback rode across the stage. Vaudeville entertainers and an opera singer also enhanced the theater's first stage show.

Performers, stagehands and even audience members endured early mishaps in the large and complex theater. Since rehearsals for the opening-day performance never fully staged a scene where horses plunged into the water tank, no one anticipated the ensuing surge of water created by the animals' dives. The swell, nearly covering the orchestra pit, generated an authentic show-stopping event; the spectacle resumed only after orchestra members had fully dried themselves and their musical instruments.

In a later horse-diving misfortune, as steeds and their riders approached the water tank, one horse slipped and fell prematurely into the water, thus altering the intricate timing of the performance. The unfortunate rider, while in the tank, suffered a broken leg after being hit by another diving horse.

Many patrons attending a first-week matinee performance never forgot the special effects developed for the mini-spectacle *The Cloudburst*. Because of a large fire in the Flats, the city had substantially increased its water pressure that afternoon. During the performance, a blast of water intended to simulate a giant deluge unintentionally poured into the orchestra pit and onto patrons unlucky enough to be seated in the first five rows.

One evening, as a horse and carriage transported a pair of escaping lovers across the big stage, the animal stumbled. The driver, hurled from the carriage onto the hard stage, broke two ribs in an unintentionally stunning special effect. During another performance, a stagehand, perched fifty feet above the performers, plunged onto the stage in full view of the horrified audience. Although knocked unconscious, he avoided serious injury. In an

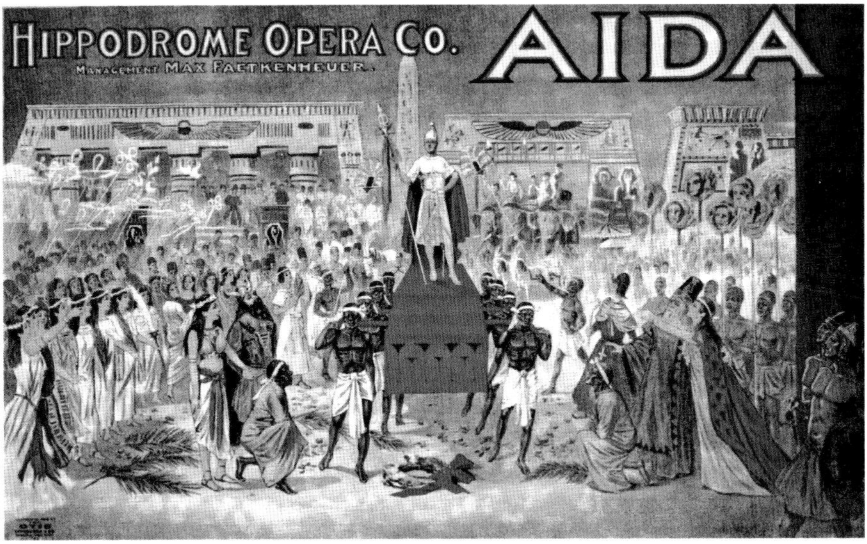

In 1908, a postcard promoted the Hippodrome Theater's own lavish production of *Aida*. *Courtesy of the author.*

incident with a much happier ending, a scenery painter dropped a can of paint on a female member of the chorus. His apology must have been very convincing; the two married each other a few weeks later.

The most tragic early incident took place on a cold morning following the completion of a performance. Carl Jasper, a talented oboe player with the Hippodrome orchestra (who had previously performed with the New York and Boston symphony orchestras), found himself locked out of his house. When the doorbell failed to operate, he pounded on the door for an hour before awakening a family member. His chill developed into pneumonia, and he died a few days later.

The Hippodrome booked its share of vaudeville acts (composed of singers, dancers, acrobats, comedians, magicians, boxing kangaroos and boomerang throwers), but few ranked among the period's top vaudevillians. The Hippodrome directly competed for talent with the powerful Keith vaudeville organization, which operated the nearby Prospect Avenue Theater. Entertainers electing to labor at the Hippodrome could expect immediate blacklisting from all Keith vaudeville houses in the country.

In 1908, a concert by Enrico Caruso commanded ticket prices ranging from two to five dollars. That year, the theater even organized its own opera company. A presentation of *Aida* included fourteen principal actors, an enormous supporting cast of five hundred and a fifty-member orchestra;

audiences paid a top price of one dollar to view the elaborate production. The opera's producers, wishing to stage a memorable event, expanded the famous Triumphant March into an hour-and-a-half spectacle. Entering by way of a ramp from the right, humans and animals walked across the stage, exited from another ramp, circled the theater through the basement and reappeared on the stage. While out of the audience's sight, science artists painted different colored spots on horses while stagehands changed elephants' baskets and humans replaced their robes, each modification contributing to the illusion of a much greater cast. Through the years, the Hippodrome also booked the Metropolitan Opera and prestigious companies from Chicago and Boston.

Special trains and trolley cars imported patrons from Toledo to the west, Erie to the east, Columbus to the south and numerous points in between. Attendance remained near capacity during the theater's first months of operation. Unfortunately, construction and operating costs greatly exceeded budgeted amounts. These overruns delayed completion of two office buildings (an eleven-floor structure on Euclid Avenue and a seven-floor building on Prospect Avenue) planned as part of the theater complex. The loss of office space rentals, combined with cost overruns and potential blacklisting of performers, forced the Hippodrome into receivership only five months after its impressive opening. Although the Shubert Theater organization, the William Morris vaudeville booking agency and two movie theater owners all submitted bids to operate the financially troubled theater, the Keith chain won the bidding contest.

The Hippodrome closed for refurbishing to bring it into conformance with Keith's high standards; the company added oriental rugs (each priced at $8,000), oil paintings and new furniture and draperies. A frustrated George Maxwell, who arrived from Boston to manage the refurbishing of the gigantic theater, walked into the manager's office two weeks before the scheduled opening and confessed, "I've just discovered eleven more rooms."

In addition to adding amenities, Keith used space beneath the stage and auditorium to construct a manufacturing and training center for vaudeville performances. The complex included a blacksmith and scenery shop; a training school for singers; a ballet master's room to instruct aspiring ballerinas; and space for dressmakers, mechanics, electricians and carpenters. Employees in the complex constructed sets for Keith's entire nationwide theater organization.

The Keith Hippodrome reopened with one of the largest vaudeville theater staffs in the world: forty ushers, ten porters, ten maids, twenty cleaners, twenty-two orchestra members, twenty stagehands, four

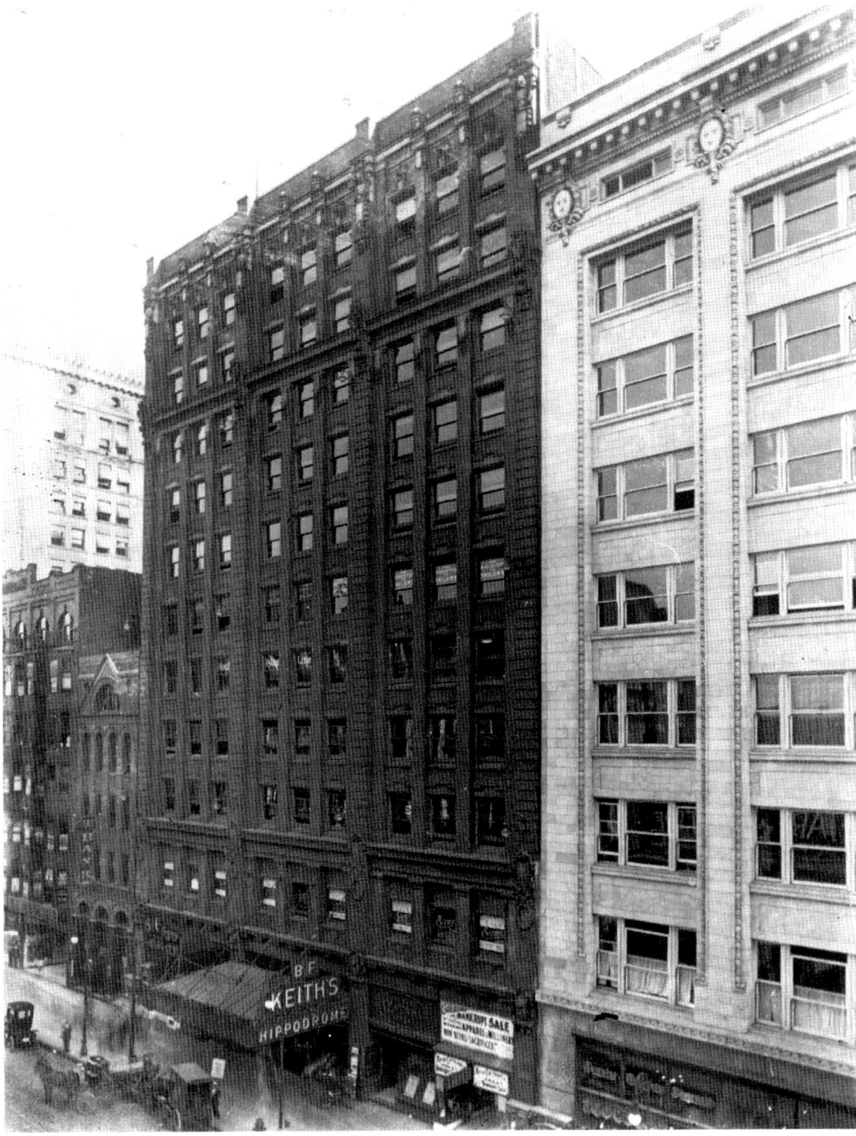

The B.F. Keith vaudeville organization owned the Hippodrome Theater from late 1908 into mid-1921. *Courtesy of Cleveland Public Library, Photograph Collection.*

house superintendents and six watchmen. Six maids, present at every performance, accessed a sewing table, needles, thread and scissors to repair tears in performers' or patrons' clothing. Equipped with smelling salts and other remedies, the maids assisted women suffering from illnesses.

During the Keith reign, the Hippodrome booked famous entertainers of the day and future superstars. Harry Houdini, Fanny Brice, Isadora Duncan, Anna Pavlova, Anna Held, John Philip Sousa, Sarah Bernhardt, Babe Ruth, Ethel Barrymore and Irene and Vernon Castle topped the list of veterans. Irving Berlin and George M. Cohan graced the Hippodrome stage during a benefit performance.

Will Rogers twirled a rope and delivered monologues about current news events prior to establishing himself as a featured *Ziegfeld Follies* performer and film star. Twenty-year-old Mae West developed into one of the most widely known entertainers of the twentieth century. The relatively unknown Sophie Tucker and Marx Brothers rose quickly to stardom. Jack Benny's performances still needed polishing prior to his emergence as an accomplished vaudeville comedian. George Jessel, already a vaudeville veteran for more than a decade, developed into a major star soon after his Hippodrome appearance.

In 1909, the Hippodrome devoted Sunday performances entirely to movies. "The Wide World in Motion" featured an array of travel films and accompanying lectures, current events, histories, dramas and comedies. One short subject displayed a slow-motion film of a bullet's path shot from a rapid-firing gun. In the summer of 1911, the theater booked its first feature-length motion pictures. During the next few years, the Hippodrome incorporated movies into the daily vaudeville program. These films ranged from short dramas to images of important boxing matches, the Indianapolis auto race and the disastrous 1913 Dayton flood.

The Hippodrome's early success benefited from the intimidating Keith organization's policy of attacking competitive threats quickly and decisively. In 1912, as the Hippodrome began a fourteen-week summer break, the nearby Euclid Avenue Opera House announced a summer vaudeville season. Almost overnight, the Hippodrome reopened with a full summer of first-rate vaudeville entertainment. In addition to taking aim at the Opera House, the Keith organization advertising discredited storefront theaters playing motion pictures: "Don't ruin your health in stuffy, store picture shows when, for the same price, you can enjoy much better entertainment in a well ventilated, cool, clean, safe theater." The Hippodrome's first-week attendance exceeded thirty-five thousand, far surpassing that of the Opera House (which terminated its summer vaudeville programs after only three weeks).

In 1913, the Hippodrome incorporated Thomas A. Edison's new Kinetophone process into vaudeville programs. The first large-scale attempt to commercialize talking movies used a cylinder phonograph connected to a projector by a belt and series of pulleys. The contraption synchronized the voices and movements of opera singers performing *Il Travatore* in what otherwise would have been a silent movie. Edison predicted every motion picture theater in the country would install his Kinetophone equipment: "Actors will speak, dogs will bark and even the moaning of the trees will be recorded and conveyed to the audience." Unfortunately, poorly trained operators failed to keep images in synchronization with the sound and insufficient amplification created poor sound quality. When a fire at Edison's lab destroyed the Kinetophone image and sound masters, the scientist abandoned his talking picture experiment.

The Hippodrome in 1913 booked the Italian silent blockbuster *Quo Vadis*. Paying a top price of fifty cents, theatergoers exceeding one-sixth of Cleveland's population traveled downtown to view Christians and Romans engaged in conflict during the time of Emperor Nero. Although the five-week, reserved-seat engagement ended because of an advanced booking of popular stage actress Marie Dressler, the film moved to the uptown Alhambra Theater for a sixth week. The following year, a three-week run of *Cabiria*, another Italian epic, entertained audiences with scenes of an erupting volcano, the destruction of a Roman navy fleet, Hannibal crossing the Alps and sacrifices of children to the god Moloch.

In 1915, the Keith organization, always seeking new ways to outmatch its competition, introduced the Hippodrome Bar by offering a free beverage each day: root beer (Monday), ginger ale (Tuesday), sarsaparilla (Wednesday), lemon juice (Thursday), grape juice (Friday) and the entire selection on Saturday. The following summer, the theater served free cold lemonade and buttermilk.

The size of the Hippodrome stage allowed the theater in 1920 to secure a booking of the original version of *Aphrodite*, an immense dramatization of an ancient Egyptian story that employed a company of eight hundred people, along with horses, camels and donkeys. Carpenters from New York arrived two months in advance of the showing to brace and reinforce the Hippodrome stage to accommodate the cast and scenery that included a forty-two-foot-high lighthouse. The colossal extravaganza generated $100,000 in receipts, a national box-office record and the largest single week in the theater's history. A scaled-down version of the spectacle later played in cities throughout the United States.

In 1921, Keith sold the theater to concentrate its efforts on the new East 105th Street playhouse and the soon-to-be-opened downtown Palace Theater. The showplace became Reade's Hippodrome; six small-time vaudeville acts and a

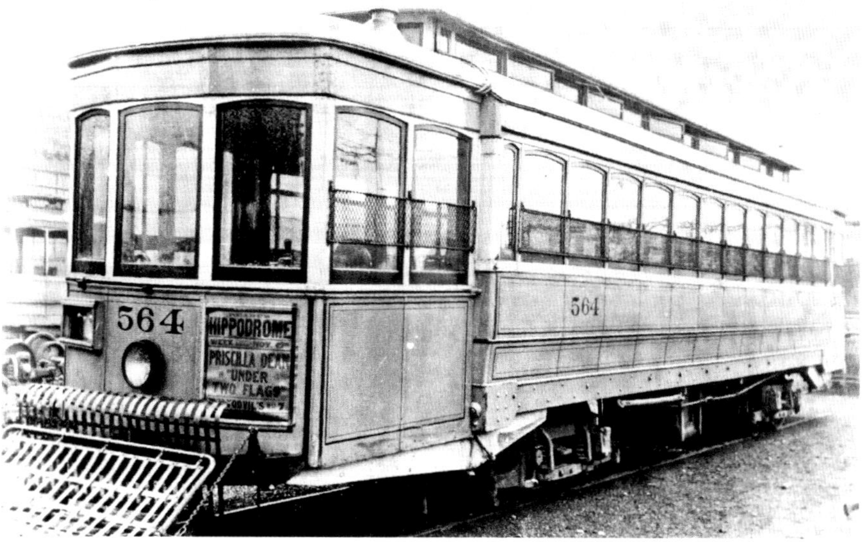

The Reade Corporation employed streetcar advertising in promoting Hippodrome attractions such as the 1922 film *Under Two Flags* combined with small-time vaudeville. *Courtesy of Cleveland Public Library, Photograph Collection.*

feature-length B movie composed the new format. Tom Mix, Hoot Gibson and Buck Jones on the screen doubled with dancers, singers and Charleston contests. In 1928, an all–motion picture format replaced vaudeville.

As early as 1929, *Plain Dealer* critic W. Ward Marsh referred to the Hippodrome as "the Hipp" in review headlines but used the more formal Hippodrome designation in the body of his text. Depending on the size of newspaper advertisements, the theater also used both names in promoting its shows. Most Clevelanders eventually chose the shorter name, referring to the playhouse as "the Hipp."

Eight years after acquiring the Hippodrome, Reade sold the theater to RKO. The new owners removed a large portion of the stage, lowered the main floor and added a new mezzanine. An increase in seating capacity to more than four thousand created the largest American theater devoted exclusively to motion pictures.

During the Depression, RKO fashioned inexpensive but newsworthy gimmicks to generate attention for its movie offerings. In 1931, employees carried bottles of aromatic ammonia (smelling salts) to revive patrons who might faint during performances of Boris Karloff in *Frankenstein* or Bela Lugosi in *Dracula*. Near the end of 1932, live entertainment briefly returned

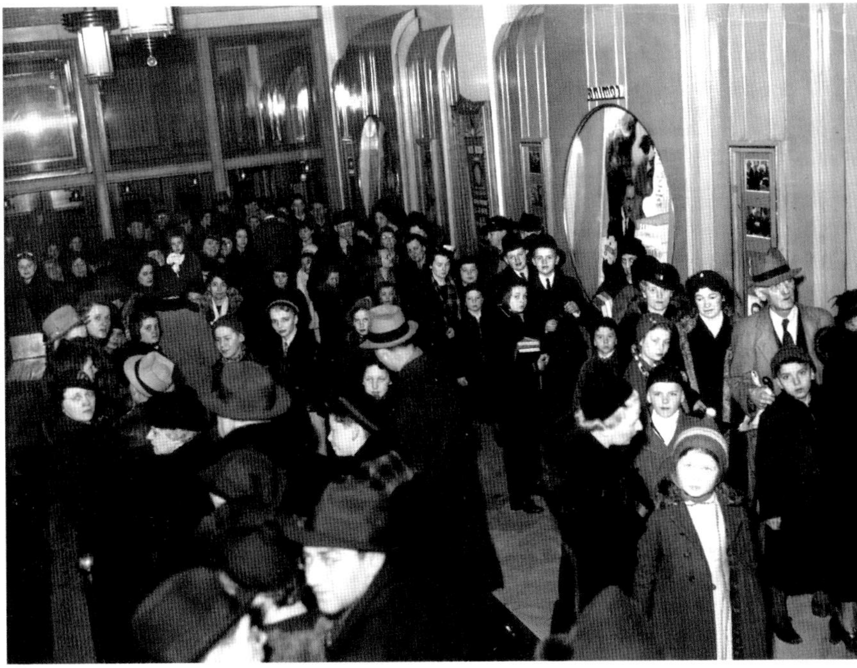

In 1938, adults and children gathered in the Hippodrome lobby prior to a showing of Walt Disney's *Snow White*. *Courtesy of Special Collections, Michael Schwartz Library, Cleveland State University.*

with first-rate headliners such as Paul Whiteman, Bill Robinson, Cab Calloway, the Mills Brothers and Guy Lombardo. In 1933, Warner Brothers leased the theater following RKO's bankruptcy.

The Hippodrome's huge movie screen, combined with the relatively new Technicolor process, at times educed surprisingly emotional responses from filmgoers. In 1941, eighty-eight minutes into a showing of *Blood and Sand*, as Rita Hayworth taunted the long-suffering Linda Darnell (wife of unfaithful Tyrone Power), the usually very acquiescent Helen Horan surprised her husband, Owen, along with about six hundred other moviegoers in the Hippodrome balcony, by standing up and shouting, "You can go to hell!" to the silver-screen image of the wayward Rita Hayworth.

As the Second World War drew to a close, news-hungry Clevelanders gathered around their radios to garner the latest war news. Hippodrome patrons remained up to date when radio station WHK used the theater's public address system to transmit two-minute news reports twice each evening. To establish the proper atmosphere during the broadcasts, the movie screen displayed a silent trailer featuring a news announcer.

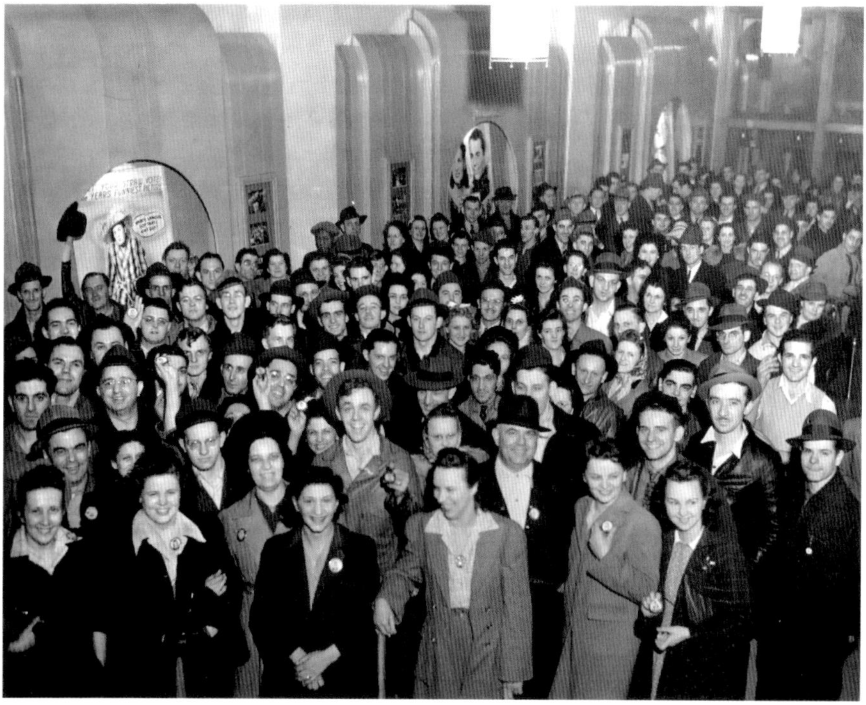

In 1943, war workers filled the Hippodrome for convenient late-evening film showings. *Courtesy of Special Collections, Michael Schwartz Library, Cleveland State University.*

Back in 1936, *Mr. Deeds Goes to Town* established a house box-office record for movies with $28,000 in receipts during its opening week. Although classic films such as *Casablanca*, *Sergeant York* and *Yankee Doodle Dandy* challenged that record, the 1943 war drama *Hitler's Children* became the Hippodrome's first film to record a $29,000 week. That same year, another war film, *Behind the Rising Sun*, generated $31,000 in receipts. Three years later, *Saratoga Trunk* soared to $35,000; *Life with Father* and *The Snows of Kilimanjaro* would later tie that mark. But a 1953 biblical blockbuster incredibly doubled the previous record holders.

The Hippodrome introduced Cleveland audiences to large-screen motion pictures with an eleven-week engagement of *The Robe*, the first movie shown in CinemaScope. Customers filled the theater, including the rarely used second balcony located above the projection booth. Here the proverbial sight of dust captured by the projector's light appeared from below the audiences' view of the movie. Opening week receipts totaled a staggering $70,000 at a top price of $1.50. In contrast, $4,000 at a

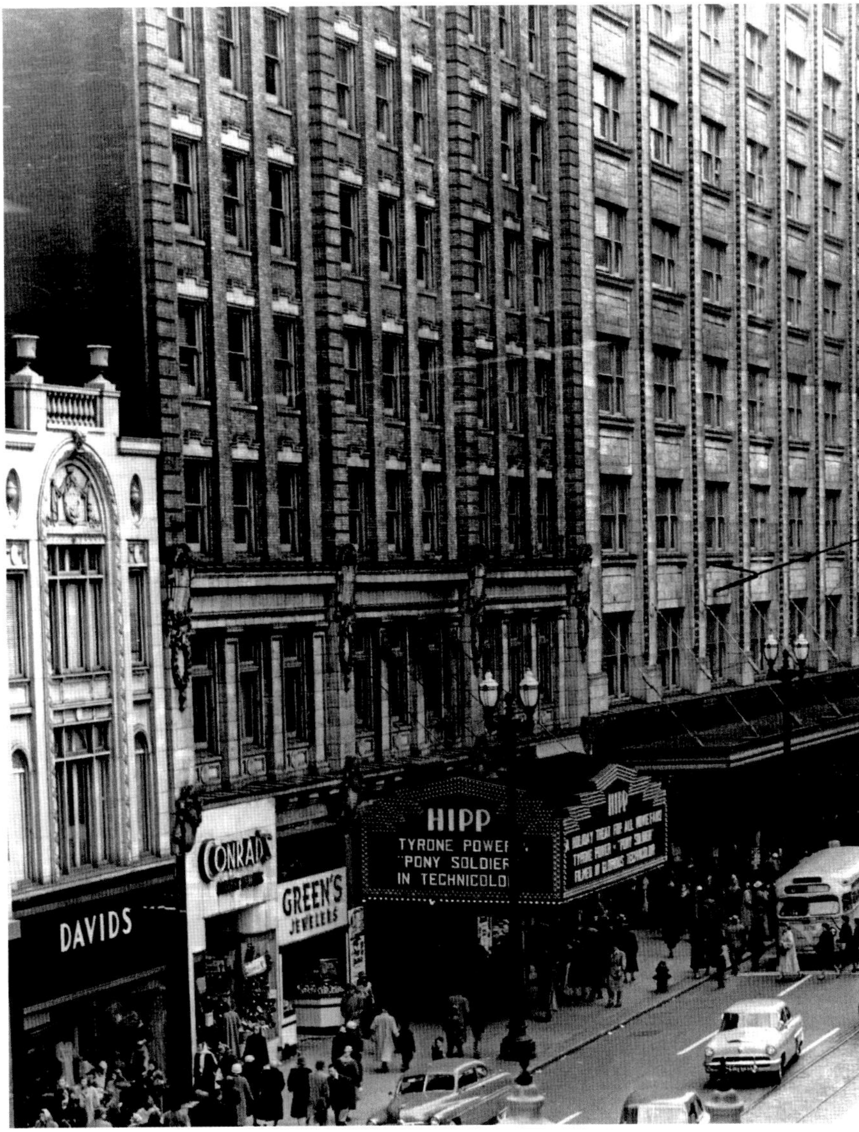

By 1952, the Hippodrome marquee reflected the theater's less formal and more popular name, "the Hipp." *Courtesy of Special Collections, Michael Schwartz Library, Cleveland State University.*

multiplex theater screen today (with much more expensive ticket prices) is considered an excellent week. *The Robe*'s entire run generated a colossal $312,000. In 1961, *The Guns of Navarone* tied *The Robe*'s eleven-week run with a substantially lower $169,000 in receipts. The 1962 reserved-seat,

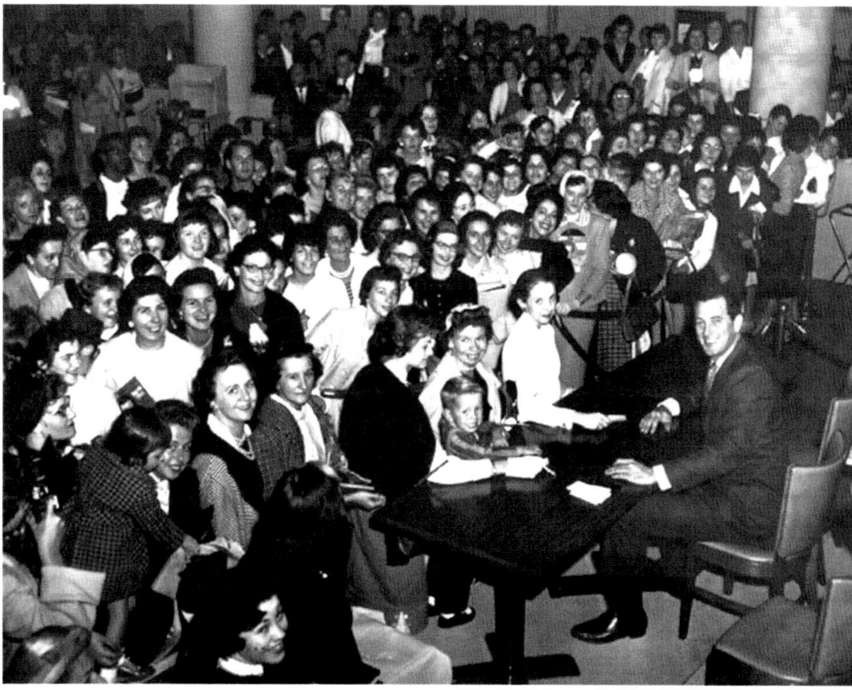

In 1953, rising star Rock Hudson signed autographs in Halle's Tea Room while promoting his new film, *The Lawless Breed*, showing at the Hippodrome Theater. *Courtesy of Special Collections, Michael Schwartz Library, Cleveland State University.*

thirteen-week showing of *The Longest Day* (the theater's longest-running movie) created total receipts of $124,000.

In the mid-1950s, live entertainment returned for the first time in years with sporadic booking of top rock acts, including Chuck Berry, the Diamonds, Frankie Lyman and the Teenagers, Clyde McPhatter and others. Enthusiastic yet well-mannered audiences provided no hint of the behavioral problems that would accompany a movie featuring rock stars.

On Sunday evening, January 20, 1957, a fight involving more than two hundred teenagers broke out in the Hippodrome balcony during a showing of *The Girl Can't Help It*. Fifteen youths required hospital treatment for cuts, bruises and, in one case, serious facial cuts. The *Cleveland Press* quoted a victim as recalling, "I turned around and something hit me. Next thing I knew, I was on the floor. All I remember is that Little Richard was singing at the time." Lieutenant Ray Moran explained, "They were hopped up on this rock and roll trash." One patrolman advised the mother of an injured boy, "Keep your kids out of a place like that."

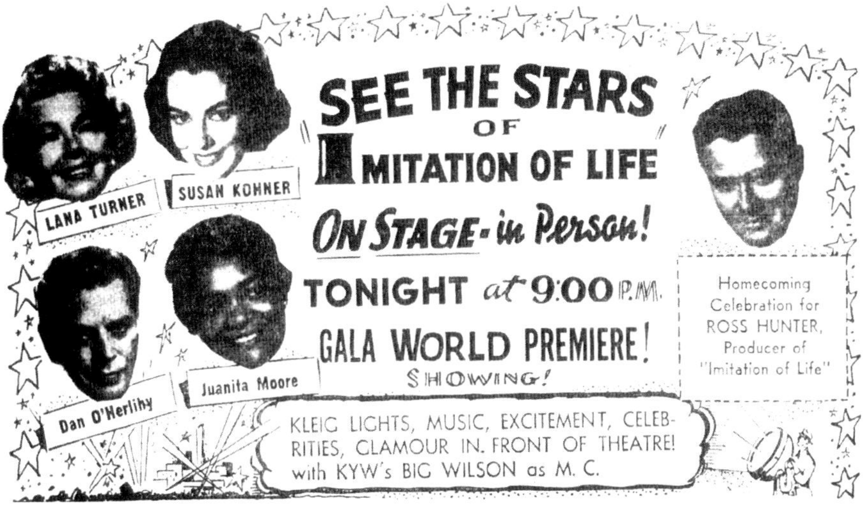

Ross Hunter, an important Hollywood producer and native Clevelander, staged the premiere showing of *Imitation of Life* at the Hippodrome Theater. *Courtesy of the* Plain Dealer.

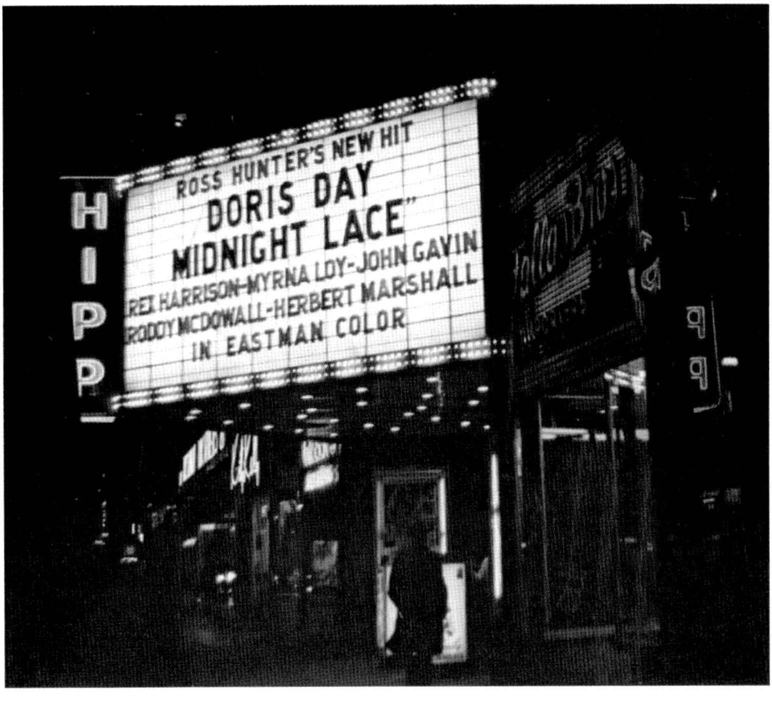

In 1960, *Midnight Lace*, another major Ross Hunter movie, received an early showing at the Hippodrome but not a premiere engagement. *Courtesy of Cleveland Public Library, Literature Department.*

Cleveland News columnist Sidney Andorn editorialized, "It's time we stopped hush-hushing these movie gang fights. It's time we stopped playing down the real villain of the brawl at the Hippodrome Sunday. The villain is the movie. The rock and roll movie with its jungle beat. The leather-jacket movie with its teen-age gangs." Andorn described the film as "a two-hour picturization of violence, brutality, sensuousness, sexationalism and pounding by gun or drum."

The newspaper columnists and police almost certainly had never viewed the movie. Rather than exploiting teenage delinquency, the film's stars (Jayne Mansfield, Tom Ewell and Edmond O'Brien) created a lighthearted comedy highlighted by cream overflowing milk bottles as Mansfield walked down the street. But the movie did contain vintage rock-and-roll performances by Little Richard, Fats Domino, the Platters, Gene Vincent and Eddie Cochran. Yet just the week before the riot, the theater played *Don't Knock the Rock* and the previous year had showed *Rock Around the Clock*, both without incident.

In a six-year period beginning in 1959, Cleveland glowed in a national spotlight as producer Ross Hunter, a Cleveland native, brought major premieres to the Hippodrome. First, Hollywood stars Lana Turner, Susan Kohner, Dan O'Herlihy and Juanita Moore attended the world premiere of *Imitation of Life*. Later in 1959, heartthrob Rock Hudson signed autographs in the Hippodrome lobby as part of the *Pillow Talk* premiere. In 1960, John Saxon, Virginia Grey and Anna May Wong presided at the first public showing of *Portrait in Black*. Four years later, *I'd Rather Be Rich* premiered with Robert Goulet and fashion designer Jean Louis as guests of honor. Louis conducted a fashion show on stage, and customers thrilled to a display of original gowns and $500,000 worth of gems used in the film. Also in 1964, but not connected with Ross Hunter, the Hippodrome hosted the world premiere of *Rio Conchos*, the movie heralding the film debut of Cleveland Browns football star Jim Brown.

Back in the late 1940s, Hollywood studios lost a hard-fought antitrust lawsuit in the Supreme Court. One of the repercussions involved the divestiture of the studio's ownership of movie theaters. Films had usually debuted at downtown theaters either owned directly by the studios or engaged in licensing agreements with them. Following the court decision, the studios agreed to divest the theaters and establish independent subsidiaries to exhibit the movies. The plan required a decade to implement, and even then, many of the newly created exhibition organizations remained sympathetic to the old, time-honored distribution system. Into the mid-

1960s, the Hippodrome remained profitable by continuing its long-established practice of featuring exclusive first-run movies primarily from the studios of 20th Century Fox, Columbia and Universal.

In 1965, the old booking arrangement collapsed. Newer theater companies, such as General Cinema, had no affiliation or past history with movie studios and forced downtown theaters to share first-run engagements with their theaters. Within a short period, old neighborhood theaters, as well as suburban cinemas, transformed themselves into showcases for first-run films. The convenience of shorter travel time, free parking and perceived safer environments devastated the downtown theaters.

The Hippodrome fought its new competition by presenting exclusive closed-circuit telecasts of a Beatles concert, auto races and the controversial stage show *Oh! Calcutta*, along with film versions of the La Scala Opera's *La Boheme*, the D'Oyly Carte's *Mikado* and a film adaptation of James Joyce's *Ulysses* accompanied by a pricy $5.50 ticket charge. These mostly successful events proved to be merely stop-gap measures to counter the otherwise plummeting attendance.

Despite stifling competition from neighborhood theaters, the Hippodrome still attracted crowds to a few "crossover" movies appealing to both white and African American audiences. In 1967, the opening week of *In the Heat of the Night* registered excellent box-office receipts of $30,000 in launching a five-week run. The next year, the seven-week engagement of *Guess Who's Coming to Dinner* opened with an equally outstanding $28,000 initial week. The movie's storyline, involving the engagement of an African American man and a white woman, did not appeal to all the patrons; stench bombs forced the evacuation of the downtown Hippodrome and suburban Stillwell and Loew's West Theaters. Beneath the seats of all three theaters, police discovered plastic bottles used in the construction of crudely made stink bombs. At the Stillwell, law officers received a threat that a more potent bomb would be exploded in the future.

The latest James Bond escapades and Clint Eastwood's "spaghetti westerns" drew good crowds, largely because the Hippodrome by now had positioned itself as Cleveland's only mainstream downtown theater. In 1970, the Hippodrome promoted its quadruple-feature composed of *A Fistful of Dollars*, *For a Few Dollars More*, *Hang 'Em High* and *The Good, the Bad and the Ugly* as "32,580 seconds with Clint Eastwood."

Unfortunately, the box-office failures tended to outnumber the successes. By the 1970s, large holes and peeling paint blighted the once-beautiful plaster walls. Dirt clung to the ceiling, and springs protruded from the theater seats.

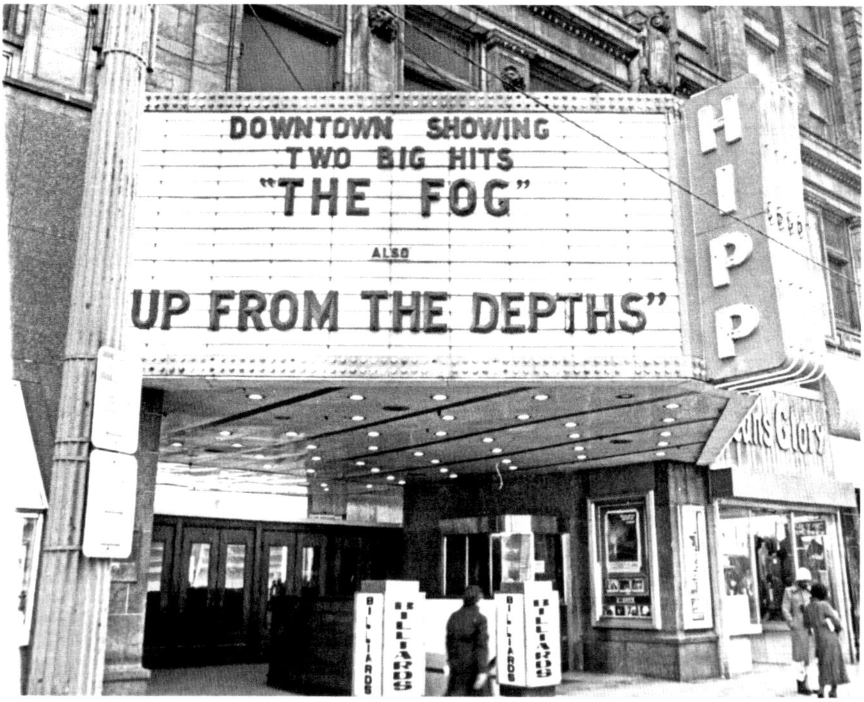

The Hippodrome closed within three months of the 1980 twin-bill booking of *The Fog* and *Up from the Depths*. *Courtesy of Special Collections, Michael Schwartz Library, Cleveland State University.*

A filthy carpet greeted customers, while a broken air conditioning system forced the use of six huge electric fans throughout the auditorium.

Even in this deplorable condition, some Hippodrome bookings generated respectable receipts, especially cross-over films such as *Shaft* and *Lady Sings the Blues*, black-orientated films and horror movies. In 1973, Bruce Lee in *The Chinese Connection* marked the first of a multitude of profitable martial arts films. A few mainstream first-run films (*Saturday Night Fever*, *Rocky II*, *Moonraker* and others), all shared with neighborhood theaters, helped to keep the Hippodrome in operation.

In the late 1970s, the once-bustling Euclid and Prospect Avenue buildings that housed the Hippodrome sat vacant. Although the Hippodrome still generated a profit, the theater's revenues alone could not justify keeping open the two otherwise empty buildings. On April 30, 1980, about sixty people attended the Hippodrome's final showing, the double feature *Scarface* and *Drum*. A parking lot now resides on the site.

Chapter 6

THE FAMILY/ORPHEUM/ ROXY THEATER

In 1907, the 715-seat Family Theater debuted on East Ninth Street. Although the playhouse survived for seven decades, not all of its history comprised the purest form of family entertainment.

The Family began as a movie theater with a five-cent admission charge, but the showplace never functioned as a conventional nickelodeon. In addition to comfortable seats, plush carpeting and a relatively large capacity, the theater exhibited a different type of movie. Using a "chronophone machine" to synchronize film with a sound disk, the Family promised "the sensation of a sensational age—motion pictures that sing and talk." Continuing its somewhat unorthodox early history, the Family added vaudeville acts after beginning as a movie theater.

In 1909, the renamed Orpheum Theater initially concentrated on vaudeville with Sundays devoted to movies. Once again a full-fledged movie theater in 1913, the playhouse exhibited a new first-run film every day, seven days a week. Within two years, the Orpheum progressed from a different movie each day to a four-week engagement of *Damaged Goods*, a film concerning a young couple who had contracted syphilis.

By the end of the decade, the Orpheum had developed into a very respectable first-run movie theater specializing in western movies starring Tom Mix, Harry Carey and William Farnum. Even with its emphasis on cowboys, the Orpheum still uncovered an occasional "sensational film" to exhibit, such as the 1919 thriller *Captured by Cannibals.* The movie promised real films of "naked, man-eating savages taken at the risk of life."

In the early 1920s, the Playhouse Square theaters had relegated the Orpheum to a second-run film house. Although the Orpheum rarely presented live entertainment, in 1929, Jean Lussier visited the theater with a unique combined in-person and film production. A year earlier, Lussier had plunged over Niagara Falls in a steel-reinforced rubber ball that he had constructed with his life savings of $1,500. He displayed the ball in the Orpheum lobby and, accompanied by films, narrated his account of the trip over the Horseshoe Falls. Lussier later moved to Niagara Falls, where he sold pieces of the ball to tourists for fifty cents. Not wanting to end his souvenir sales when the material composing the ball ran out, he substituted pieces of rubber tires to sell as keepsakes.

In 1930, following a redecoration and installation of sound equipment, the Orpheum reopened as the Roxy movie theater. Except for a brief experimentation with live burlesque shows, the Roxy remained a double-feature movie house for three years. In 1933, the Roxy constructed a new stage and runway, added cushioned seats and built dressing rooms in the adjacent Hotel Mecca. The theater reopened as a burlesque house where top bananas, baggy-pants comedians, striptease artists and vaudeville performers replaced movies.

Comics developed routines based on topical subjects, parodies of current song hits, fashion trends and sketches lampooning quack doctors, henpecked husbands, shotgun weddings, politicians, pawnbrokers, stenographers and most every subject in between. Some of the comics continued for four or five decades, entertaining new generations of burlesque audiences.

Adding to the allure, candy sellers promenaded down the aisles encouraging customers to purchase overpriced boxes of sweets that might include a five-dollar bill or a Bulova watch. As the years passed, the concessionaires dispensed with candy to hawk racy pictures. Police censors visited the Roxy every week but found little to condemn except for an occasional loose brassiere worn by a chorus lady.

The shows, often adding vaudeville acts, extended continuously from 11:00 a.m. to 11:00 p.m. with midnight performances on Saturdays. A forty-four-cent admission charge generated enough revenue to pay for a top act and eighteen singing and dancing chorus girls who each earned twenty dollars per week. In the 1930s, New York Yankee teammates Lou Gehrig and Joe DiMaggio visited the theater when the Indians hosted the Yankees. Former trapeze artist and later beloved circus clown Emmett Kelly launched a short-lived burlesque career at the Roxy. Ann Corio and Hinda Wausau, two of burlesque's most popular beauties, paid regular visits to the Roxy.

Yet most of the Depression-era performers and their unique dances are long forgotten; examples include Chicago's Marion Morgan with her machine gun dance, Dorothy Wahl and the black panther dance, Hilda Allison's voodoo torture dance and, perhaps the most creative of all, Molly Manor and the dance of the frozen fruit basket.

After concluding her striptease act, Princess Yvonne used "mental telepathy" to read the minds of Roxy audience members. Gypsies danced in costumes constructed from an old drop curtain once used at the nearby Bandbox nightclub. As a vaudeville entertainer, Estelle Montillo balanced furniture on her head.

Plain Dealer critic Glenn C. Pullen integrated his sardonic commentary into reviews of the stage shows. He noted exotic dancer Laverne "would be a Mae West double if she wore more clothes." Reviewing a Mother's Day show, Pullen observed, "It takes a lot of imagination to find any connection between Nora Ford's Mother's Day dance and mothers. If her mother saw her discarding her garments all over the stage, she would be sent to bed without any supper." He reported that Della Carroll, who advertised herself as a princess, "demonstrated a disrobing technique never learned in Buckingham Palace." When Cleveland hosted a large convention, Pullen predicted "conventioneers to the city will remember Moana Leslie's 'Bridal Veil Strip' long after the conference is forgotten." During this period, the Roxy adopted the slogan "bring the ladies—but not the kiddies."

While newspaper critics supplied their readers with reviews and critiques, the Roxy utilized another source to gain an understanding of the shows' quality. Every Friday afternoon, eighty-year-old Isabel Kane visited the theater to view the new show and offer management advice on what worked well and what needed improvement. Decades earlier, Isabel (the former Bijou Russell) had been a performer supporting some of the biggest acts in vaudeville: George M. Cohan, Pat Rooney Jr., Trixie Friganza and others.

In the late 1930s, the Roxy incorporated second-run films (but not of an adults-only nature) into burlesque programs to create longer shows that reduced the number of live performances from five to four per day. During a short period in 1938, the theater eliminated stage performances completely to concentrate on movie attractions. The film *Miracle of Life* presented a detailed account of the birth of a child, and critics described the obscure *Sex and Love Madness* merely as a "sex film." By the end of the year, burlesque combined with second-run films staged a strong comeback. The format continued into 1945, when movies disappeared and entertainers reverted to the demanding five-a-day (six on Saturdays) performance schedule.

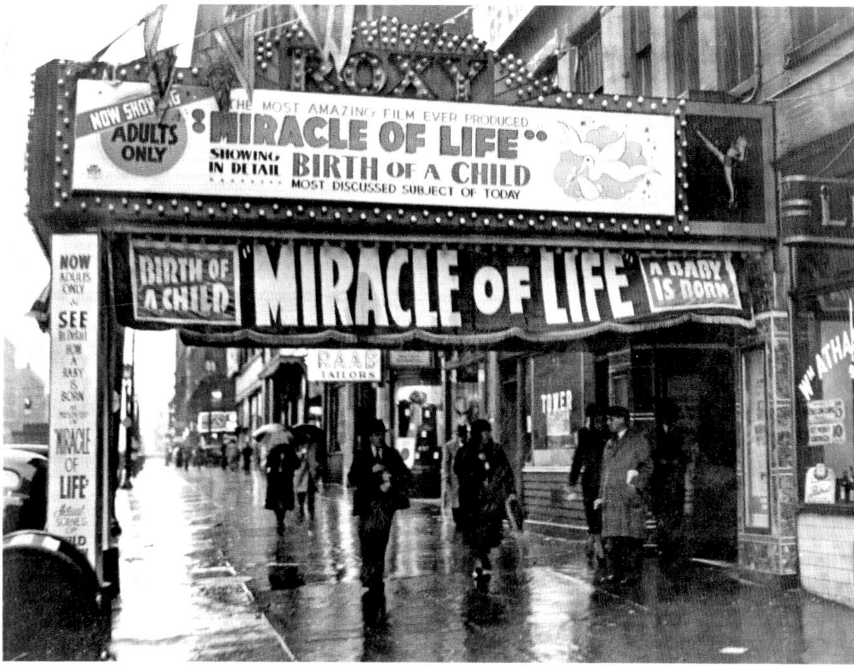

The Roxy returned to its movie roots in 1938 with the showing of *Miracle of Life*. *Courtesy of Special Collections, Michael Schwartz Library, Cleveland State University.*

In the late 1930s and early 1940s, the Roxy's golden age for showcasing new talent, Red Buttons (a later television comic and Academy Award–winning dramatic actor) and Tony Award winner Robert Alda refined their talents on the tiny East Ninth Street stage. Alda later recalled dining at the nearby Chef Hector Café because "I was so broke that I usually lived on spaghetti." Roxy performers also included upcoming television personalities Phil Silvers and Pinky Lee. Joe DeRita, a reoccurring Roxy guest, turned to films in the 1940s and 1950s and then joined the Three Stooges.

Veteran burlesque performers Joe Yule and Mickey Katz also graced the Roxy stage. Yule, the father of Mickey Rooney, appeared in movies from 1939 until he died in 1950. Katz (the father of Joel Grey and grandfather of Jennifer Grey) played in orchestras at Cleveland's Loew's State, RKO Palace, Park Theater, Golden Pheasant Restaurant, Alpine Village Nightclub, Manger Hotel and Goodtime cruise ship. Katz later worked with Spike Jones and as a recording artist and club performer.

In 1953, early television superstar Jerry Lester, performing at the Sky-Way Lounge, noticed the Roxy had booked his old friend Harry Lifty.

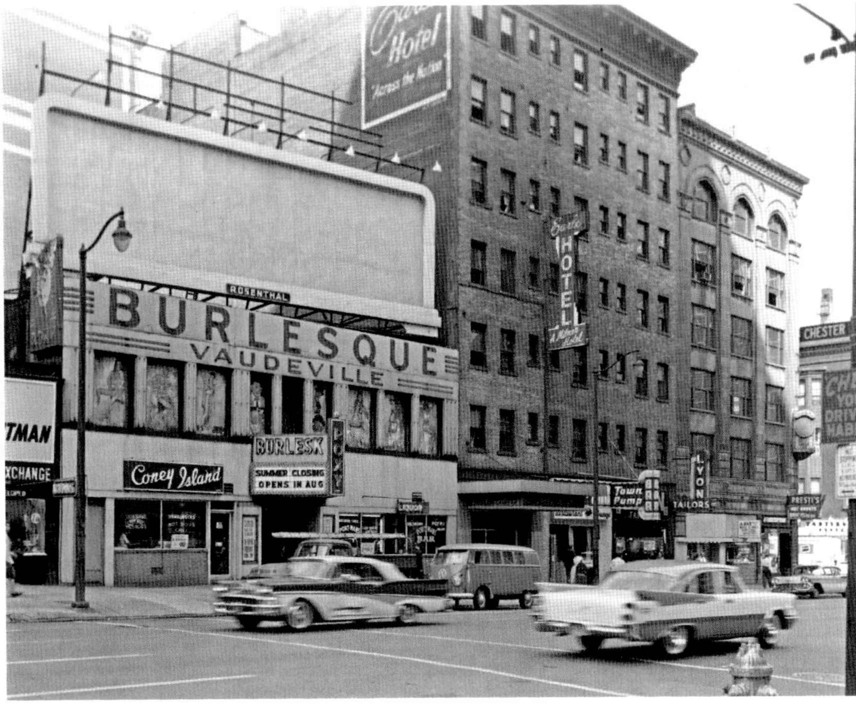

In the 1950s, the Roxy continued in operation as the last remaining Cleveland burlesque theater. *Courtesy of Cleveland Public Library, Photograph Collection.*

Lester delighted the burlesque audience by climbing onto the Roxy stage to exchange a few jokes with Lifty.

From the 1950s into the mid-1960s, Roxy patrons relished the bumps and grinds of Tempest Storm, Blaze Starr, Justa Dream, Irma the Body, Cupcake Cassidy, Sally the Shape, Naughty Valetta, White Fury and her Twin 44's and hundreds of other strippers. Superstar Tempest Storm's traveling wardrobe included ten negligees, each composed of twenty-five yards of silk.

In the mid-1950s, films briefly returned to the Roxy when some of the era's most successful strippers displayed their routines in a series of movies, among them *Teaserama* (Tempest Storm), *Striporama* (Lili St. Cyr and Georgia Southern) and *Buxom Beauties* (Tempest Storm, Lili St. Cyr and Blaze Starr).

Beginning in 1964, the Roxy added adult movies to the live burlesque programs. Roxy patrons viewed silver-screen classics such as *My Bare Lady*, *The Lullaby of Bareland*, *Nature Family Robinson* and *Career Girls at a Nature Camp*. As films progressed from adults-only to triple-X rated, audiences became substantially tougher. In 1971, following one evening's final performance, thieves hid in the theater and later carried away a set of double X–rated movies and the film projectors. The next year, again following the Roxy's closing for the day, four sticks of dynamite fastened to the basement ceiling ripped a four- by five-foot hole though the lobby floor. Although police never conclusively established the motive, many believed the Roxy's format switch to all-male X-rated movies triggered the explosion. By this time, live entertainment had disappeared.

In 1973 and 1974, Roxy manager Thomas H. Flynn endured frequent arrests while defending Clevelanders' rights to view obscene movies. His detainments started during the Roxy's Ohio premiere of *Deep Throat*. Police raided the theater, seized the film and arrested Flynn, who, within an hour, had posted bond and reopened the Roxy with a second print of the film. Vice squad members promptly repeated the raid, seize and arrest sequence. The next day, the exercise reoccurred when Flynn obtained a third print of the controversial film. Along with front-page publicity, the three raids directly earned extra box-office receipts. Since the vice squad had not secured search warrants, Flynn charged the officers the steep five-dollar admission (a substantial increase over the usual three-dollar charge) every time they entered the theater in their attempt to close it down.

Following *Deep Throat*, Flynn's arrests took place in such rapid succession that a judge bundled together four separate obscenity cases in one hearing. Flynn paid a $300 fine and incurred a one-year probation sentence for his exhibition of *The Devil in Miss Jones*, *It Happened in Hollywood*, *Behind the Green Door* and *Memories within Miss Aggie*.

By the time the Roxy exhibited *Teen-Age Cheerleaders*, courts had ruled that police could only confiscate one copy of a film for use as evidence. While detectives removed a film reel from one projector, Flynn placed the succeeding reel, obtained from a second copy of the movie, onto another projector; the audience experienced no interruption even though the police exited with a copy of the film. Expressing little irritation with the law, Flynn commented on his latest arrest: "Every time they confiscate a film, my business increases because people find out it's a dirty movie."

In 1975, for the first time in four years, live strippers returned, while pornographic movies again supplemented the performances. The following year, the Roxy posted frequent sold-out signs for amateur strippers from local colleges. But on November 6, 1977, four decades of burlesque entertainment or adult film programming ended as the Roxy closed to make way for construction of a new office building. On its final day, the theater exhibited two X-rated movies, *Innocent Girls* and *Company Hits*.

Chapter 7

THE PRISCILLA/BANDBOX/ LITTLE THEATER

Debuting in 1910 near the northeast corner of East Ninth Street and Chester Avenue, the 1,200-seat Priscilla Theater attracted immediate (and often unfavorable) attention by installing an outdoor electric sign proclaiming PRISCILLA in five-foot letters while using colored lights to enhance background images of a trapeze performer, juggler and dancing chorus girl. The Priscilla specialized in small-time vaudeville, usually not even bothering to identify the names of performers in the theater's advertisements. A troupe of baboons once composed the headline act.

Mimicking many of the period's vaudeville theaters, the Priscilla integrated movies into its lineup of attractions. The innovative *Cleveland Monthly* offered "a motion picture record of local events." Soon after, the Priscilla devoted Sundays entirely to movies. In 1917, the theater combined vaudeville with "photo dramas" consisting of short comedies, westerns, dramas, cartoons and newsreels. Accompanied by a full orchestra, full-length movies made an appearance in the summer of 1918. But the Priscilla never graduated into a major movie theater and eventually abandoned films altogether to concentrate on girlie shows (*Carnival of Nude Models*, *Frisco Shimmy Dancers*, *Jazz Babies*, *Whiz Bang Girls* and numerous similar productions). Reviewing a weekly stage show, a *Plain Dealer* critic accurately summed up the entire history of the theater: "There are no particular high spots on the Priscilla bill this week, but for all that, it's right good entertainment."

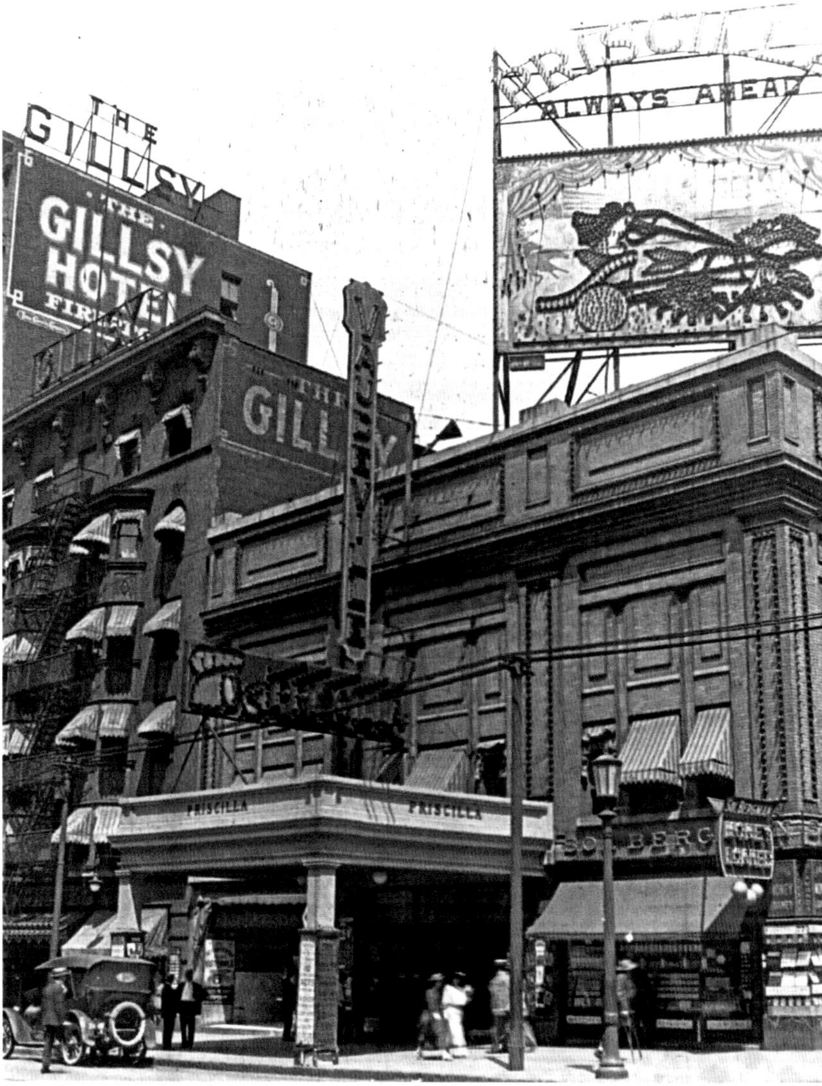

A large electric sign (top right), on East Ninth Street atop the Priscilla Theater, created attention and controversy. *Courtesy of Cleveland Public Library, Photograph Collection.*

In 1922, the Bandbox nightclub, decorated in gaudy red banners and tinsel trimmings, replaced the Priscilla. Although the Bandbox sometimes exhibited films of boxing matches, the club demonstrated little interest in movies expect for a peculiar showing of *Rolling Down to Rio with Secretary of State Hughes*, a film depicting navy life aboard the battleship *Maryland.*

When the Empire Theater (located a few blocks south on East Ninth Street) closed for the 1923 summer break, the theater's treasurer used his wife's influence (she produced chorus numbers for the Bandbox) to obtain summer employment in a nightclub revue. Frozen with fear during his stage debut, he fainted in front of the audience. Fortunately, Buddy Abbott cured his stage fright before becoming the famous comedy partner of Lou Costello.

One week after the Bandbox closed in 1927, a short-lived but significant movie house replaced the club. According to the owners, the mission of the Little Theater of the Movies, Cleveland's first art theater, was the exhibition of "ultra-artistic and modernistic movies which, because of their limited appeal, are never shown in commercial movie houses." As one example, the theater presented *Rustic Romance*, "a tragic-comedy in which fowls and animals have the leading roles." The bookings, primarily from Russia, Germany, France and Italy, also featured a limited number of American offerings. A three-piece orchestra, composed of a piano, violin and cello, provided accompaniment for the films. In addition to enjoying the off-beat movies, Cleveland's intelligentsia gathered in the lounge to partake of two additional benefits: smoking free cigarettes and consuming complimentary soft drinks.

Failing as an art house after only a few months, the theater changed its name to the Little Theater and presented live plays. Following nine weeks of Shakespearean productions, the showplace experimented with new dramas along with staging trusty revivals. The theater presented a six-week run of French dramatist Edouard Bourdet's *The Captive*, one of the first productions of the work in the United States.

On May 20, 1928, the Little Theater staged the world premiere of playwright Patrick Kearney's adaption of Sinclair Lewis's novel *Elmer Gantry*. Even prior to the first performance, the Cleveland Federation of Churches deemed the production "sacrilegious and way beyond the boundaries of common decency." The organization strongly suggested that the city ban every performance. Edwin D. Barry, Cleveland's safety director, asked Kearney if Gantry had ever been convicted of any of his scandalous affairs and appeared confused when the playwright explained the novel and his adaptation consisted only of fictional characters. Barry warned Kearney that he would attend the opening performance and arrest him and the cast if the play violated Cleveland's laws against licentious and blasphemous stage presentations.

After the play's debut, Barry and a select blue-ribbon panel of four censors compared notes while standing in front of a vacant store on East Ninth Street.

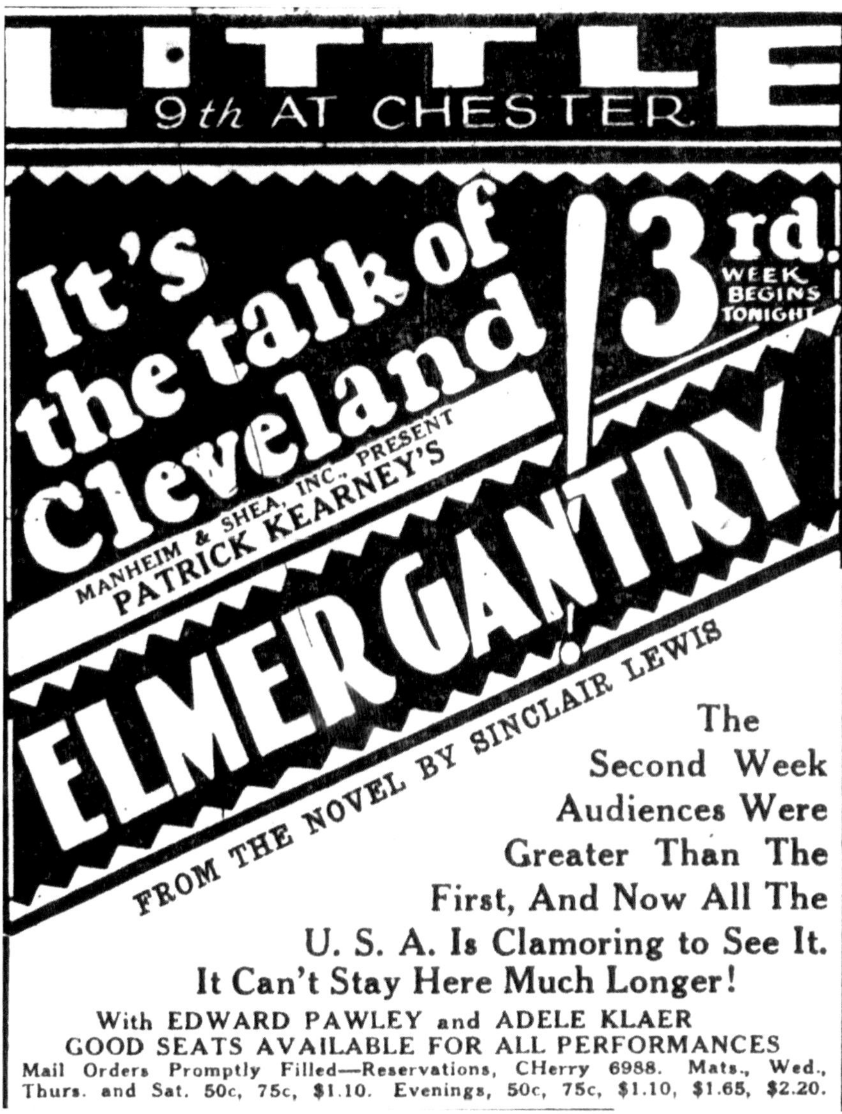

The stage version of *Elmer Gantry* received its world premiere at the Little Theater. *Courtesy of the* Plain Dealer.

The group unearthed no serious objections and merely recommended toning down three of the love scenes. Nevertheless, the attempted ban generated front-page publicity, resulting in sold-out performances. Large crowds at the box office often forced pedestrians traveling on busy East Ninth Street to walk into the street while passing the theater.

Even after gaining the city's approval, *Elmer Gantry* faced another significant hurdle. Lead actress Regina Wallace, chosen from more than two hundred performers who auditioned for the part, decided after her initial performance that she did not like the character and withdrew from the show. A replacement, on stage after less than twenty-four hours' notice, functioned admirably even while holding the script in her hand during her first appearance. Meanwhile, Kearney implemented many revisions to his script, including a completely rewritten third act. Following a three-week run at the Little Theater, *Elmer Gantry* moved to the uptown Alhambra Theater for another two weeks prior to its successful New York City debut.

The Little Theater remained in existence for about one year. In 1928, the Empress burlesque house, which opened on Christmas Day, shut down within a month. An office building replaced the theater.

Chapter 8

THE MILES/CARTER THEATER

In 1913, the growing East Ninth Street entertainment district added the Miles Theater, a hybrid playhouse presenting two daily marathon five-hour programs consisting of a first-run movie and small-time vaudeville. Customers entered the two-thousand-seat playhouse from either East Ninth Street or Huron Road. At peak times, male employees assisted female patrons in navigating through long ticket lines, shielding the ladies from the inevitable and disagreeable pushing and shoving.

The theater's attractive Louis XIV–style interior featured a cohesive design from its chairs and tables to the proscenium arch and masonry embellishing the box seats. Velour curtains, with deep gold galloons, decorated boxes containing upholstered mahogany chairs. Murals portraying French castles and garden scenes pervaded the theater, whose prevailing colors were ivory, gray, rose and gold, accented with a soft-green velvet carpet.

The *Plain Dealer* reported that the Miles would play only high-class movies, with "none of the blood-curdling pictures that send youngsters out in the park shrubbery to hold up the hapless passerby." Yet in its first year of operation, *The Drug Terror* sensationally depicted underworld activities with "authentic scenes and incidents" highlighting the evils of cocaine. By 1914, movies had completely replaced vaudeville on Sundays.

In 1923, the Columbia Burlesque Circuit assumed control of the Miles, renaming it the Columbia Theater. During its burlesque period, the theater hosted comedian Joe Yule and jazz musician Eddie Heywood Sr., whose son would later record the 1950s pop hits "Canadian Sunset" and "Soft Summer

Breeze." Charleston and Black Bottom contests attracted spirited audiences throughout the 1920s. The Columbia closed after staging seven years of entertaining yet nondescript burlesque shows. On the final day of operation, management presented a free pair of silk stockings to every female patron.

As the Great Lakes Theater, the old Miles showcased double-feature movie bills from mid-1930 into 1932. In 1933, the showplace became the Carter, its fourth identity, and continued the movie format with an "adults-only" designation often accompanying the films. After two years, the theater briefly reverted back to its original name and again presented vaudeville and movie combinations. In the mid-1930s, the playhouse again changed formats as it functioned as the Federal Theater, producing plays as a WPA project. An admission of $0.25 ($0.50 for reserved seats) helped the government pay actors' wages of between $93 and $103 per month. The offerings included *Triple-A Plowed Under*, a play concerned with the rise and fall of government farm bills, and *The First Legion*, which documented spiritual agonies during the Depression. Government

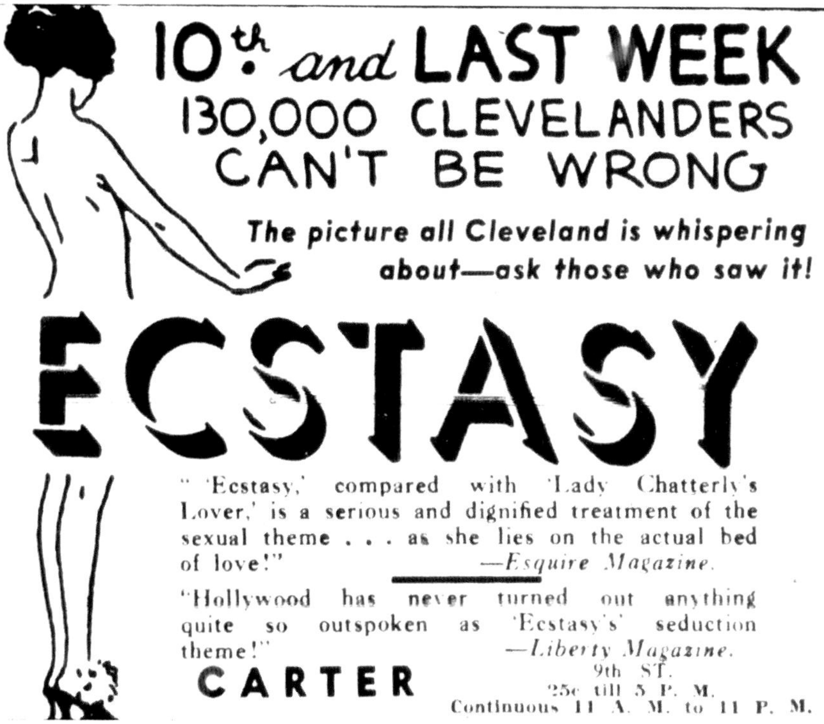

Following a ten-week run at the Carter Theater, Cleveland movie houses continued to book *Ecstasy* for the next ten years. *Courtesy of the* Plain Dealer.

officials in Washington, D.C., temporarily closed the theater, claiming it needed reorganization, but the Federal never reopened.

Three years of adult-themed movies followed the Carter's 1936 reopening. In 1937, the ten-week run of *Ecstasy*, a Czech film, created a sensation. Two years earlier, United States censors had banned the film from the entire country, believing "it would be a great detriment to American morals." The film's highlights included sixteen-year-old Hedy Kiesler (later known as Hedy Lamarr) swimming in the nude and frolicking naked through the countryside. Even worse, although only showing the actors' faces, the movie hinted at sexual intercourse and female orgasm. Following its engagement at the Carter, *Ecstasy* generated long runs for years in numerous theaters throughout the city. In 1943, the film even played at the prestigious Hanna Theater, where midnight showings accommodated war workers.

Other Carter film hits included *10 Days in a Nudist Camp* (combined with an in-person visit from "Miss Sunshine") and three-week runs of *Slaves in Bondage* (a film concerned with exploitation of prostitutes), *Forbidden Adventure* (a movie that depicted monkey worshipers) and *Marijuana: The Weed with Roots in Hell.*

Between 1939 and 1959, the Carter offered mostly conventional second-run double features with heavy measures of westerns and crime thrillers. In

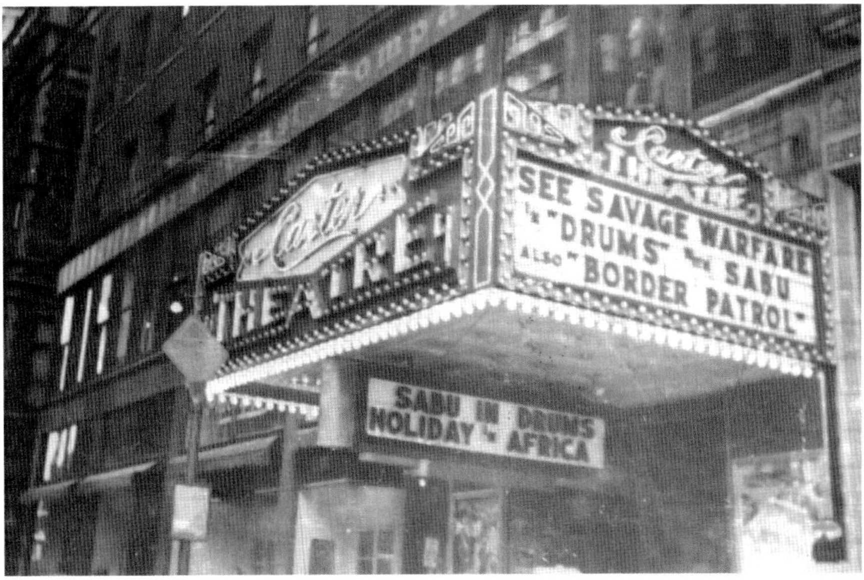

In 1948, the Carter Theater exhibited one of its typical double-feature bookings. *Courtesy of Cleveland Public Library, Literature Department.*

1944, sparks drawn into a theater intake fan from a burning rubbish pile, situated in an adjacent alley, ignited a fire that required evacuation of all twelve of the theater's customers.

In the 1950s, the theater remained open twenty-four hours a day, transforming itself into a combination movie playhouse and homeless shelter. The *Plain Dealer* portrayed the Carter as "a flophouse with a soundtrack." The theater closed on May 31, 1959, when the auditorium's roof collapsed during a showing of the triple feature *Land of the Pharaohs*, *Helen of Troy* and *Siege of Red River*. No injuries occurred since the Carter stood completely devoid of patrons at the time of the roof mishap.

Chapter 9

THE STANDARD AND STRAND THEATERS

As the popularity, length and price of movies all increased, a new generation of larger and more comfortable theaters superseded the outmoded nickelodeons. The Standard (1914) and Strand (1915) Theaters, both located near the intersection of Prospect Avenue and East Ninth Street, epitomized this growing trend.

Prior to the Standard Theater's opening, the owners completed several exploratory trips to New York City to investigate the latest ideas in movie theater design and decoration. They promised the Standard would offer "every modern feature for comfort and beauty." On June 12, 1914, the seven-hundred-seat Standard debuted as the city's largest playhouse devoted strictly to movies. Constructed at the rear of a nine-year-old office building, the venue fronted Prospect Avenue, one block west of East Ninth Street. The lobby, attractively festooned with trellis work surrounded by thousands of artificial flowers, generated a stunning impression. Creamy white walls with blue panels, each edged in silver, and seats upholstered in leather beautified the auditorium.

First-run film offerings initially changed three times each week, but feature-length movies composed only part of the Standard's attraction to filmgoers. Shortly after its opening, the theater launched the first Cleveland showing of *The Million Dollar Mystery*, an intriguing twenty-three-episode serial shown simultaneously in theaters across the country and serialized in more than two hundred newspapers, including the *Plain Dealer*'s Sunday magazine. The producers intentionally did not complete the final chapter, asking movie fans to submit, in fewer than one hundred words, their suggestions for the serial's conclusion. The best entry would win $10,000; promotional advertising promised "$10,000 for 100 words." Unfortunately, the Standard did not produce the winning entry.

Only a year after its opening, the Standard became Cleveland's first theater to exhibit movies (other than special attractions) for an entire week. Joseph Grossman, the theater manager, proudly announced Cleveland's arrival as a "full-week-run city," taking its place with New York, Chicago, Los Angeles and Detroit. Pessimistic friends advised Grossman he would fail within thirty days. But the Standard obtained first-run engagements of Theda Bara movies (about five per year) when the vamp reigned as the biggest box-office draw in the country. Prior to most performances, the Standard required police assistance to regulate sidewalk congestion created by Bara's fervent fans.

Never taking large audiences for granted, Grossman devised popular contests to generate interest in the theater's movies. In 1918, he created a lip reading contest with the goal of identifying all the words spoken by William S. Hart in the final reel of *The Bargain*. Patrons mailed in their lists hoping to claim a cash prize of ten dollars, five dollars or three dollars to be awarded to the three patrons submitting the largest number of authenticated words. One contestant unsuccessfully claimed the ten-dollar first prize by submitting a paperback version of a dictionary; he maintained that all the words spoken by Hart would be found in the book.

In 1920, the Standard encouraged viewers of *A Modern Salome* to compose an essay of no more than two hundred words explaining the major lesson taught by the film's story. The winner received fifty dollars, while other contestants won passes to the theater. In fact, everyone submitting an entry received at least one pair of tickets.

In 1921, less than five years after the Standard's supposedly risky experiment of booking full-week movies, a sensational promotion propelled *Shipwrecked Among the Cannibals* into a three-week engagement. Advertising claimed, "One overnight bag would carry the entire wardrobe of 5,000 cannibals." The Standard placed notices in Cleveland's newspapers apologizing if, due to the immense crowds, any patron had his or her clothing torn or disarranged and promised the manager would make a full settlement for damages. Requiring less dramatic publicity, that same year Priscilla Dean and Lon Chaney in *Outside the Law* also generated a fine three-week run.

Competition from Playhouse Square soon relegated the Standard to second-run status. Beginning in 1924, the theater changed films five times each week. A mere decade after its 1914 opening, owners contemplated razing the theater to reconfigure its space for commercial purposes. But the Standard received a new lease on its life that lasted another sixty-eight years.

During the 1930s and 1940s, the theater booked second-run double features with a heavy emphasis on Randolph Scott westerns. In 1949, the Standard briefly promised "big-time burlesque" as live musical follies plus a double-feature movie program, composed of unidentified movies, became the bill of fare.

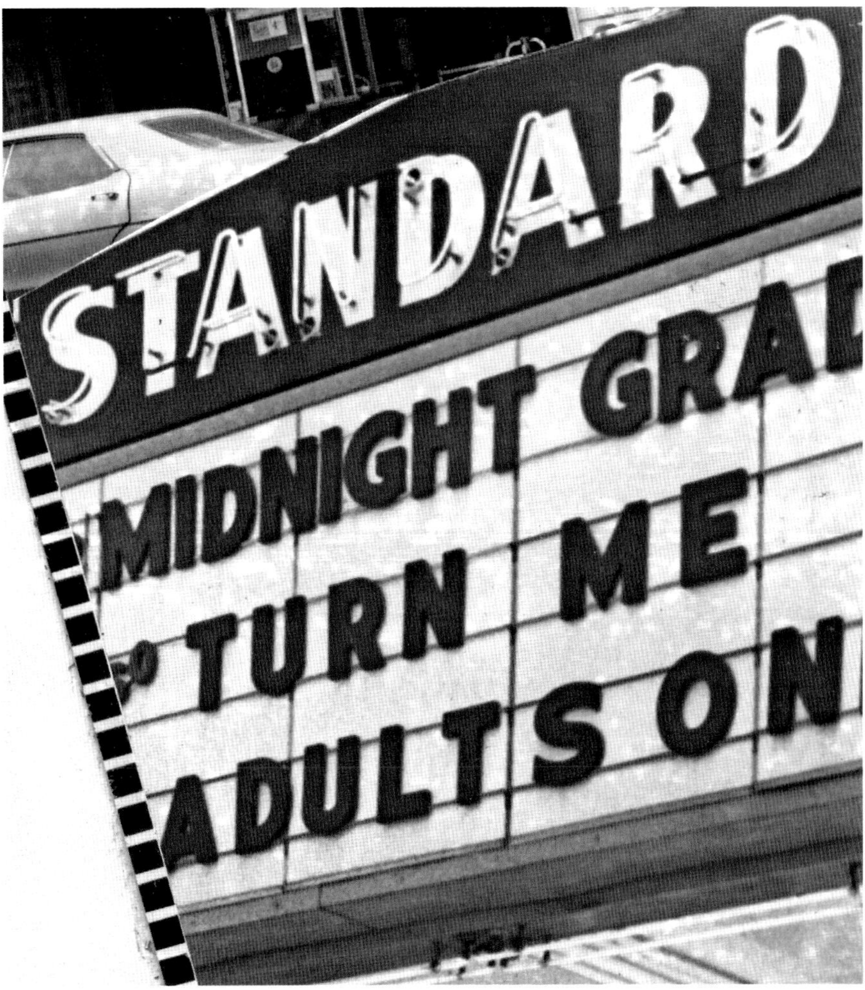

By the late 1950s, the Standard had already started its exhibition of soft-porn films. *Courtesy of Cleveland Public Library, Photograph Collection.*

In the early 1950s, the Standard uncovered a small market for subtitled Czech and German movies. But by the end of the decade, the theater had shifted to much spicier film attractions. In 1959, an assistant police prosecutor and two members of the downtown vice squad viewed two soft-porno films (*Lovers Incorporated* and *The Lonely Sex*) and allowed their continuation only when the Standard agreed to cut a few seconds from the movies. Six years later, Peter Bellamy, in reviewing the Danish film *Days of Pleasure, Nights of Madness*, noted, "If all the movies were as tasteless as this one, sex and sin would go out of style." The critic claimed the color cartoon marked the high spot of the evening's entertainment.

As nudity and sex pervaded mainstream films in the late 1960s, the Standard turned to hard-core pornographic movies and, in 1976, changed its name to the Lido Theater. Tattered and uncomfortable seats, a threadbare lobby and poor interior and exterior lighting now characterized the once-beautiful theater. After a six-year existence, the Lido closed in 1982, the last of Cleveland's downtown porno theaters.

Changing its name back to the Standard, the theater reopened as a replacement for the demolished Hippodrome. From the Hipp's demise on May 1, 1980, to the Standard's rebirth on June 11, 1982, no mainstream movie house operated in downtown Cleveland for the first time since the nickelodeon days. The refurbished Standard reopened primarily to exhibit action and horror movies, with its principal patrons consisting of businessman intent on viewing two hours of murder and mayhem. Martial arts films joined the mix in 1983; the following year, teenagers swarmed the theater to view *Breakin'*, a break-dance film.

In 1995, the Standard closed to make way for a 450-seat playhouse. Completed in 1997, the Art Deco theater had been built to attract a comedy club and restaurant, but it has never been occupied.

On November 6, 1915, the exquisite Strand Theater, a neighbor of the Standard, debuted on the main floor of the Erie Building located on the southeast corner of East Ninth Street and Prospect Avenue. Owners of the 660-seat theater called it "the house beautiful." Ivory lattice frames enclosed beautiful mural paintings delicately shaded by soft white, green, red or blue lighting. The combinations of color accents changed nightly. After journeying through a long and wide lobby, patrons entered an auditorium lighted by white Japanese lanterns. Ornamental plaster, cornices and molding pervaded the showplace while stars twinkled from the ceiling.

The Strand exhibited first-run movies until the opening of the Playhouse Square theaters. Experiencing declining attendance as a second-run theater,

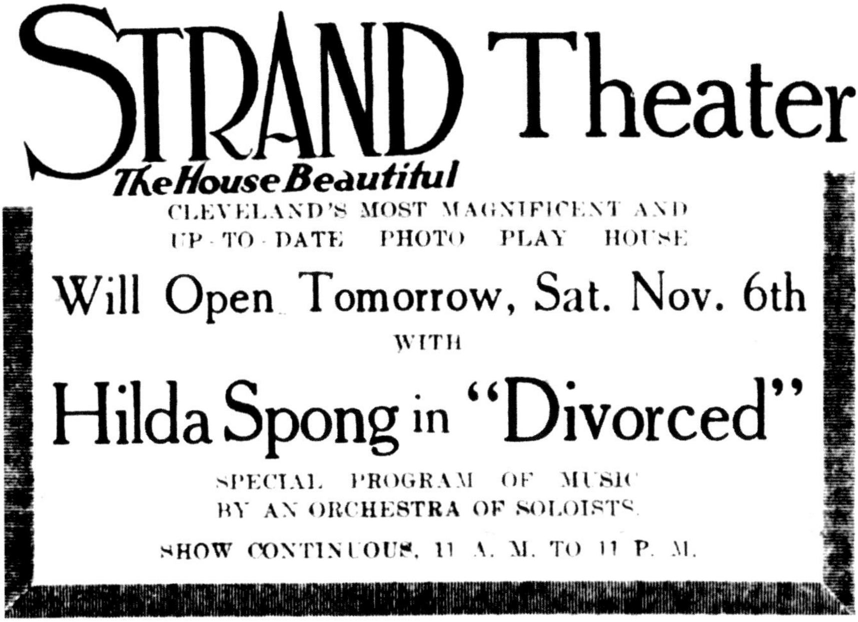

In 1915, the Strand Theater debuted to great fanfare. *Courtesy of the* Plain Dealer.

the Strand turned to Russian and German movies along with American B movies such as *Assassin of Youth* (exploiting the dangerous effects of smoking marijuana) and *Mars Attacks the World* (a compilation of previously shown Flash Gordon serial episodes). In 1939, the theater combined *Sins of Love* (shown two years earlier at the neighboring Carter Theater) with *False Shame* (an obscure twelve-year-old German import) and an on-stage appearance by Radio's Friendly Advisor—a man of a thousand experiences. Shortly after this odd triple feature, the twenty-five-year-old theater closed to accommodate commercial space.

Chapter 10

THE MALL AND LOWER MALL THEATERS

The tiny three-hundred-seat Mall Theater, located on Superior Avenue near Public Square, debuted in 1909. Manager Louis Becht probably never imagined that performing his administrative duties at the theater would entail three arrests. First, Cleveland police held Becht in custody on a charge of unlawful exhibition of films of the Jack Johnson v. James Jackson Jeffries 1910 boxing match, the fight that inspired the Broadway play and movie *The Great White Hope*. Becht incurred his second and third detentions for violating Cleveland mayor Newton D. Baker's ban of all movies depicting any type of crime. Acting as his own one-man board of censors, Baker stated, "I will not tolerate the showing of films that tend to degrade instead of elevate." Becht's second arrest involved presenting *The Adventures of Lieutenant Petrosino*, an account of a real-life New York City detective's fight against organized crime. The manager's final police encounter occurred when a character in a film fired a pistol.

Seven years after the Mall's opening, a pair of playhouses replaced the relatively new theater. Taking advantage of the decline in elevation between Euclid and Superior Avenues, a creative architect designed a duplex movie house with one theater situated on top of the other. From Superior Avenue, patrons entered the six-hundred-seat Lower Mall Theater, located just two doors east from the former Mall Theater. The larger nine-hundred-seat Upper Mall Theater, fronting Euclid Avenue, even included a balcony.

The Upper Mall booked five-reel, first-run movies starring some of the biggest box-office attractions of the period: Douglas Fairbanks, Billie

Burke, Francis X. Bushman, William S. Hart and others. The Superior Mall specialized in one- and two-reel films, including Keystone Cop comedies, the adventures of Mutt and Jeff, cartoons, travelogues, newsreels, short subjects and O. Henry stories. Although the two theaters exhibited different films, one fifteen-cent ticket could be used at either the Euclid or Superior Avenue theater, or at both. Patrons wishing to view the films at both theaters merely walked up (or down) a marble staircase.

The Upper Mall and Lower Mall are often cited as the first duplex theater in the nation. Yet the short-lived Oxford Theater, debuting four years earlier and a few blocks to the west on Ontario Street, actually introduced the twin cinema concept not only to Cleveland but also, according to the theater's manager, to the entire country. A fireproof curtain dividing the Oxford auditorium allowed the presentation of two different movies at the same time. One admission charge covered both films.

By 1919, the Loew's chain had purchased the Upper Mall and Lower Mall Theaters and exhibited the same movie in both venues. During the showing of Alice Brady in *The Red Head*, Loew's admitted all redheaded females free of charge and awarded "the reddest of the redheads" a five-dollar prize. The two theaters closed briefly during the Depression.

In 1945, the Lower Mall became a foreign movie house, exhibiting films from England, Italy, France, Sweden, Germany, Russia and Japan. On December 26, 1946, Laurence Olivier's classic British import *Henry V* began a seven-week, reserved-seat, road-show engagement at a top price of $2.50. One Olivier fan, very averse to loud noises, inquired if the film contained any scenes involving guns. When informed that bows and arrows were the major weapons in the time of Henry V, she asked if the arrows created much racket. The film returned about a year later for an encore two-week road-show presentation.

In 1947, the downtown Lower Mall and uptown University Theater shared an exclusive eight-week first-run showing of *The Best Years of Our Lives*. Combined, the two theaters contained about 1,600 seats, less than half the capacity of the Hippodrome, State or Palace Theaters. But smaller studios, such as Samuel Goldwyn, experimented with exhibiting films in smaller theaters to create longer runs coupled with higher admission prices.

In the late 1940s and early 1950s, the Lower Mall capitalized on a growing interest in movies imported from Italy by staging a ten-week run of *Paisan* and an eleven-week showing of *Bitter Rice* (moved to the downtown Esquire Theater for a twelfth week). A seven-week road-show presentation of *Cyrano*, an eight-week engagement of the French melodrama *The Sinners*

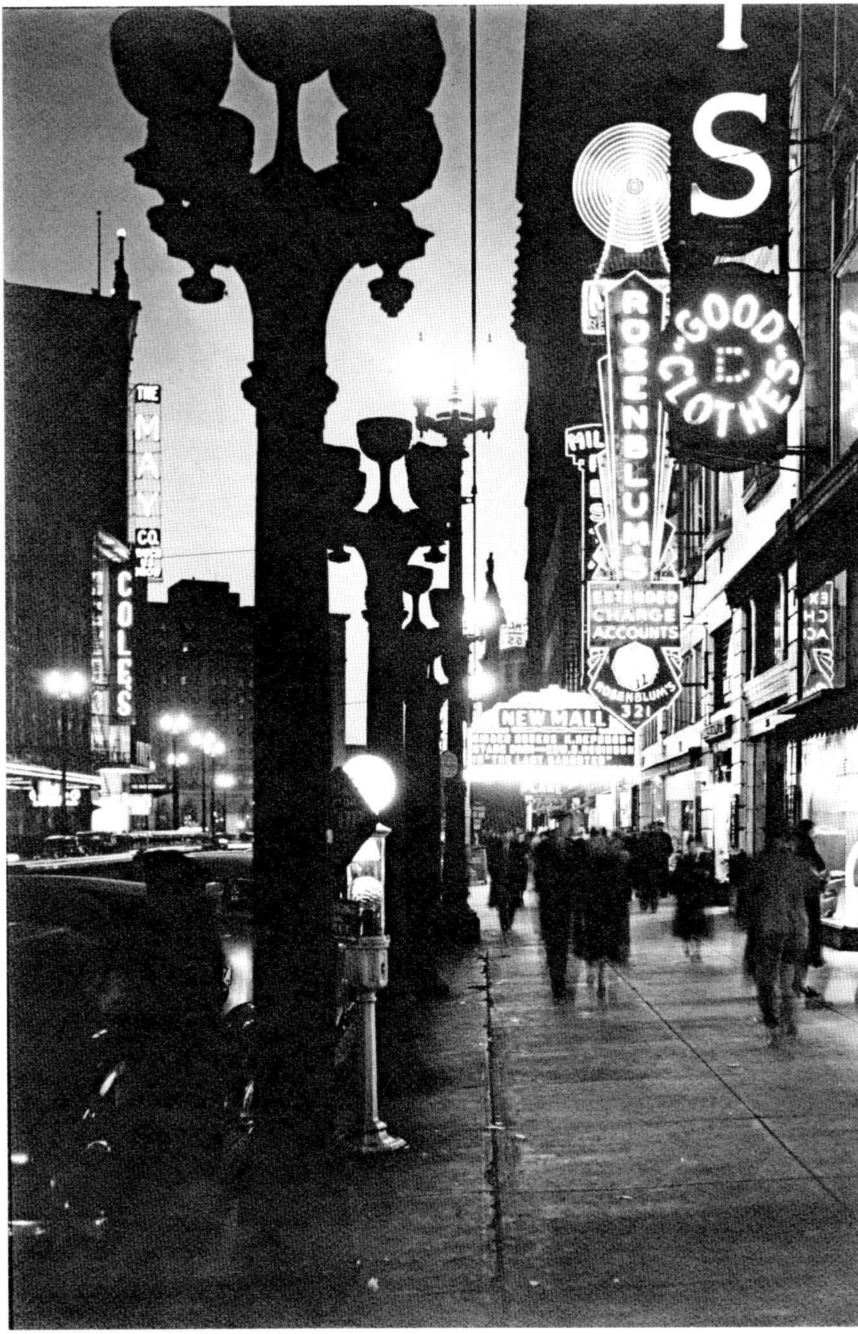

In March 1938, the Upper Mall Theater seamlessly blended in with storefronts on lower Euclid Avenue. *Courtesy of Cleveland Public Library, Photograph Collection.*

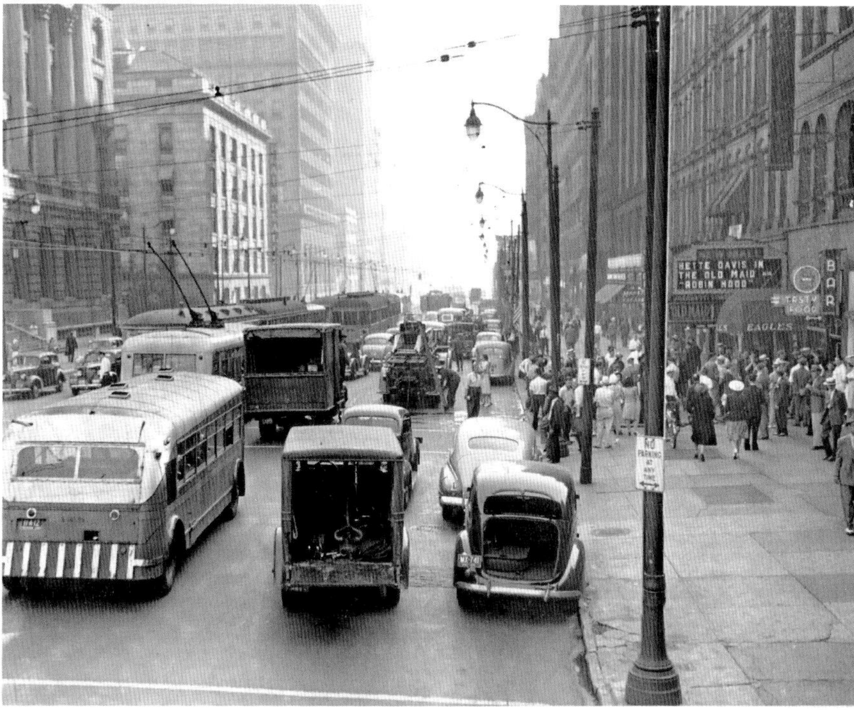

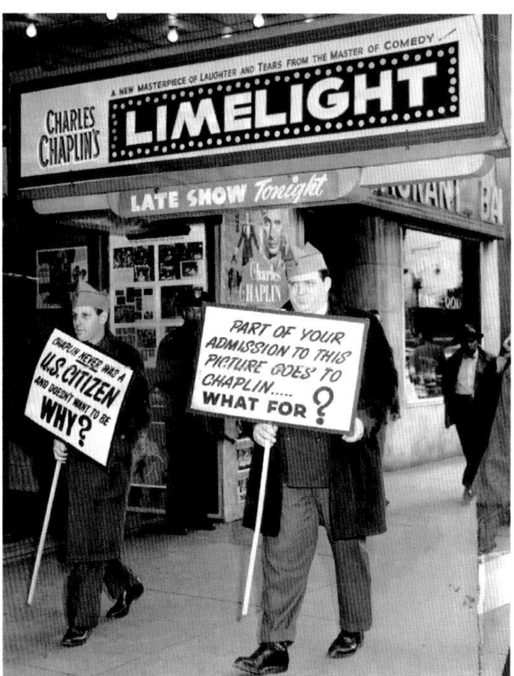

Above: Photographed in the 1940s, the Lower Mall (right) resided on busy Superior Avenue. *Courtesy of Special Collections, Michael Schwartz Library, Cleveland State University.*

Left: In 1953, during the four-week run of *Limelight*, American Legion members picketed the Lower Mall Theater in protest of Charlie Chaplin's perceived un-American activities. *Courtesy of Special Collections, Michael Schwartz Library, Cleveland State University.*

and extended first-run showings of Walt Disney's "true-life adventure" films *The Living Desert* and *The Vanishing Prairie* all assisted in creating a very successful period for the theater. Yet in the 1950s, the Lower Mall faced strong competition from four new rivals: the Heights Art Theater, the Continental Art Theater and the Cedar Lee and Colony Theaters.

In mid-1953, as a result of this new competition, the Lower Mall supplemented its art movie bookings with conventional second-run double features, often showing the same films as its sister Upper Mall Theater. In 1954, the Lower Mall presented an eleven-week second-run showing of William Holden's naughty film *The Moon Is Blue* following its first-run engagement at the Hippodrome.

On August 31, 1960, both the Upper and Lower Mall Theaters closed. The Lower Mall, soon to be converted into a parking garage, ended its existence with the double feature *Naked Road* and *Prime Time*. The Upper Mall concluded with *Man on a String* and *The Young Land* prior to its conversion into about ten thousand square feet of office space used to double the size of the Women's Federal Savings and Loan office.

Chapter 11

THE STILLMAN THEATER

The 1916 debut of the 1,800-seat Stillman Theater marked the arrival of the first true movie palace in downtown Cleveland. Patrons entered the theater, styled in Italian Renaissance motif from the Louis XVI period, through three beautiful foyers separating Euclid Avenue from the auditorium. Ornamental plaster and cameo-like medallions blended perfectly with a green and white color scheme. At the rear of the upper mezzanine, a series of specially designed smoking boxes prevented smoke and odor from escaping into the seats below. An innovative satin movie screen created a brilliance and definition new to Cleveland. Ushers dressed in dark green uniforms used converted military "swagger sticks," with lamps added to the handles, to escort patrons to their seats.

Outside, a "sidewalk automatic bulletin" advised Euclid Avenue pedestrians of the current film (feature attraction, news, cartoon, short subject, etc.) and the hour and minute of the next scheduled film. Automatic ticket-selling machines and change makers assisted in moving long lines of moviegoers into the theater. Hyman L. Spitalny's twenty-five-piece orchestra supplied the accompaniment for first-run silent films starring Rudolph Valentino, Charles Chaplin, Greta Garbo, John Gilbert, Mary Pickford, Douglas Fairbanks, John Barrymore, Harold Lloyd and numerous others.

Entrepreneur Emanuel Mandelbaum, who emigrated from Austria-Hungary to Cleveland at the age of fourteen, built the Stillman. A former cigar maker, Mandelbaum also constructed the Knickerbocker Theater on Euclid Avenue about seventy blocks east of downtown. Rumors of the

Stillman's sale surfaced within a year of its debut; potential purchasers included the foremost vaudeville, movie and legitimate theater organizations (Keith, Fox and Shubert). In 1917, the Loew's movie theater chain acquired the Stillman as its first Cleveland showplace and remained the owner until the theater closed in 1963.

Not all of the theater's excitement and intrigue took place on the movie screen. In 1918, while standing in the Stillman's ticket line, Eva Kaber and a hit man bargained over the terms for the murder of her husband; she offered $5,000 and suggested the hit man use an automobile to run over her spouse, but the two never came to a suitable agreement. Eva resorted to poisoning her husband but succeeded only in turning him into an invalid. Next, she hired two assassins to stab her husband to death, a task they successfully accomplished. Convicted of murder, she died in prison.

Although Loew's chose the State Theater to debut the majority of its most popular films, the smaller Stillman reigned as the theater of choice for many prestigious long-run films. In 1917, the Stillman staged its first road-show presentation, Cecil B. DeMille's *Joan the Woman*, a drama portraying Joan of Arc. In 1921, Rudolph Valentino's breakout film *The Four Horsemen of the Apocalypse* completed a six-week road-show engagement. During the 1920s, the Stillman booked eight other road-show movies: *The Three Musketeers*, *Scaramouche*, *The Covered Wagon*, *The White Sister*, *The Hunchback of Notre Dame*, *Secrets*, *Dorothy Vernon of Haddon Hall* and *Broadway Melody*. The majority of these films played four- to six-week engagements.

In 1928, the Stillman installed the first air conditioner in an Ohio theater. The new technology still needed considerable fine tuning, so ushers checked temperature gauges in various parts of the theater, reporting to the engineer when the cooling dropped below a reasonable comfort level.

Also in 1928, more than 250,000 people packed the theater to view Cleveland's first showing of *The Jazz Singer*, often depicted as the first talking movie. Actually, the Stillman had demonstrated Vitaphone sound films in the spring of 1927 but without financial success. Since downtown theaters showed little interest in talkies, a steady stream of Vitaphone movies played the uptown Circle Theater beginning a full year prior to *The Jazz Singer*'s debut. In addition to not inaugurating the Vitaphone revolution, the Al Jolson blockbuster utilized sound for only six songs and about two minutes of dialogue; the remainder of the eighty-nine-minute film contained standard silent footage.

As the Roaring Twenties neared their conclusion, Cleveland's business community considered Euclid Avenue frontage near East Ninth Street

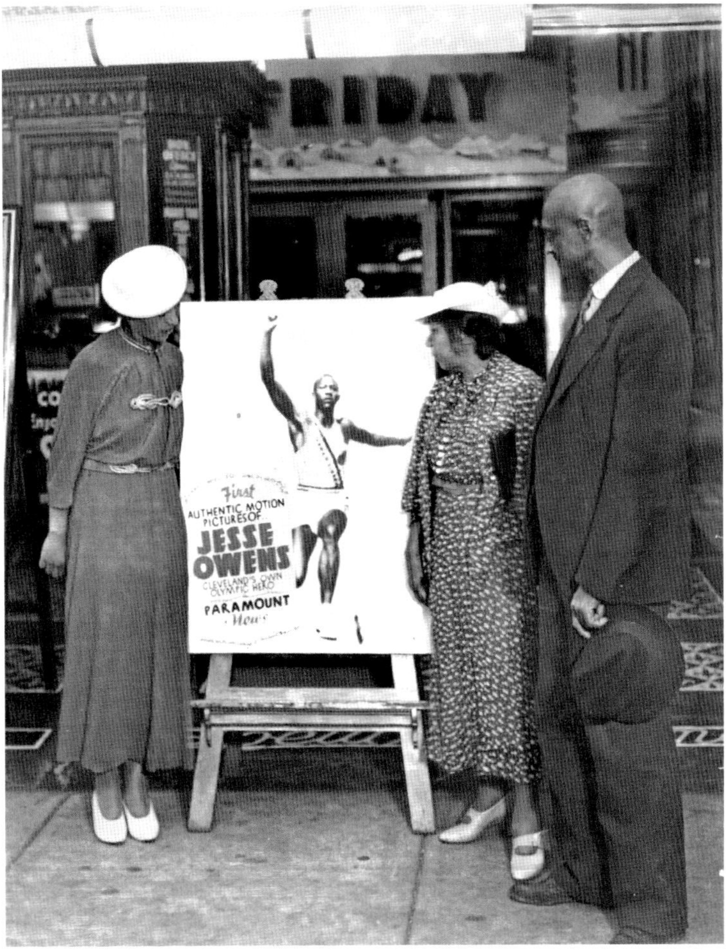

In 1936, the Stillman displayed films of Jesse Owens's remarkable Olympic performances. Owens's parents (right) visited a movie theater for the first time in their lives. To the left is Owens's wife; their union lasted forty-five years until Jesse's death. *Courtesy of Special Collections, Michael Schwartz Library, Cleveland State University.*

much too valuable to use as a theater lobby. Consequently, on August 23, 1928, Loew's announced it would close the Stillman in about three weeks to provide the adjoining Statler Hotel with additional space. In 1963, following a thirty-five-year delay, Loew's and the Statler executed the plan.

In 1933, Loew's implemented an innovative new booking strategy for the State and Stillman Theaters. Following an initial showing at the much larger State Theater, many films moved to the smaller Stillman to extend their downtown engagements. Loew's earned additional revenue while longer runs increased the public's curiosity and desire to see the movie. The Marie Dressler and Wallace Beery movie *Tugboat Annie*, the first of these "move over" films, played its first week at the State and the second at the Stillman.

In the 1940s, Loew's integrated the reopened Ohio Theater into the "move over" mix. The downtown run of the 1944 thriller *Gaslight* illustrates how the company successfully implemented the booking logic. The opening week at the State generated a very strong $20,500 in receipts. Rather than holding *Gaslight* for a second week, Loew's replaced it with *And the Angels Sing*, which produced an excellent $19,000. Meanwhile, *Gaslight* moved to the Stillman for its second and third weeks, generating receipts of $11,500 and $8,500, both above the Stillman's breakeven point of about $6,000. Rather than gambling on a potential fourth-week loss at the Stillman, *Gaslight* moved to the smaller Ohio for its fourth and fifth weeks; the film produced receipts of $6,500 and $4,000, both above the Ohio's breakeven point of about $3,500. Without the moves to the Stillman and Ohio, the profitable five-week run of *Gaslight* would have been concluded after one or two weeks at the State. The rationale anticipated today's bookings in multiplex theaters. Many movies debut on multiple screens, but the number of screens is reduced as attendance declines.

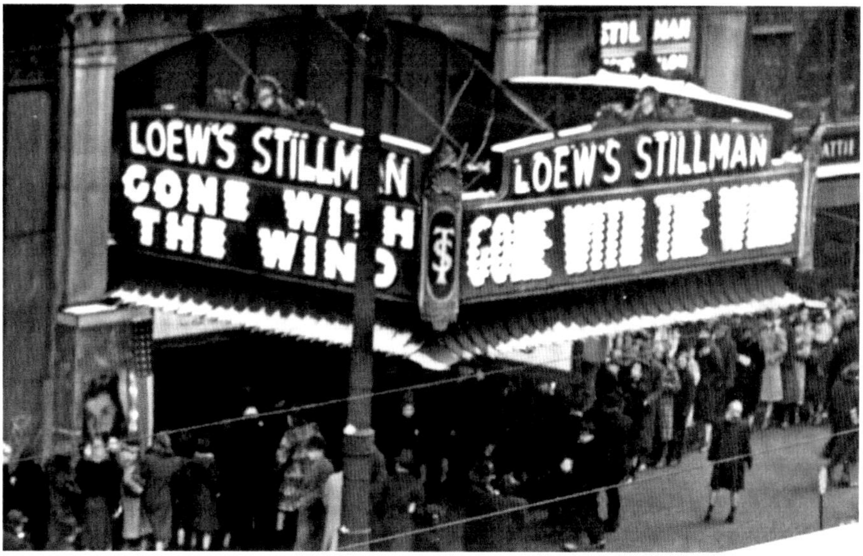

Many of the biggest blockbuster movies of the era, including *Gone with the Wind*, debuted in Cleveland at the Stillman Theater. *Courtesy of Special Collections, Michael Schwartz Library, Cleveland State University.*

By the 1940s, most movies slated for long runs started at the Stillman Theater; studios sacrificed a potentially huge first week at the State for the publicity and prestige of a longer run in the smaller Stillman. Prime examples of this strategy include an eleven-week first-run engagement of *Psycho*; ten-week showings of *Gone with the Wind*, *Ivanhoe* and *The Country Girl*;

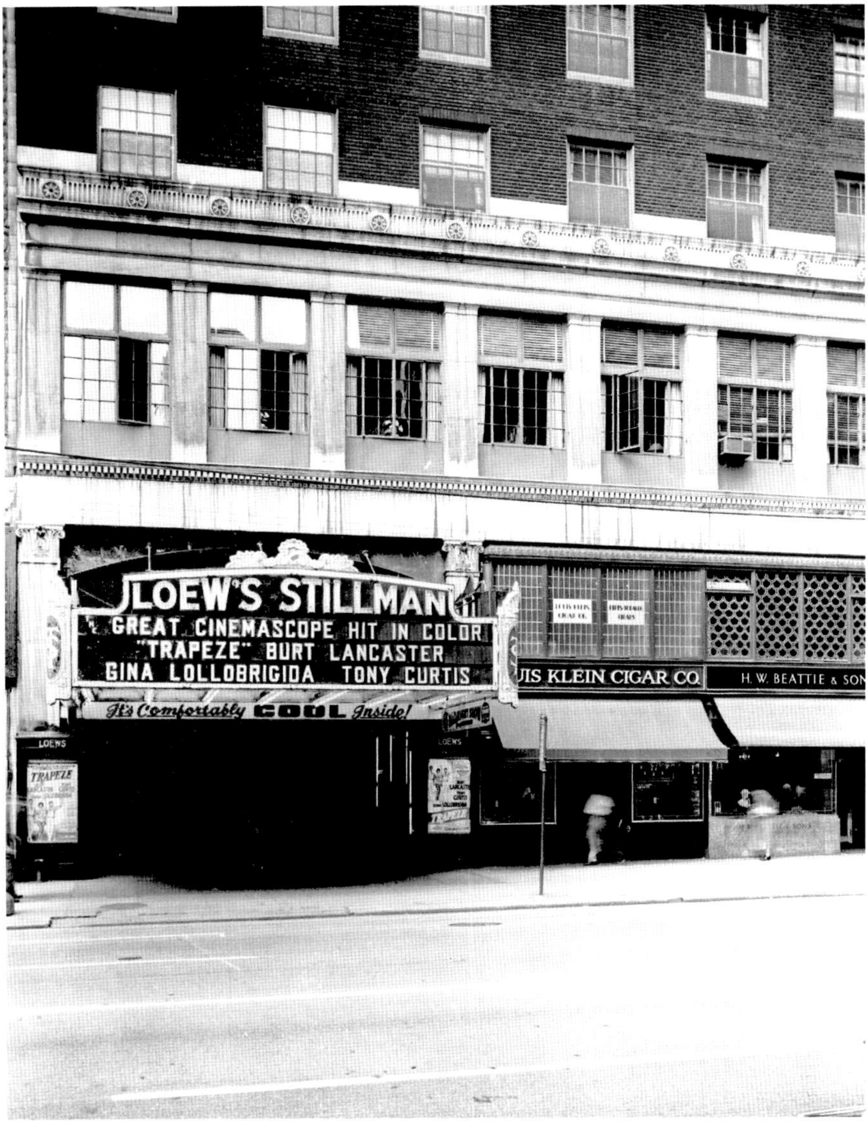

In the 1950s, the Stillman Theater enjoyed excellent turnouts for many popular films, including *Trapeze*. *Courtesy of Special Collections, Michael Schwartz Library, Cleveland State University.*

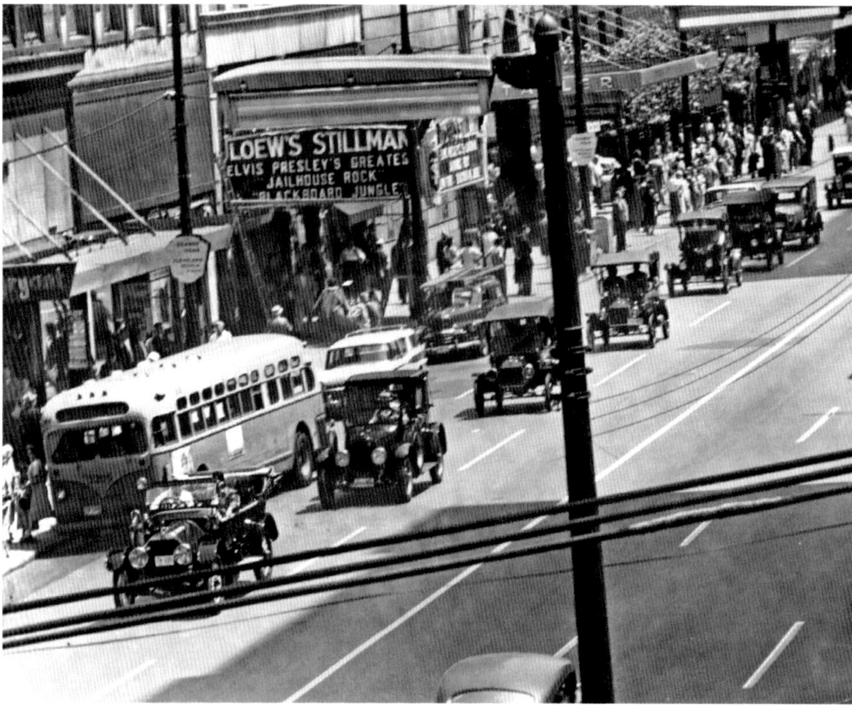

On June 4, 1959, a parade honoring the fiftieth anniversary of Ford Motor Company's victory in a New York to Seattle endurance run passed in front of the Stillman Theater. *Courtesy of Cleveland Public Library, Photograph Collection.*

a nine-week run of *To Catch a Thief* (the final two weeks at the Ohio Theater); and numerous engagements of six to eight weeks.

In 1951, the Stillman hosted the United States premiere of *An American in Paris*. Just one week following this seven-week run, the theater initiated a seventeen-week engagement of *Quo Vadis* (the Stillman's all-time longest-running movie), sharing a simultaneous world premiere with St. Louis, San Francisco, Atlanta, Memphis, Pittsburgh and New York City. Employing the "move over" philosophy, *Quo Vadis* completed an eighteenth week at the Ohio Theater.

In addition to long-run engagements and moves from the State Theater, the Stillman also booked numerous B movies not strong enough for exhibition at the huge State Theater. To create a successful B movie run, exhibitors used a special blend of imagination and creativity. In 1956, the Stillman's crew painted hundreds of UFO signs on downtown sidewalks to publicize the movie *Unidentified Flying Objects: The True Story of Flying Saucers*, a

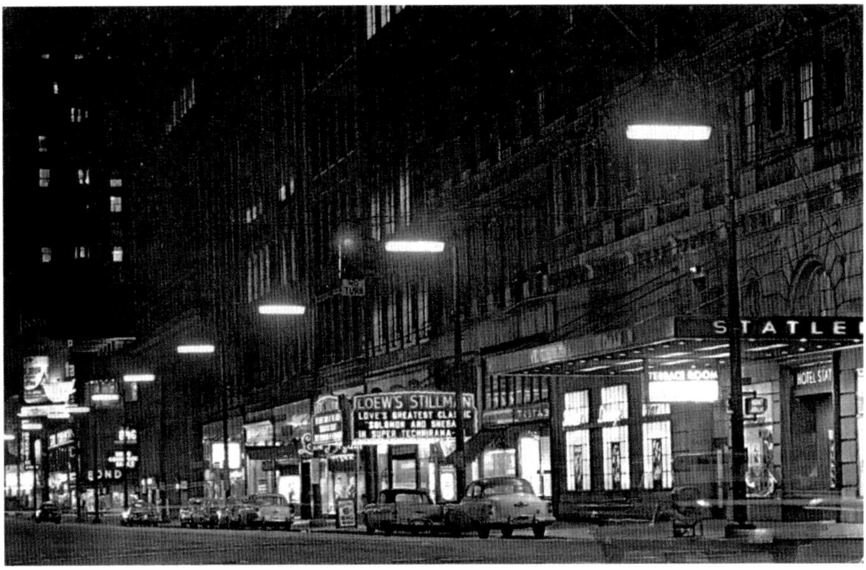

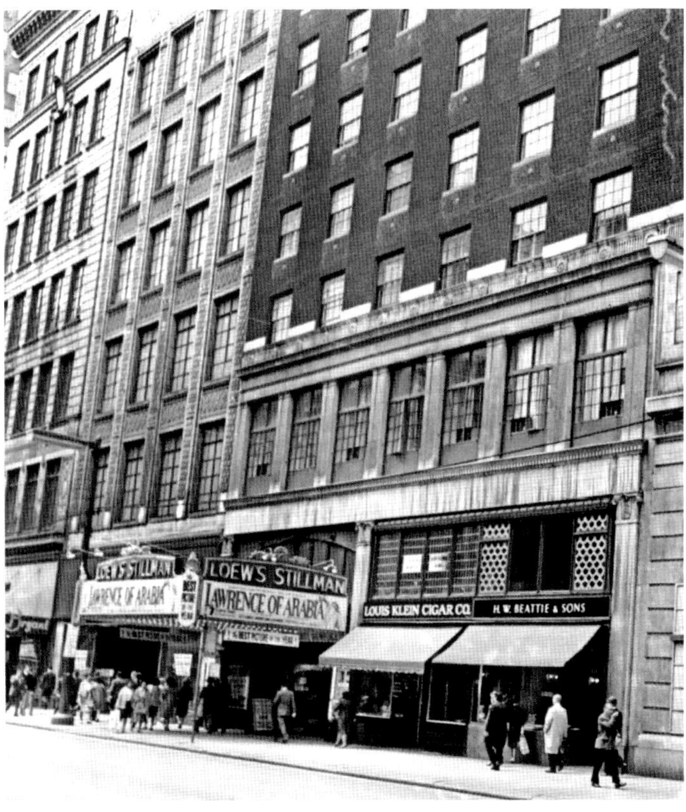

Above: In late January 1960, *Solomon and Sheba* continued in the sixth week of a seven-week engagement at the Stillman Theater. *Courtesy of the author.*

Right: The Stillman's final movie, the first-run showing of *Lawrence of Arabia*, continued for sixteen weeks. *Courtesy of Special Collections, Michael Schwartz Library, Cleveland State University.*

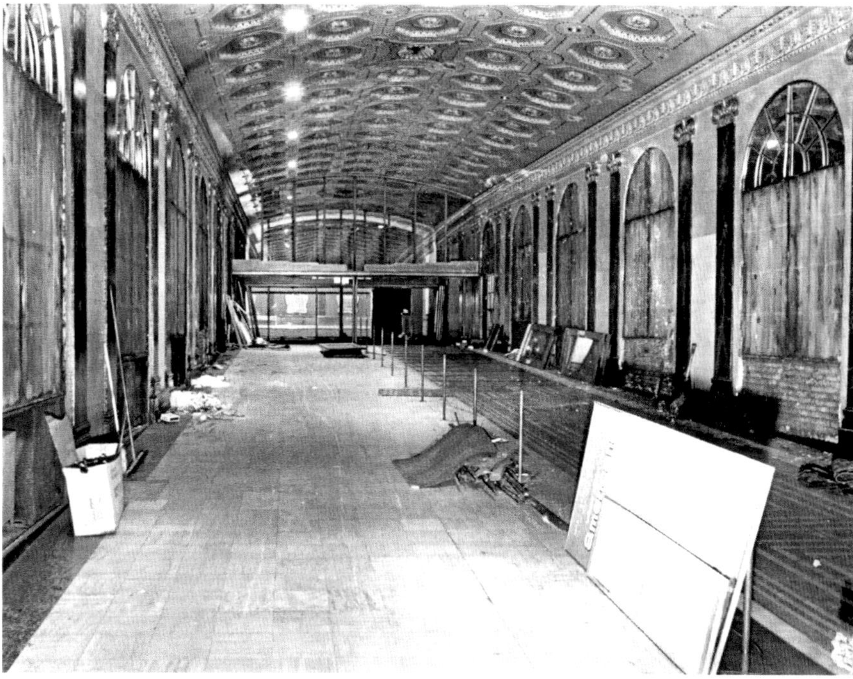

The Stillman Theater lobby is in the initial stages of demolition; the site is now the entrance ramp to a parking lot. *Courtesy of Special Collections, Michael Schwartz Library, Cleveland State University.*

film combining documentary footage with a fictional story. At the end of the engagement, the Stillman management regrettably realized that they had no idea how to remove these painted markings. After two weeks of frustrating and unsuccessful experimentation, the team finally discovered that scrubbing the sidewalks with hot water and a wire brush would accomplish the task.

In 1960 alone, the Stillman Theater booked extended first-run engagements of the major hits *Solomon and Sheba*, *The Apartment*, *Psycho* and *The World of Suzie Wong*. Nevertheless, only three years later, the showplace closed. The still beautiful theater's final movie, a first-run road-show engagement of *Lawrence of Arabia*, played for sixteen weeks. Following the Stillman's closing, art dealers purchased the theater's furniture and paintings. The Loew's chain reused the seats, carpeting and projection equipment in other theaters.

The Statler Hotel converted the Stillman site into a parking garage. The former lobby area functioned as an entrance ramp, while the old auditorium served as the garage and an expansion of the hotel's ballroom. Instead of promoting movies, the theater marquee publicized PARK in three-foot-high red letters. More than a half century after the Stillman's demise, the marquee still exists and continues to advertise the parking garage. Portions of the theater's once-ornate lobby carvings remain visible from the Euclid Avenue entrance to the parking facility. Ironically, the life of the garage has now exceeded that of the theater.

Chapter 12

THE EUCLID THEATER

Few movie houses have a history as short and strange as that of the Euclid Theater. Debuting on April 20, 1919 (Easter Sunday), the two-thousand-seat theater advertised itself as the city's largest and most magnificent motion picture playhouse. Patrons endured long ticket lines to enjoy movies and scrutinize the interior of this superb new theater. A twenty-five-member orchestra provided the musical accompaniment for the period's leading silent movies. Yet a mere two weeks after its stunning debut, the owners announced the property had been sold to a developer who planned to raze the pristine playhouse.

Located on the northeast corner of Euclid Avenue and East Ninth Street, the site had previously housed another entertainment venue, Cleveland's Cyclorama. Seated in a large, circular auditorium, audiences witnessed a huge fifty-foot-high by four-hundred-foot-long canvas painting revolving around them along with a domed ceiling representing the sky. Debuting on November 6, 1886, a blend of actors' narratives, sound effects and lighting created theatrical reenactments of the Civil War battles of Lookout Mountain, Mission Ridge and Chattanooga. To one side, the large mural depicted the rock palisades of Lookout Mountain; to the other side, the city of Chattanooga.

Railroads transported carloads of curious visitors to the Cyclorama from nearby cities and towns including Akron, Canton, Erie, Youngsville, Lorain, Warren, Kent, Galion, Bellevue, Norwalk, Zanesville and Coshocton. Following a long run, the Civil War extravaganza ended;

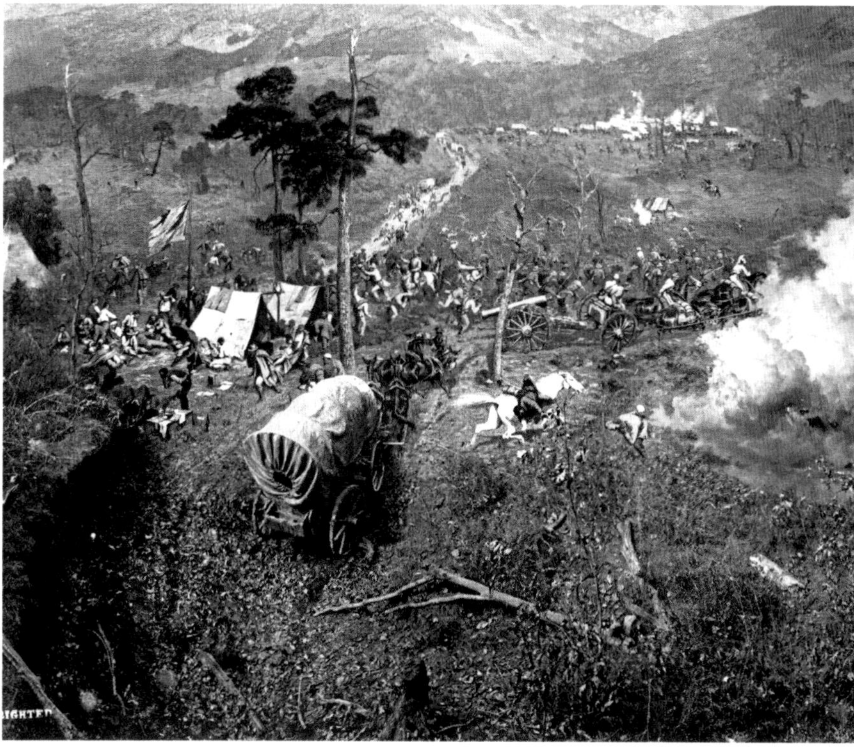

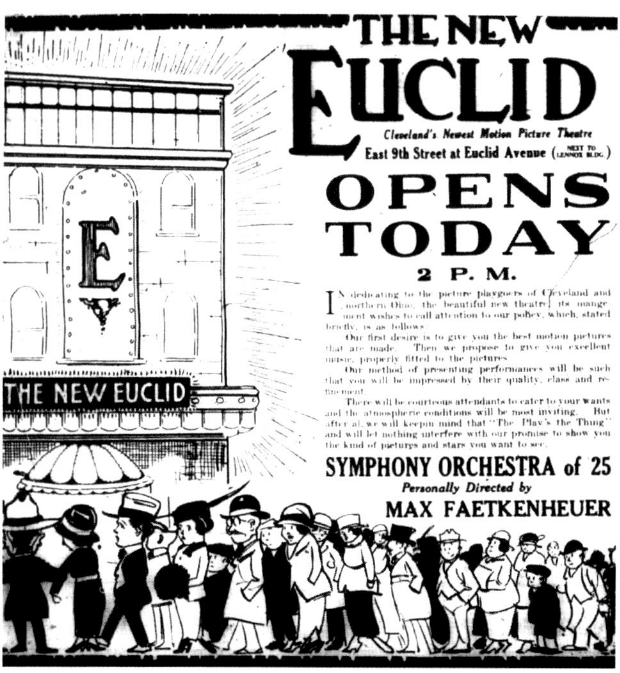

Above: Depicted in this photograph is a small portion of the mammoth painting used as a setting for a Civil War battle in Cleveland's Cyclorama Theater. *Courtesy of Cleveland Public Library, Photograph Collection.*

Left: The stunning Euclid Theater experienced a very short life on the corner of Euclid Avenue and East Ninth Street. *Courtesy of the* Plain Dealer.

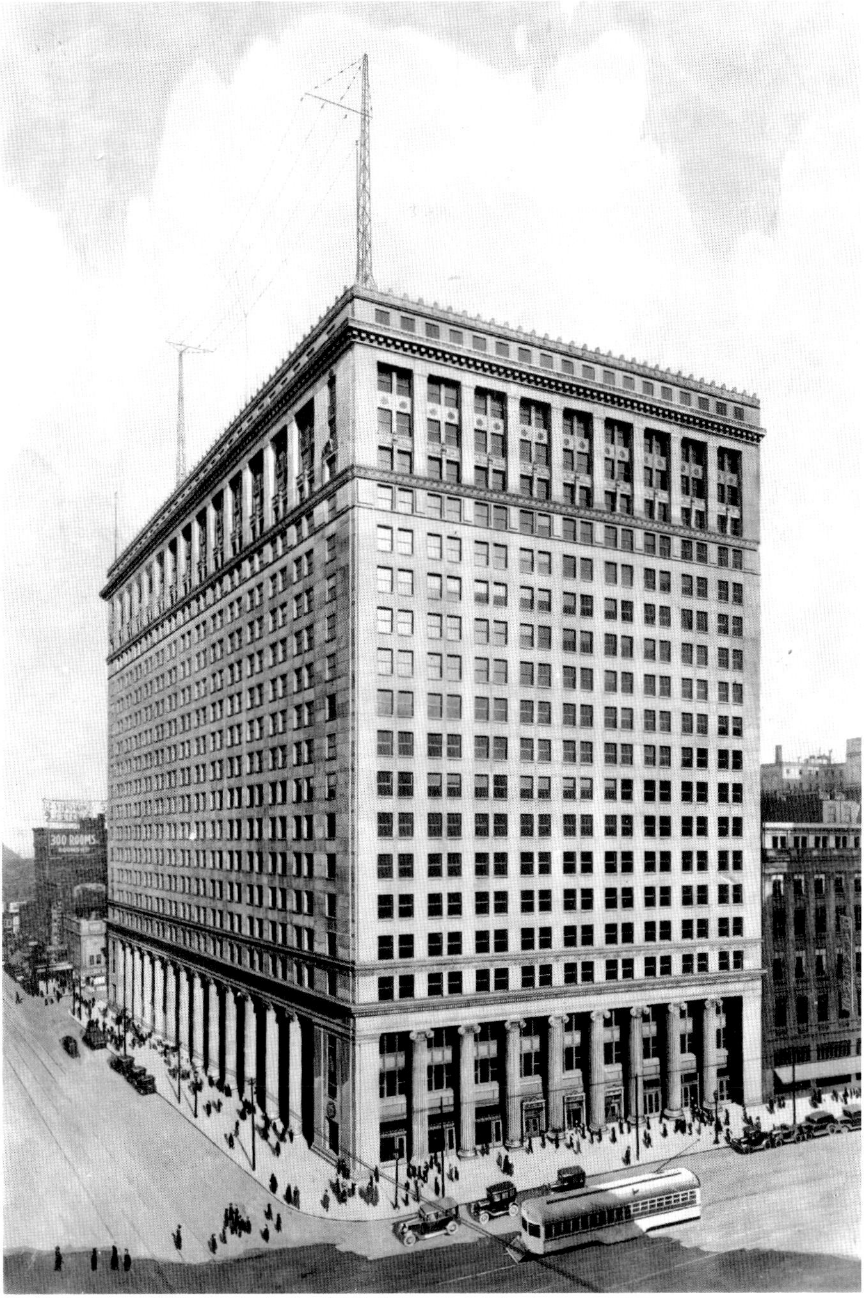

Construction of the still-existing Union Trust Building forced the demolition of the Euclid Theater. *Courtesy of Cleveland Public Library, Photograph Collection.*

the city of Buffalo inherited the huge mural after it had been dismantled in Cleveland. Productions of *Jerusalem on the Day of the Crucifixion* and *The Battle of Gettysburg* extended the Cyclorama's life in Cleveland into 1895. The building next housed Bicklorama, a sales outlet and training school for Winton bicycle riders. Razing of the building allowed for the construction of the Euclid Theater.

From an East Ninth Street entrance, Euclid Theater's customers traveled through a corridor, festooned with brown tile and mirrored walls, leading into the main lobby. There a fountain, sitting at the foot of a marble staircase, directed patrons to the mezzanine and balcony. Green leather upholstered seats accented the theater's major colors of blue, French gray and gold. By August 1919, Loew's Theaters had assumed management of the doomed playhouse located within one hundred yards of the equally beautiful Loew's Stillman Theater.

Sacrificed for the construction of the still-existing Union Trust Building, the Euclid Theater closed on May 11, 1922, following a showing of Rudolph Valentino in *The Sheik*. Loew's most likely would have never built the State and Ohio Theaters had the Euclid Theater not been razed. Thus, Playhouse Square Center's current configuration of theaters is a direct consequence of the Euclid Theater's untimely demise.

Chapter 13

THE STATE THEATER

Anticipating the premature closing of the beautiful Euclid Theater, Loew's constructed an even larger and more stunning movie temple in Playhouse Square, Cleveland's new theater district. Loew's understood the value of fronting playhouses on busy and prestigious Euclid Avenue; the company had already operated the downtown Mall, Euclid and Stillman movie theaters on Euclid Avenue, as well as the Alhambra and Park film houses on the same street just west of University Circle.

As coveted Euclid Avenue frontage quickly disappeared, Loew's erected the 3,446-seat State Theater auditorium on land directly behind the yet-to-be-built Palace Theater. The auditorium connected to the theater's Euclid Avenue entrance through a series of three continuous foyers totaling 320 feet in length and stretching 47 feet in width. The huge entranceway incorporated Vermont marble, terrazzo in ivory and gold, a large fireplace and red carpets and draperies trimmed in gold. Four 50-foot oil murals by American modernist painter and muralist James Daugherty also embellished the lobby. Considered to be the largest theater lobby in the world, the combined foyers still stretch the entire distance past the neighboring Palace Theater's lobby, auditorium and stage house.

Thomas B. Lamb, one of the twentieth century's leading creators of lavish movie theaters, designed the new showplace. Often described as Italian Renaissance, the theater actually integrated Roman, Greek and European Baroque designs that incorporated stately mahogany columns and one of the country's finest coffered ceilings. Marcus Loew, president of Loew's

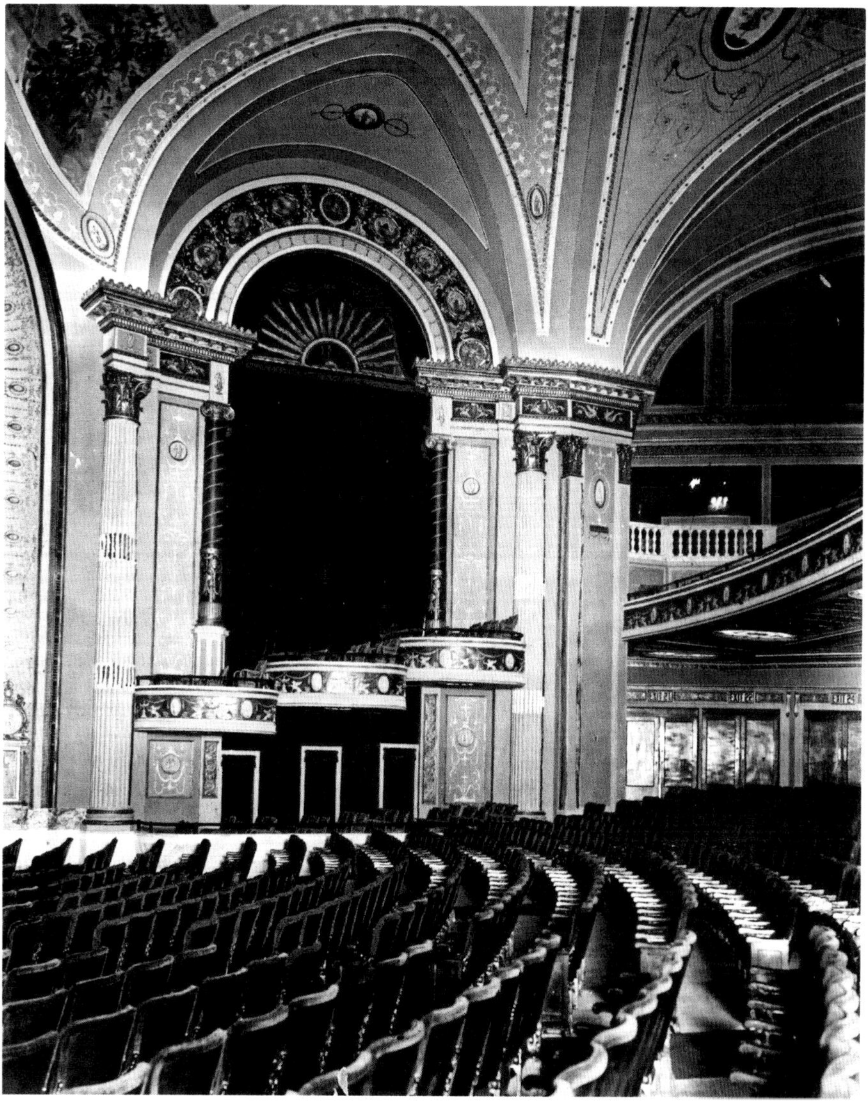

The State Theater's 3,446-seat auditorium complemented the beauty and vastness of the lobby. *Courtesy of Special Collections, Michael Schwartz Library, Cleveland State University.*

Theaters, considered the State's debut important enough to transport two train cars filled with MGM silent film stars to Cleveland for the opening night festivities taking place on February 5, 1921.

Although constructed as a movie theater, Loew's quickly discovered that the State also required supplementary attractions to fill the large auditorium.

Responding to this added necessity, Hyman L. Spitalny's theater orchestra produced pre-film concerts; mini–stage productions and fashion shows helped increase attendance, as did guest appearances by major silent film stars including Theda Bara and Mae Murray.

Beginning in 1922, the Shubert organization leased the State for twenty-three weeks to carry on its ill-conceived vaudeville competition with the Keith circuit. Clevelanders enjoyed the antics of up-and-coming performers (the Marx Brothers and George Jessel) while still taking pleasure in performances by old-time vaudeville duos such as Weber and Fields and Buck and Bubbles.

As dance orchestras increased in popularity, the State contracted multiple-week bookings with Guy Lombardo, Fred Waring, the Hotel Winton Orchestra, Janet Alder's Girl's Band and the Circle Terrace Orchestra. In the late 1920s, aspiring newcomers Ginger Rogers and Ray Bolger performed on the State stage. On Sunday mornings, the Euclid Avenue Baptist Church (nicknamed John Rockefeller's church) held Bible classes and speaker presentations at the State. The theater also hosted a special service in memory of the late president Warren G. Harding.

In the 1930s, movies combined with top-of-the-line live acts helped the State remain in operation during the depths of the Depression. The performers included Bob Hope, Jack Benny, Glenn Miller, Milton Berle, Jimmy Durante, Judy Garland, Edgar Bergen, Cab Calloway, Ted Lewis, Eleanor Powell, the Mills Brothers, Bill Robinson and the Paul Ash Orchestra.

In early 1933, a growing number of patrons complained that they had lost wallets or the contents of purses while attending performances at the State, especially during busy weekend evenings. On the Saturday evening of February 11, theatergoers flocked to the State to enjoy a popular booking composed of a live performance of *Showboat* starring Helen Morgan and the film *Hot Pepper* featuring Lupe Velez and Edmond Lowe. The audience garnered more excitement than they had anticipated that night. Undercover police canvassing the crowded lobby recognized and arrested a team of three professional pickpockets. As one of the trio attempted to flee, a police officer used a blackjack to knock him unconscious in front of thousands of people using the lobby to enter or exit the theater during a break in performances. The two males possessed very little money when arrested, but their female counterpart had stashed a large amount of funds under her armpits.

In 1936, the film *San Francisco*, the first movie to complete a two-week engagement at the State, continued at the Stillman for two more weeks. In the late 1930s, large gains in attendance signaled the imminent end of the Depression's doldrums. In 1938, 12,600 people jammed the State in one

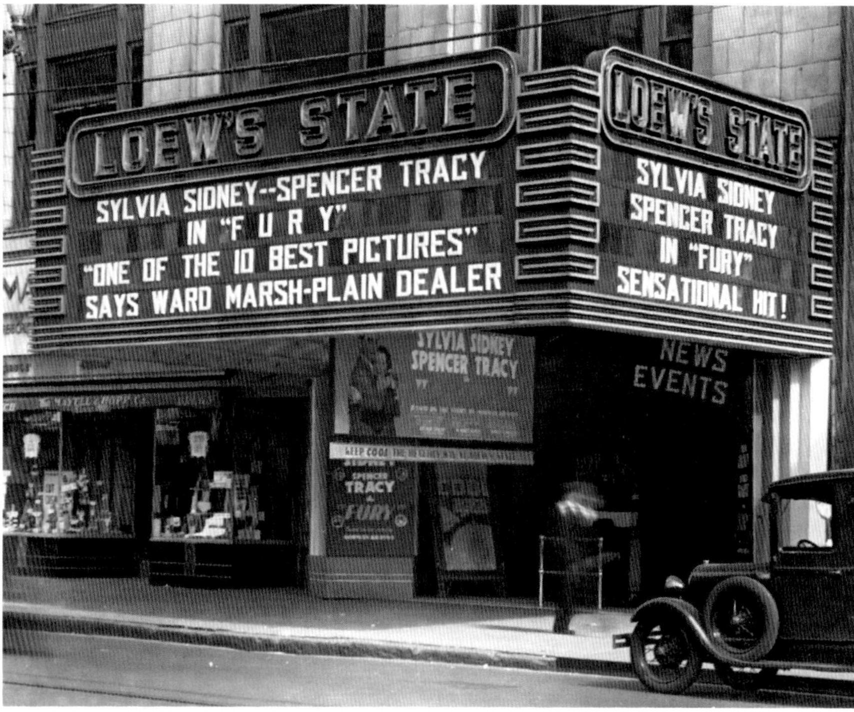

In June 1936, the State Theater presented *Fury*, a film that helped propel Spencer Tracy into a major box-office star. *Courtesy of Cleveland Public Library, Photograph Collection.*

day to view *Boys Town*, starring Spencer Tracy and Mickey Rooney, while 13,225 attended, in a single day, the Nelson Eddy and Jeanette MacDonald film *Sweethearts*.

In 1941, Bob Hope entertained State audiences prior to a midnight preview of his latest film, *Nothing but the Truth*. Spending a few days in Cleveland, Hope also conducted a live national radio broadcast from the Music Hall and delivered the opening ceremonial kickoff in a Cleveland Rams football game against the defending champion Chicago Bears. His kick soared between seven and ten feet before tumbling to the ground.

In the 1940s, the State had returned to its roots as primarily a movie theater, although its guest star list still featured very formidable entertainers: Mickey Rooney, Jane Powell, Mario Lanza, Kathryn Grayson, the Ink Spots, Jack Carson and Sammy Kaye. In 1943, the film *Stage Door Canteen* held for three weeks before moving to the Stillman for two additional weeks. The next year, *Going My Way* remained for four weeks prior to the Stillman hosting the fifth, sixth and seventh weeks.

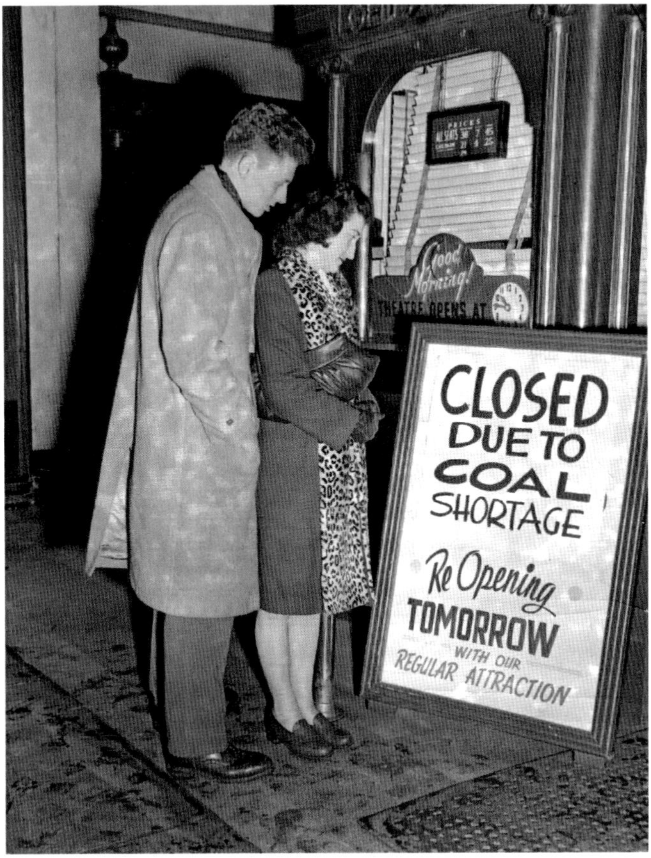

Right: On February 1, 1945, a disappointed couple intending to see Judy Garland and Margaret O'Brien in *Meet Me in St. Louis* discovered a closed theater, hampered by a coal shortage. *Courtesy of Special Collections, Michael Schwartz Library, Cleveland State University.*

Below: The Cleveland Public Library created displays featuring tie-ins with movies playing in downtown theaters. In 1946, an exhibit promoting *The Harvey Girls* included movie stills and books relating to railroads, restaurants and the western United States. *Courtesy of Cleveland Public Library Archives.*

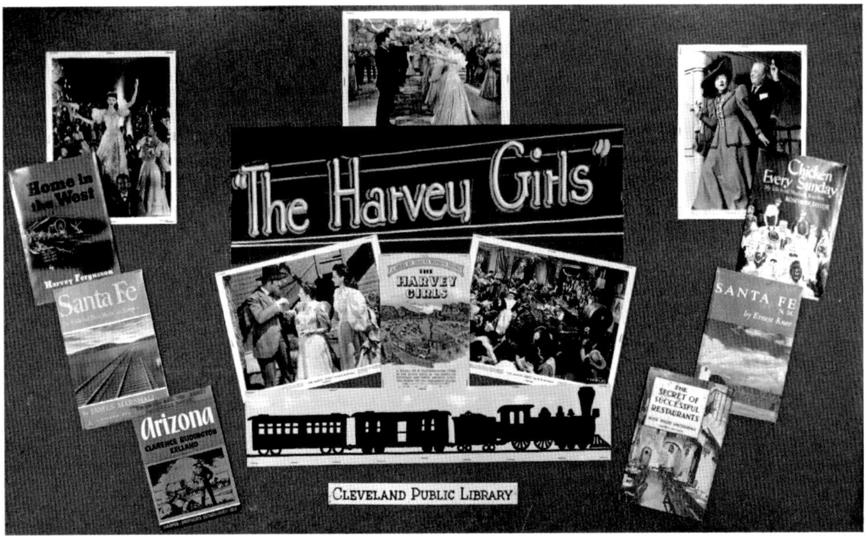

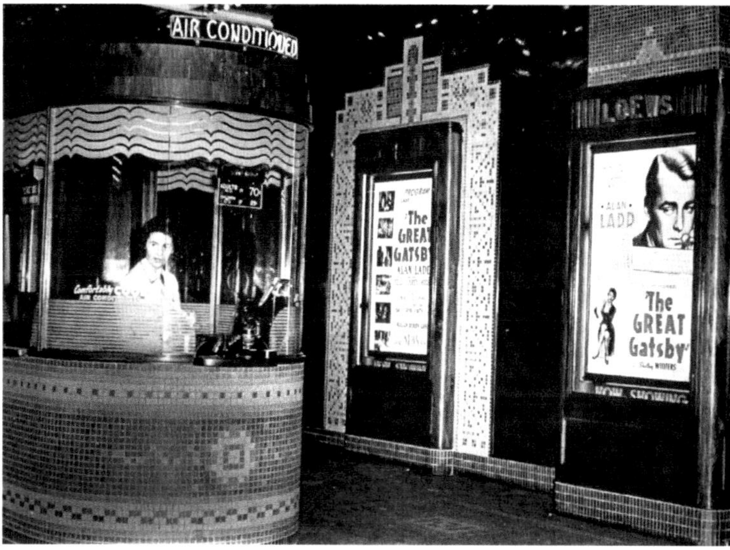

In 1949, Alan Ladd's version of *The Great Gatsby* played for a week before moving to the Ohio Theater for a second downtown week. *Courtesy of Cleveland Public Library, Photograph Collection.*

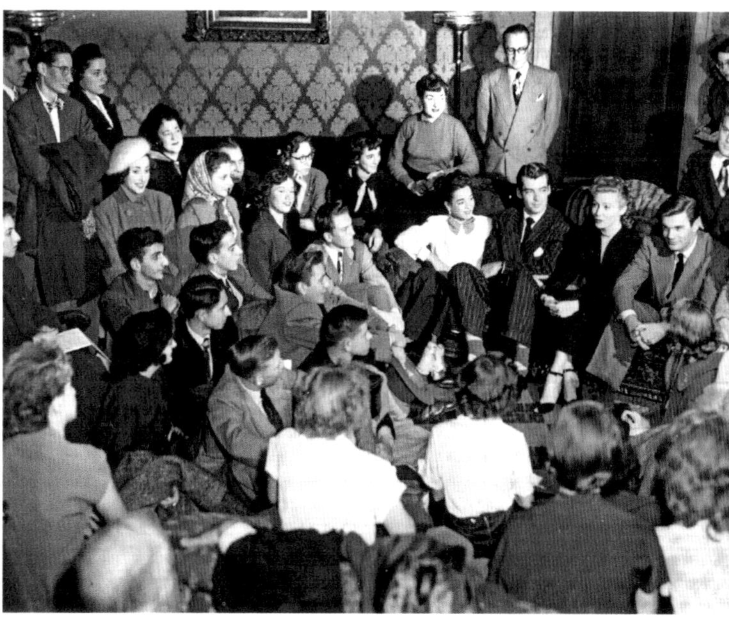

In the State lobby in 1949, sixty-five students and teachers from high school drama classes chatted with five rising screen stars seated to the right: Lita Baron, Rory Calhoun, Rhonda Fleming, Louis Jourdan and John Agar. *Courtesy of Special Collections, Michael Schwartz Library, Cleveland State University.*

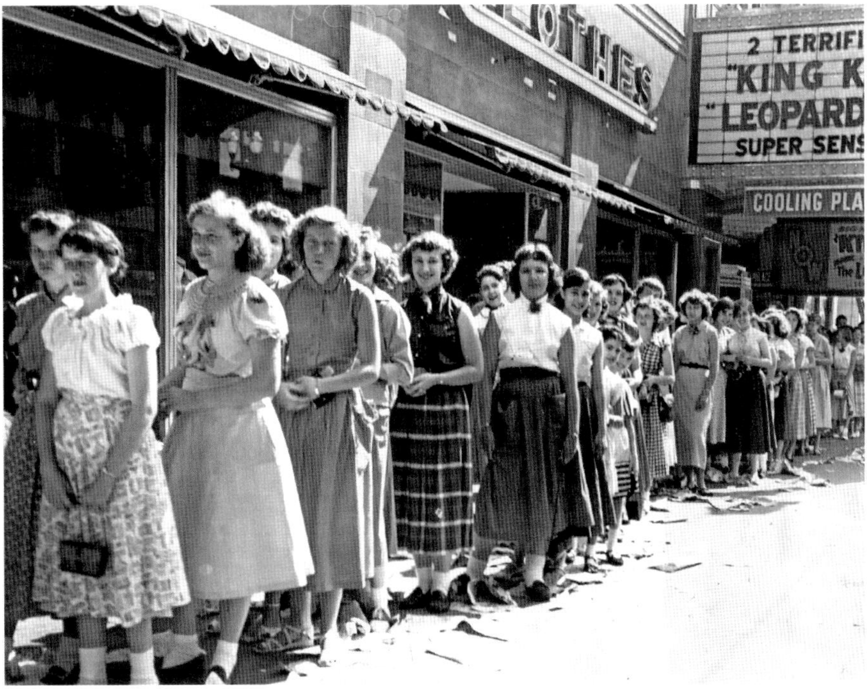

On June 27, 1952, patient teenage females stood in a three-block line to purchase tickets for a live performance by singing sensation Johnny Ray. *Courtesy of Special Collections, Michael Schwartz Library, Cleveland State University.*

Actress Betty Garrett, visiting Cleveland in 1955 to both promote her new film *My Sister Eileen* and accompany her husband, Larry Parks (playing at the Hanna in *Teahouse of the August Moon*), recalled introducing the duo's new nostalgic vaudeville act at the State Theater back in 1949.

In the 1950s, guest appearances became even less frequent. Rising stars Debbie Reynolds, Tony Bennett and Eydie Gorme performed on the State stage, as did pop singers Patti Page, Guy Mitchell, Les Paul and Mary Ford, Johnny Ray, the Four Lads and Bill Haley and the Comets. Bob Hope's in-person visits promoted his films *The Seven Little Foyes*, *That Certain Feeling* and *Paris Holiday*, while Doris Day plugged *Julie*. In 1953, *Knights of the Round Table*, an early CinemaScope production, became the State's first five-week run with an additional two rounds at the Stillman.

Through the decades, the State's huge lobby (capable of accommodating four thousand people) served as a venue for special exhibits, displays and events. In the 1920s, the Loew's organization used the lobby to stage after-hours employee dances and picnics attended by the entire range of staff

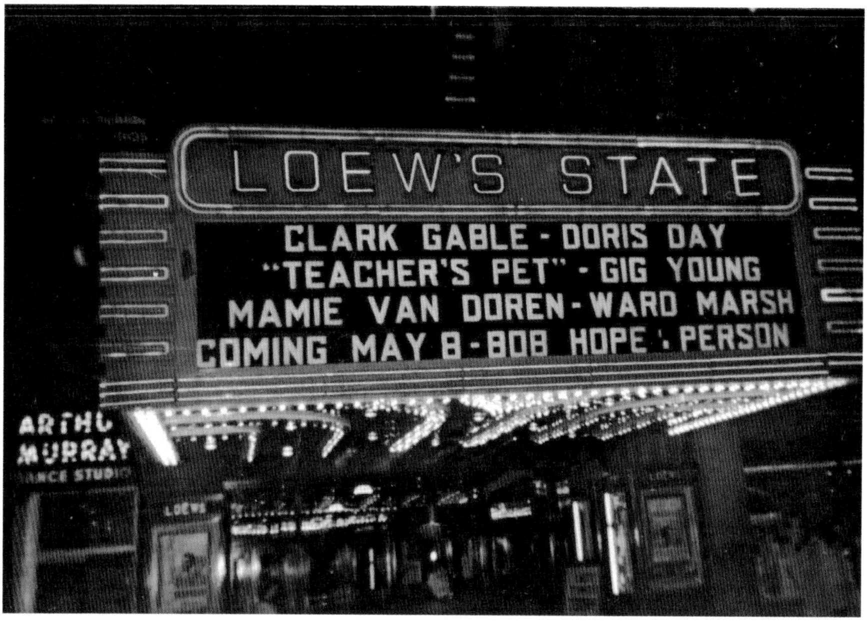

In 1958, Clark Gable and Doris Day starred in the hit film *Teacher's Pet*. Next, Bob Hope would appear in person to promote his movie *Paris Holiday*. *Courtesy of Cleveland Public Library, Photograph Collection.*

members, from managers to ushers. Radio station WTAM broadcasted programs from a studio in the lobby. The Rose Royal Midgets held a reception for one thousand area orphans, and Cleveland schoolchildren displayed dolls, colored baskets and play houses that they had created on school playgrounds. The lobby also hosted an exhibit of sculptures and pictures of firefighters and fire horses and a display comprising sheet music, photographs and manuscripts representing chamber music, orchestral scores, songs and piano pieces created in Cleveland.

In the 1930s, the State promoted the Buster Keaton film *Parlor, Bed Room and Bath* by constructing a parlor, bedroom and bathroom in the lobby. An exhibit showcased new products developed by Cleveland companies. A flower show featured a display of applications of electricity in gardening; an electric soil sterilizer that supposedly eliminated weeds developed into the show's highlight. Families enjoyed a model of the Chesapeake and Ohio Railway system originally displayed at the Chicago Century of Progress exposition.

During World War II, the Red Cross, marines and coast guard all used the lobby to enlist volunteers for service, while more than four hundred people registered for war-related employment after viewing recruiting displays. The merchant marine presented a war show in conjunction with National Maritime Day. Another organization used the lobby to collect old phonograph records to be shipped to members of the American military overseas. An "Army at War" art exhibition displayed 118 oil, watercolor and sepia drawings and paintings by American artists assigned to theaters of war throughout the world. Other lobby displays centered on optics, electronics and a four-thousand-pound jet-propelled bomb expected to be dropped on Japan. From the nose of a B-17 bomber, a simulated aerial view of Tokyo and a conversation between a pilot and bombardier highlighted another lobby display. In two years of war bond drives, Clevelanders purchased $5,500,000 worth of bonds in the State lobby.

In the 1950s, along with fashion and flower shows, the Ohio Desk Company displayed modern executive furniture in conjunction with the film *Executive Suite*. In 1957, the army transported a Nike missile to the lobby. But the lobby

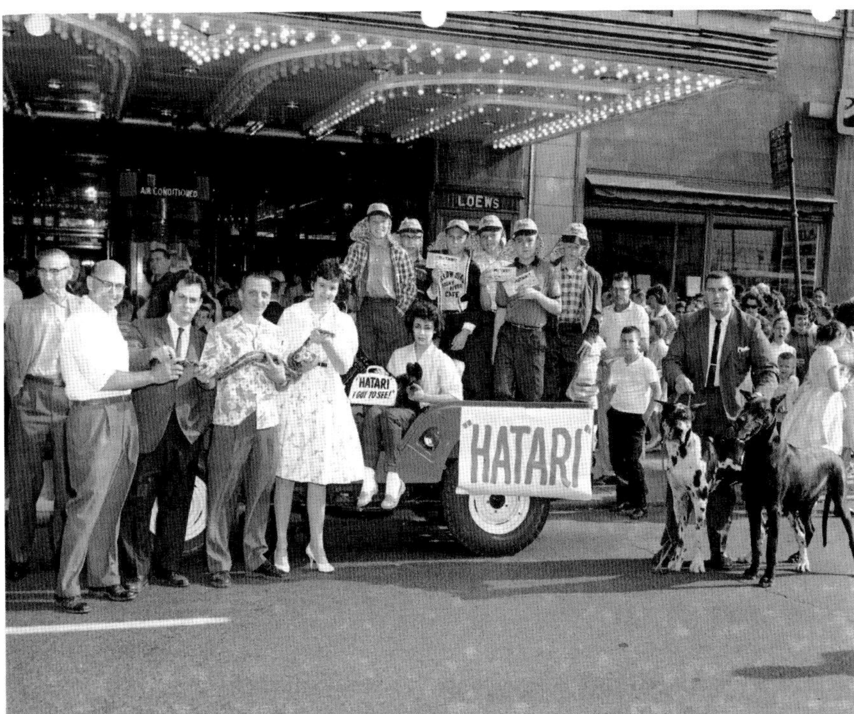

On June 9, 1962, guests at an invitational screening of *Hatari* interacted with an eight-foot boa constrictor, a three-foot woolly monkey and two 180-pound Great Danes. *Courtesy of Cleveland Public Library, Photograph Collection.*

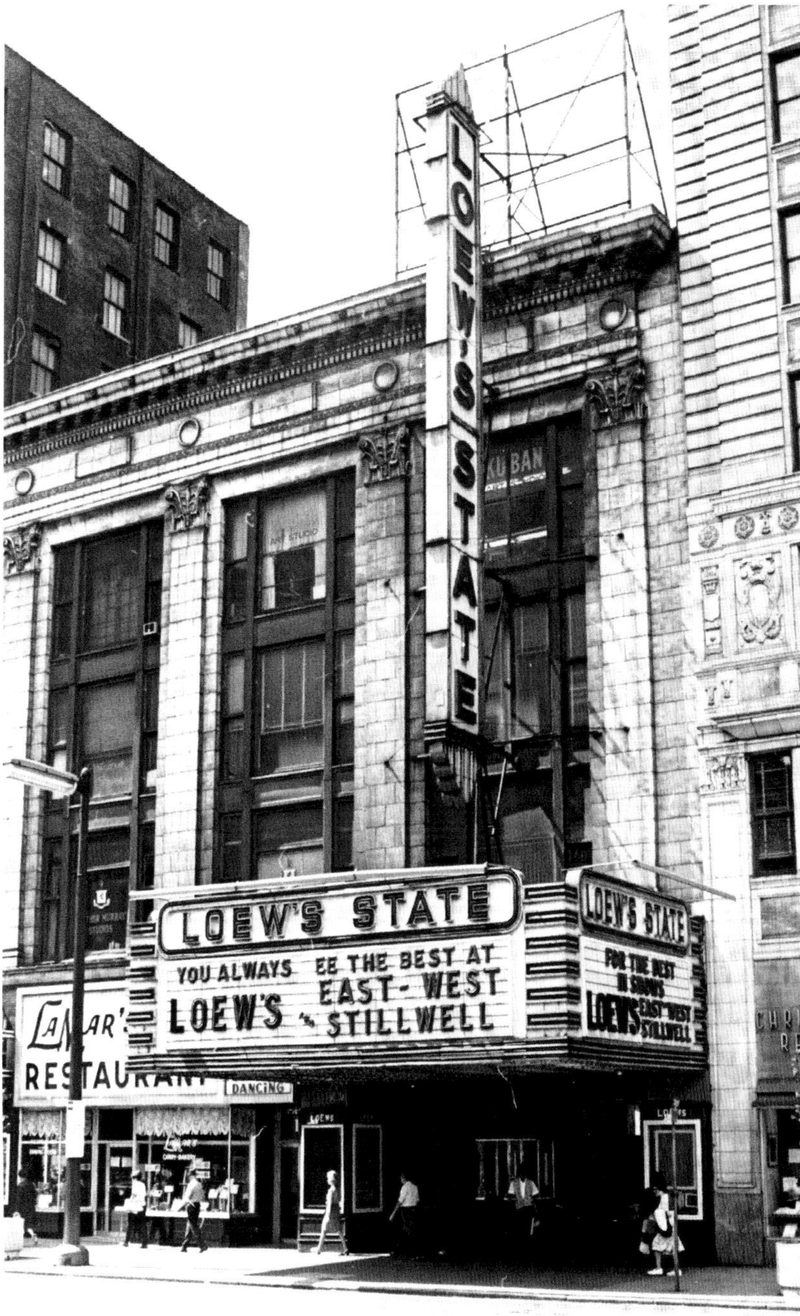

With no remaining downtown Loew's theaters, the marquee of the abandoned State Theater advertised the company's new suburban locations. *Courtesy of Special Collections, Michael Schwartz Library, Cleveland State University.*

exhibits didn't always function exactly as intended. In 1953, while viewers of the crime film *Vice Squad* examined a display of guns, burglary tools and other criminal paraphernalia, someone stole a .32-caliber automatic gun from the display. In the 1970s, preservationists used the lobby as a catalyst to rescue the State and Ohio Theaters from a waiting wrecking ball.

In the mid-1960s, the loss of mainstream first-run engagements created box-office receipts that plunged faster and further than earlier declines attributed to television. But even as attendance plummeted, one major exception demonstrated that Clevelanders would still patronize downtown movie theaters. In 1965, the State shared *Thunderball* with the neighborhood Shaker and Vogue Theaters. Because of the film's popularity and the State's much greater size, the first week box-office receipts of $55,000 easily outdrew its two competitors' take of $35,000 each. In fact, *Thunderball* produced the largest weekly receipts for a movie-only event in the theater's history. The James Bond thriller continued for eight more profitable weeks at the State, one of the few bright spots during a period of almost consistent losses.

In order to remain in business, the State desperately needed exclusive bookings. In desperation, the owners of the theater closed off large portions of the auditorium, converted projection equipment to accommodate Cinerama and exhibited four road-show presentations: *Grand Prix*, *Far from the Madding Crowd*, *2001: A Space Odyssey* and *Ice Station Zebra*.

Box-office receipts, even from the road-show films, failed to stop the downward spiral. In 1969, the State and Ohio Theaters closed on the same day, leaving the Palace as the only remaining Playhouse Square movie theater still in operation. In a dramatic understatement, *Variety* remarked that the closings "somewhat dims the razzle-dazzle of Playhouse Square."

In 1970, the gloomy path toward probable demolition continued. Classified newspaper ads offered the State Theater's contents for sale—ornamental mirrors, carved tables and chairs and other furnishings—all at bargain prices. Meanwhile, *Life* magazine featured James Daugherty's no longer visible mural *The Spirit of Cinema-America* as a two-page pull-out cover on its February 27, 1970 issue. The accompanying story documented the sale of the fifty-two-acre Paramount studio, along with the company's artifacts and treasures. The title, "Goodby [*sic*] to the Glory Days," seemed just as appropriate for Cleveland's downtown movie theaters.

About this time, former Seattle resident Ray Shepardson relocated to Cleveland to work as a Cleveland Public Schools administrator. After discovering the abandoned theaters while seeking a venue for a meeting, Shepardson resigned his school position to found the Playhouse Square

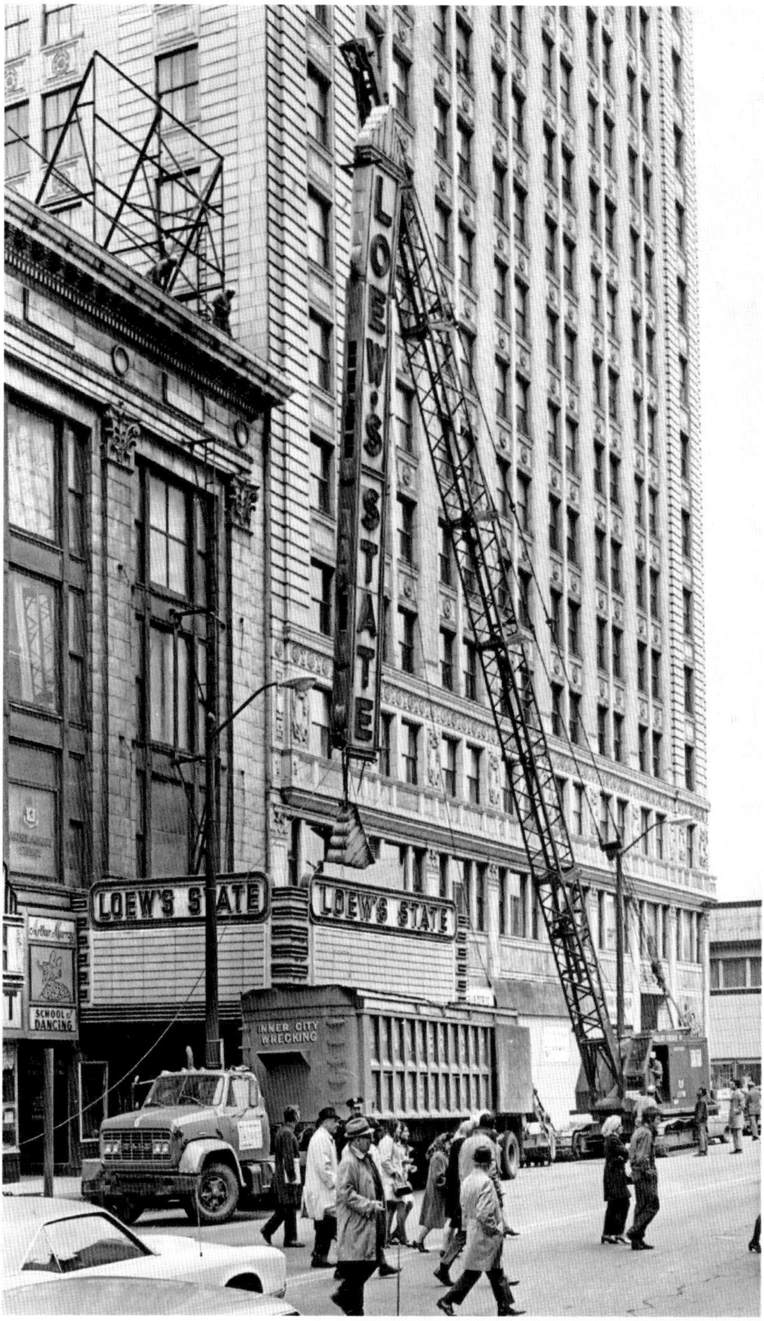

In 1972, the expected demise of the State Theater began with the removal of the marquee and a large neon sign. *Courtesy of Special Collections, Michael Schwartz Library, Cleveland State University.*

Association. The organization's objectives, viewed as unrealistic dreams by most observers, centered on rescuing, restoring and returning the Playhouse Square theaters to their former relevance.

By 1972, the association had grown to 438 members, each paying $120 per year. The diversified group included doctors, lawyers, dentists, local celebrities, a cocktail waitress and even a San Francisco–based photographer who discovered the association while visiting Cleveland. The association's staff comprised six people: Shepardson; a membership sales person; a community and business relations liaison; a box-office person; a maintenance man; and a combination secretary, bookkeeper and promotion assistant. No one on the staff, including Shepardson, possessed any expertise in booking theatrical events or saving theaters from demolition. In an era before computerized fundraising, senior citizens living in the downtown Bohn Tower looked up telephone numbers and placed them on three- by five-inch cards for use by telemarketers.

The seemingly inevitable announcement arrived on May 25, 1972: both the State and Ohio would be razed to construct an eighty-eight-thousand-square-foot parking garage. "We just can't go on forever keeping these buildings empty," the property owners lamented. A wrecking ball, parked behind the theaters, stood prepared to begin the demolition. Fortunately, a group of civic activists joined forces with Shepardson to save the State and Ohio from extinction.

Since the State and Ohio auditoriums lay in ruins, the Playhouse Square Association used the State Theater lobby for occasional fundraising balls and bashes and rented the space for commercial activities, including a group of hula dancers promoting travel to Hawaii.

Restoring a theater requires extraordinary expertise and sizeable expenditures of money, but even the initial task of convincing a skeptical public that restoration made sense proved to be a daunting task. By the 1970s, downtown Cleveland supported a large workforce that abandoned the central city every afternoon at 5:00 p.m.; many, if not most, viewed the downtown movie theaters as dinosaur-like relics of a bygone era. Yet on April 18, 1973, the credibility of restoring the theaters took an enormous leap forward as a 360-seat makeshift cabaret opened its doors in the State lobby where a concession stand once stood.

Preparing for the cabaret opening, volunteers had removed eight layers of paint from the marble baseboards and fifty gallons of dirt from just one fan used in the steam heating system. Electricity, shorted out by mice dining on the insulation, had been repaired. Construction workers built

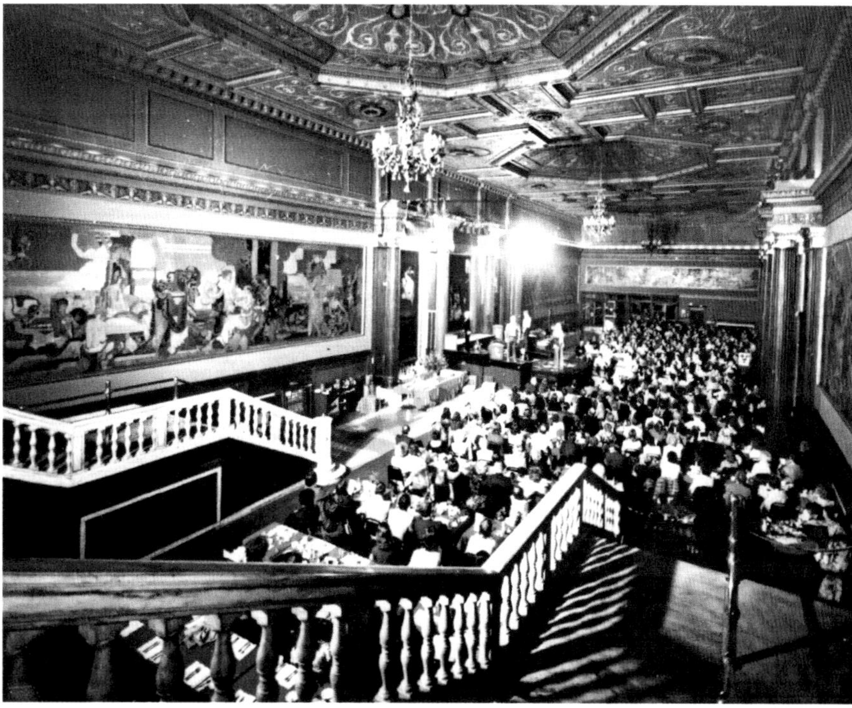

The surprising two-year run of *Jacques Brel Is Alive and Well and Living in Paris* demonstrated that Clevelanders would support downtown entertainment. *Courtesy of Cleveland Public Library, Photograph Collection.*

the stage using aluminum once supporting the State's conventional movie screen and scaffolding from the Cinerama screen. Seats obtained from the closed Black Angus Restaurant had been put in place. Three crystal and brass chandeliers, once beautifying the Commodore Perry Hotel in Toledo, enhanced the nostalgic feeling of the new cabaret.

The planned three-week engagement of *Jacques Brel Is Alive and Well and Living in Paris*, the cabaret's first production, continued for two years. The 522 riveting performances of the musical revue, comprising twenty-seven songs performed by a four-member cast, attracted 140,000 people paying between $7.75 and $11.75 to enjoy a buffet dinner and view the show; total box-office receipts reached $1.5 million.

The lobby cabaret continued by presenting new shows in 1975 and 1976. In the late 1970s, Chita Rivera, Della Reese, Mel Torme, Ray Charles and other major stars performed in a refurbished (but not yet restored) auditorium.

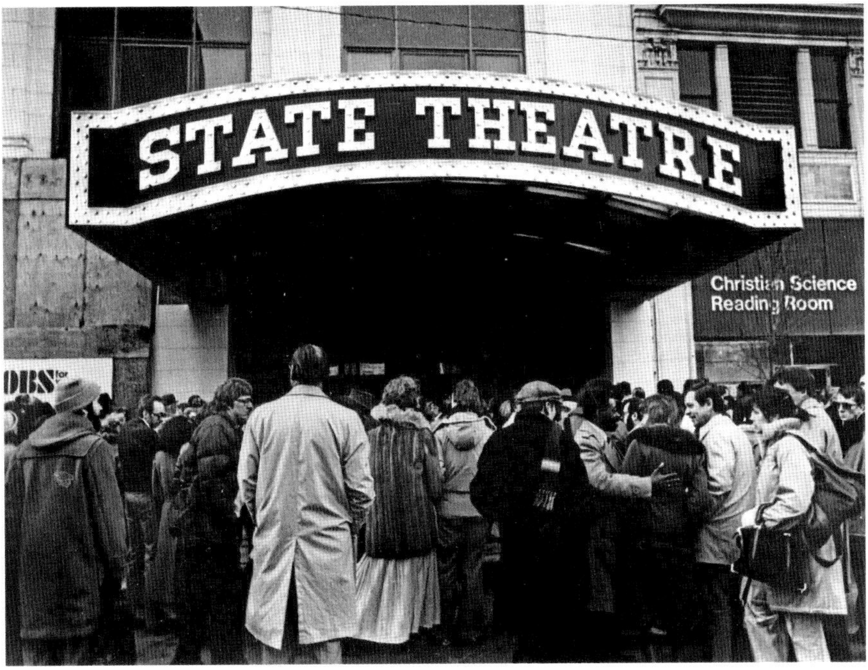

Above: On March 4, 1980, a crowd outside the State Theater watched as magician Harry Blackstone Jr. (performing at the neighboring Palace Theater) lighted the rebuilt marquees of the State and Ohio Theaters. *Courtesy of Special Collections, Michael Schwartz Library, Cleveland State University.*

Right: *Stompin' at the State* entertained audiences for fourteen months. *Courtesy of Special Collections, Michael Schwartz Library, Cleveland State University.*

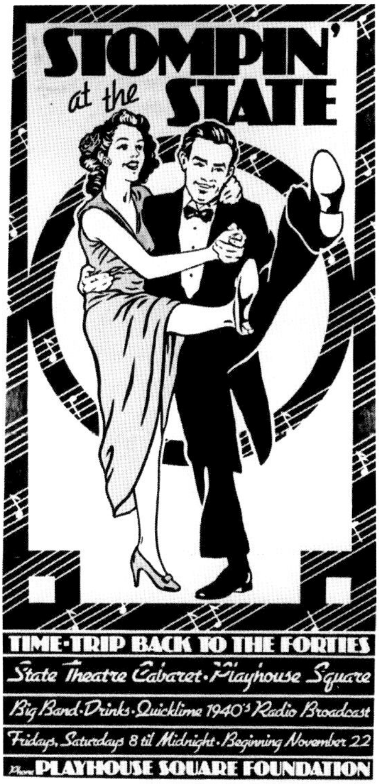

In 1980, the Playhouse Square Association transformed the State Theater lobby into a 1940s nightclub complete with a live orchestra, dance floor, jitterbug contests, conga lines snaking through the lengthy lobby, dime-a-dance girls, cigarette girls and a simulated radio broadcast. The Glenn Miller Orchestra highlighted the opening night production. Advertised as

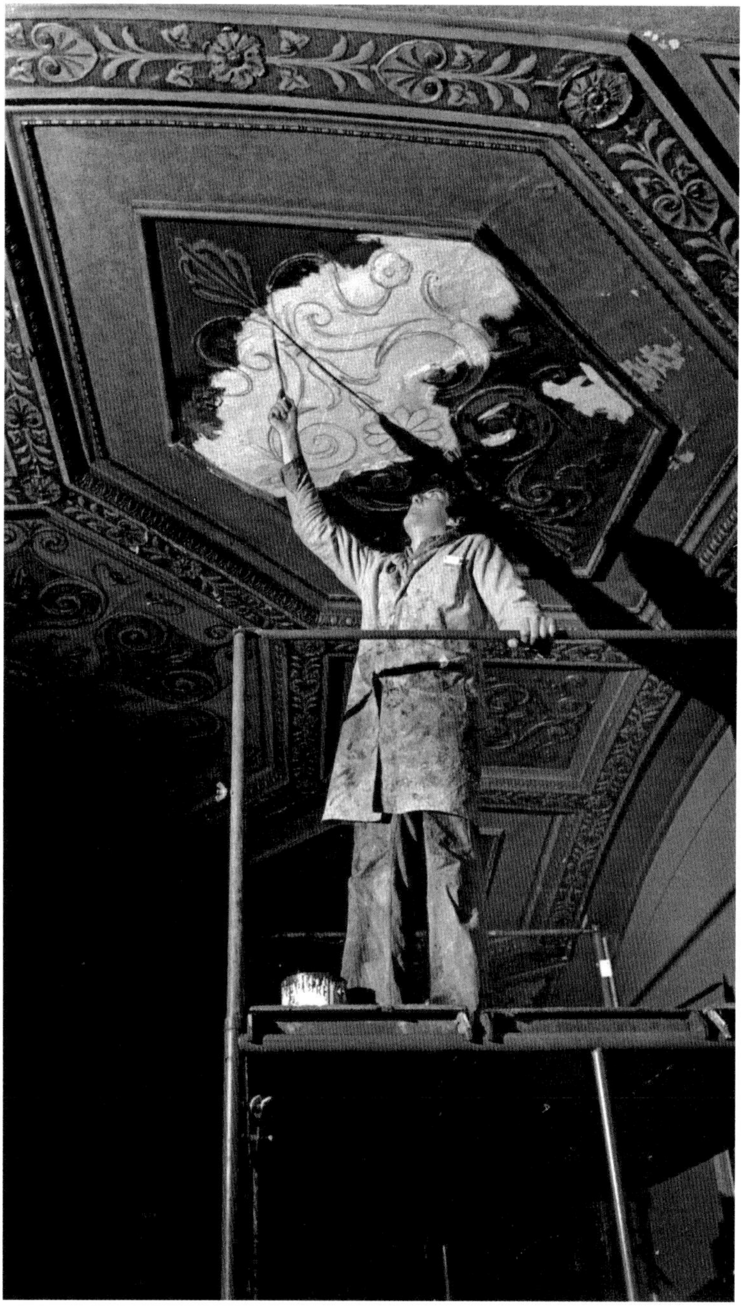

Meticulous restoration, combined with modern technology, led to the State Theater's 1984 reopening as a state-of-the-art entertainment venue. *Courtesy of Cleveland Public Library, Photograph Collection.*

"four hours of nonstop entertainment," the club remained in operation from 8:00 p.m. to midnight. Many female audience members attended clad in long dresses and feathered hats, while males wore military uniforms. College students, not yet born when nightclubs reached their peak popularity in the 1940s, composed more than 20 percent of the spectators and indicated that a renovated Playhouse Square could draw its share of youthful audiences. Booked for eight weeks, *Stompin' at the State* continued for more than fourteen months.

The beautifully renovated State Theater, including a completely new state-of-the-art stage house, reopened in 1984 with a first-night celebration highlighted by Steve Allen, Mike Douglas, Diahann Carroll and Roberta Flack. Two days later, the State hosted a week-long tour by the Metropolitan Opera and soon served as the home for the fledgling Cleveland Ballet and Cleveland Opera.

Through the years, the State's large seating capacity, enormous stage and modern stage house provided a perfect setting for the Cleveland debut of many important Broadway productions: *Phantom of the Opera*, *Cats*, *Les Miserables*, *Miss Saigon*, *The Lion King*, *Wicked*, *Jersey Boys* and others. Legendary performers graced the State stage in an array of Broadway shows: Yul Brynner (*The King and I*), Anthony Quinn (*Zorba*), Mickey Rooney (*Sugar Babies*), Mary Martin and Carol Channing (*Legends*), Joel Grey (*Cabaret*), Tommy Tune (*My One and Only*), Robert Goulet (*South Pacific*), Chita Rivera (*Can Can*) and Debbie Reynolds (*The Unsinkable Molly Brown*).

Concerts by Frankie Valli, Diana Ross, Jerry Seinfeld, Robin Williams, Tony Bennett and David Copperfield drew capacity crowds, as did the Kirov Ballet, Joffrey Ballet, American Ballet Theater and Virsky Ukrainian National Dance Company. Tributes to Elvis Presley and the Beatles, along with popular hip-hop and jazz concerts, attracted large audiences. The Cleveland Ballet and Cleveland Opera prospered prior to succumbing to financial difficulties, while younger audiences enjoyed *Sesame Street Live*, *Winnie the Pooh*, *Alvin and the Chipmunks* and other productions. Today, the State Theater, the largest of the Playhouse Square venues, continues to host a wide spectrum of entertainment offerings.

Chapter 14

THE OHIO THEATER

In 1921, *The Return of Peter Grimm*, the Ohio Theater's premiere presentation, involved a man who returned from the dead. The fantasy became somewhat of a reality in foretelling the history of the theater itself, which experienced three separate "deaths": as a legitimate theater, a nightclub and a movie playhouse. Finally, in 1982, the Ohio triumphantly returned to launch its fourth life as an integral member of the Playhouse Square Performing Arts Center.

During the planning of the State Theater, designer Thomas Lamb converted a section of otherwise wasted space into the smaller Ohio Theater. Mimicking the State, the Ohio's long 280-foot lobby connected the Euclid Avenue entrance to the theater's auditorium. The lobby ranked second in length to the next-door State Theater and was the world's longest lobby devoted to a legitimate theater.

Divided into two sections, an outer lobby extended eighty feet from Euclid Avenue into a two-hundred-foot interior grand lobby containing antiques, paintings, a huge fireplace, paneled woodwork, a red carpet and drapes and green and ivory decorations. The lobby prominently displayed three significant murals created by Italian artist Sampitrotti: *Venus: Her Birth from the Waves* (west wall), *Venus: Her Triumph* (east wall) and *Venus: Her Consecration* (south wall). Placed in the middle of the lobby, a set of bells obtained from an Italian monastery signaled to theatergoers the beginning of performances and ending of intermissions.

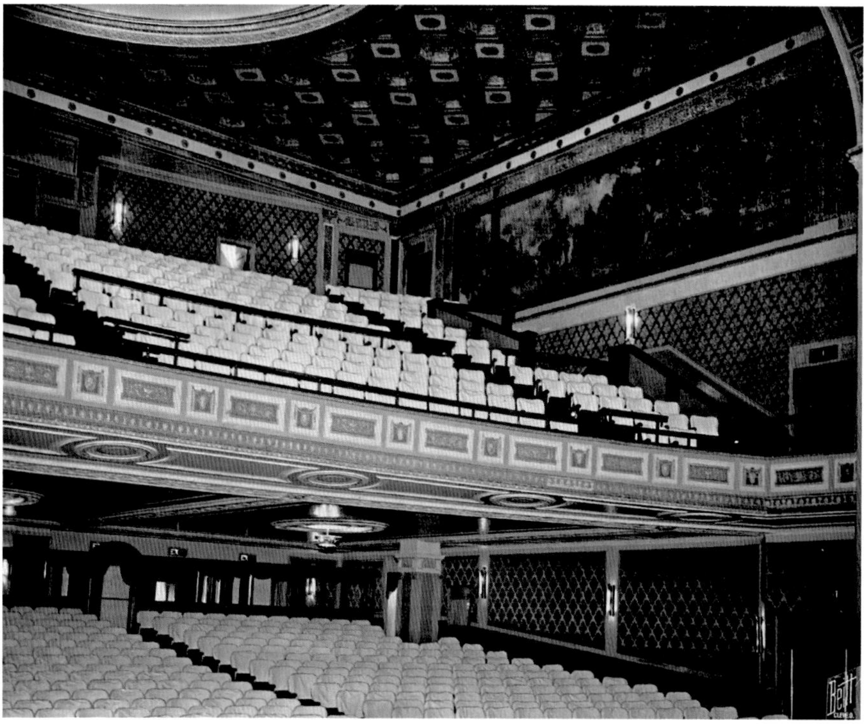

The Ohio Theater auditorium, built for live stage presentations, ranked among the most attractive in the nation. *Courtesy of Special Collections, Michael Schwartz Library, Cleveland State University.*

The 1,338-seat auditorium, patterned in a fourteenth-century Venetian style, featured soft green, tan, gold and ivory as major colors. The forty- by eighty-foot stage rivaled the size of the main floor seating area. Beautiful twin stairways led to the upstairs mezzanine and a balcony containing a crystal chandelier from the home of a nobleman living near Milan and paintings by Pizzi depicting the joys of pastoral life. The major ladies' room, attractively highlighted with cream walls, featured blue and rose furniture in the style of Louis XVI.

A week prior to its grand opening, the Ohio priced tickets for the initial performance at ten dollars at a time when typical admission prices ranged from fifty cents to three dollars. In a unique lottery arrangement, remaining first-night tickets declined in price by one dollar each day. The Ohio Theater showcased productions from the Klaw-Erlanger theatrical organization, while the competing Hanna Theater, which would debut just forty-three days after the Ohio's opening, obtained its shows from the Shubert circuit.

The beginning of the Roaring Twenties, saddled by a poor national economy, had not yet bellowed very loudly when the Ohio Theater debuted in 1921. Producers severely curtailed Broadway tours due to the overall sluggish economy, rapidly rising transportation costs and increased competition from radio and, within a few years, sound movies. High prices limited attendance on the shows that did tour; in Cleveland, the least expensive seats tended to sell much faster than pricey three-dollar tickets. Yet Robert McLaughlin, the Ohio's experienced and multi-connected manager, kept the theater operating nearly every week during the decade.

From the Ohio's opening into the early 1930s, the greatest dramatic actors of the period appeared on its stage: Ethel Barrymore, Judith Anderson, Helen Hayes and others. Performers gracing the stage also included George M. Cohan, Fanny Brice, Jack Benny, Fred Astaire, Eddie Cantor, W.C. Fields, George Jessel, Ed Wynn and the Marx Brothers. Musicals and revues filled the theater with the melodies of George and Ira Gershwin, Rogers and Hart, Irving Berlin, Jerome Kern, Oscar Hammerstein, Sigmund Romberg and Victor Herbert.

In 1922, George Abbott, an actor, writer, director and "show doctor" (a person who fixes productions that require script or plot alterations to succeed), made his first appearance at the Ohio as an actor in the comedy *Dulcy*. Sixty-five years later, Abbott returned to direct a revival of his show *Broadway* and celebrate his 100th birthday. Abbott lived past the age of 107; he died while drafting changes for an anticipated revival of *The Pajama Game*.

Clevelanders witnessed early editions of two future Broadway classics. In 1925, the success of a pre-Broadway road production of *No, No, Nanette* spawned a second touring company. Both versions played the Ohio Theater prior to New Yorkers viewing the show. Before the year ended, the Ohio had booked a third touring edition. In 1927, Jerome Kern and Oscar Hammerstein's landmark musical *Show Boat* opened at the Ohio two weeks following its premiere performance in Washington, D.C., and one month prior to its Broadway debut.

Creative promotional schemes, often involving contests appearing in Cleveland's newspapers, accompanied many of the touring shows. But a 1929 publicity stunt may have partially backfired when the Ohio's management established a temporary first-aid facility for patrons who fainted while viewing performances of *Dracula*. During the five-week engagement, a large amount of passing out occurred near the end of the shows, possibly because each person administered to by the first-aid center received a "faint check" good for a free admission to another performance.

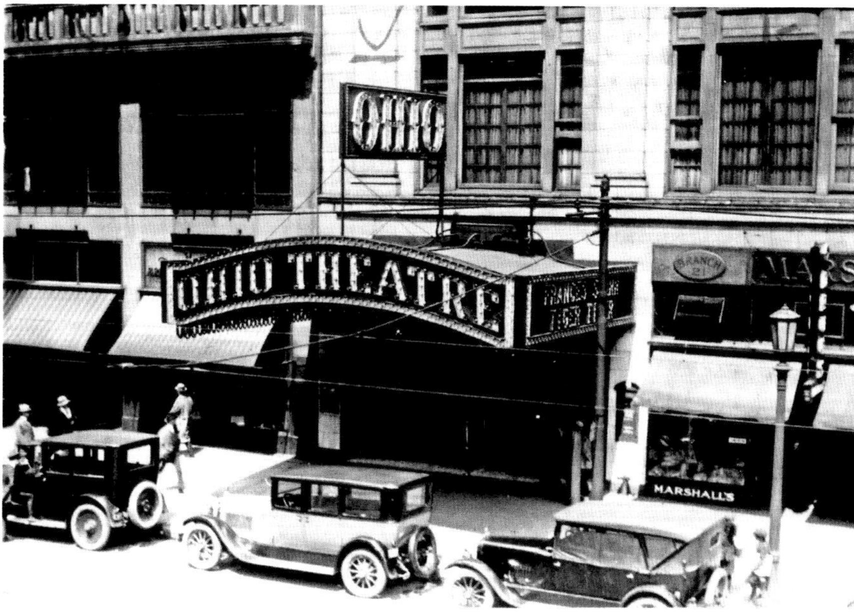

In April 1924, Francis Starr appeared in *Tiger, Tiger* at the Ohio Theater. William Boyd, her costar, subsequently played Hopalong Cassidy in sixty-six movies. *Courtesy of Special Collections, Michael Schwartz Library, Cleveland State University.*

The lengthy productions of Eugene O'Neill, *Strange Interlude* (in 1929) and *Mourning Becomes Electra* (in 1932), both beginning at 5:30 p.m., required dinner intermissions that created weighty etiquette dilemmas for Cleveland socialites. Fashionable ladies pondered the appropriateness of wearing formal dinner attire to a theater performance beginning before six o'clock. A Halle Department Store consultant revealed how she personally planned to resolve the quandary: she would wear a lace jacket until the intermission and then remove the jacket to reveal a sleeveless dinner gown.

For several seasons, summer stock companies augmented with guest stars presented outstanding summer repertory programs. With prices never exceeding $1.50, patrons enjoyed plays featuring Broadway stars Alfred Lunt, Lynn Fontanne, Walter Huston, Leo Carrillo and Ruth Gordon; silent film celebrity Dorothy Gish; and aspiring future screen luminaries Spencer Tracy and Melvin Douglas.

Although not constructed as a movie playhouse, the Ohio Theater exhibited five of the most prestigious road-show film presentations of the 1920s: *The Ten Commandments*, *Ben-Hur*, *Beau Geste*, *Old Ironsides* and *King of Kings*. More than a generation later, remakes of three (*The Ten Commandments*,

Ben-Hur and *King of Kings*) would entertain audiences again as road shows in the very same theater.

The Depression further reduced the availability of Broadway productions; even highly successful New York shows did not attempt tours. The Ohio Theater consequently remained dark for months at a time.

In 1932, the theater exhibited a small number of tours and three road-show movies: *Grand Hotel*, *Strange Interlude* and *The Sign of the Cross*. Also that year, an offspring of one of MGM's most recognized celebrities appeared for a week in the Ohio lobby to promote his new movie. The six-month-old cub of Leo the Lion plugged *Tarzan the Ape Man*, a film in which he had a significant role, playing at the neighboring Allen Theater.

The next year, three road-show film presentations (*Rasputin and the Empress*, *Cavalcade* and *Dinner at Eight*), each surviving for only two weeks, composed the theater's only bookings. Two more road-show movies, *Queen Christina* and *The House of Rothchild*, failed in 1934, as did a financially disastrous summer schedule. A money-losing, two-day engagement of the biblical fantasy *The Green Pastures* crushed further short-term attempts to rejuvenate the Ohio. On October 24, 1934, the playhouse closed, waiting for renewed prosperity to revive the legitimate theater. For the Ohio, the wait would continue for nearly a half century.

A multitude of rumors quickly spread regarding the fate of the abandoned playhouse, the most credible being a conversion into a nightclub, beer garden, cabaret or Folies Bergere venue. On October 22, 1935, the Art Deco–style Mayfair Casino nightclub, patterned after Manhattan's French Casino, debuted in the former theater. Advertisements, targeting the top hat and formal gown crowd, touted the main-floor lobby's circular bar as the longest in the world. A "sky bar," situated at the former balcony's highest point, offered another alternative for purchasing drinks that included Champagne cocktails priced at seventy-five cents. The remodeled theater auditorium incorporated dinner tables, a new circular stage and a third bar. The new owners constructed kitchen facilities underneath the still-existing former theater stage.

A staff of 16 bartenders and 112 servers catered to customers during busy periods. The club offered dinner from 5:30 p.m. to 10:00 p.m. and supper from 10:00 p.m. to closing. Many dinners could be purchased for $1.50, but an expensive filet mignon cost $2.25. The wine list included Bordeaux and burgundies, Champagnes, sherries and Italian, Hungarian and California ports. The oldest available bottle, a 1920 Hungarian wine, sold for $6.00. The most expensive bottle of Champagne, Pol Roger from 1926, cost $12.00.

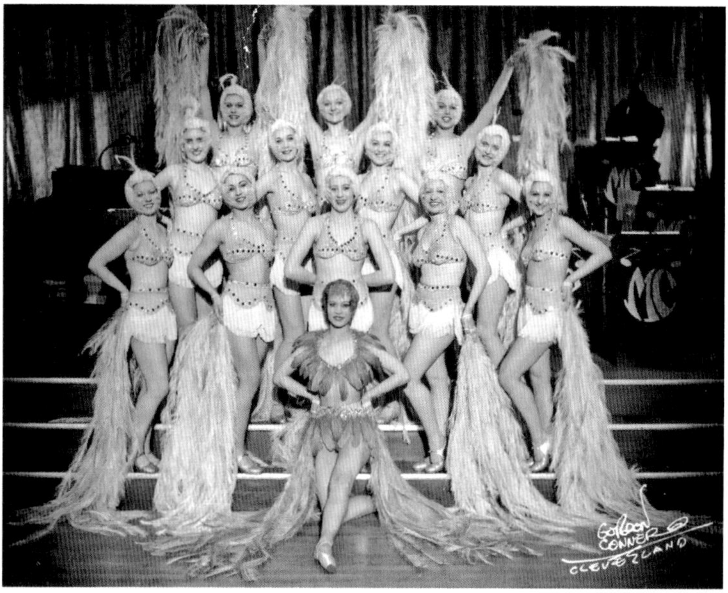

During the Depression, the Mayfair Casino temporarily transformed the Ohio Theater into a swank supper club offering nightly stage shows. *Courtesy of Special Collections, Michael Schwartz Library, Cleveland State University.*

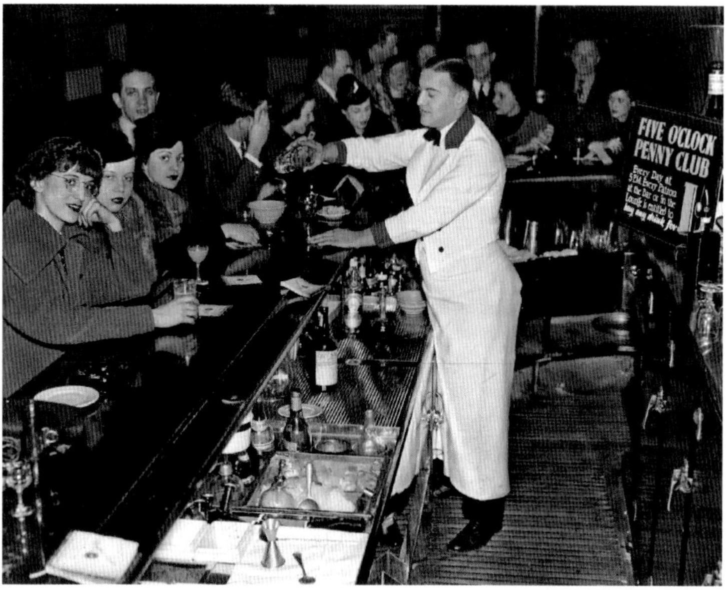

The Mayfair Casino's large staff of bartenders worked in various locations throughout the nightclub. *Courtesy of Special Collections, Michael Schwartz Library, Cleveland State University.*

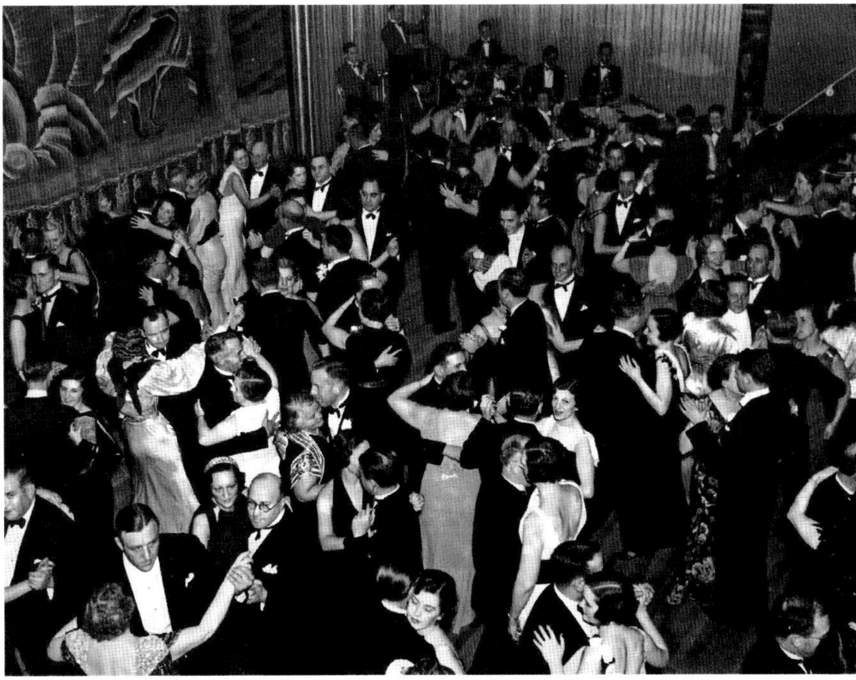

Mayfair Casino patrons enjoyed dancing to some of the nation's top orchestras. *Courtesy of Special Collections, Michael Schwartz Library, Cleveland State University.*

Three dance orchestras provided entertainment, without a cover charge, in various parts of the nightclub. A mere one dollar admitted patrons to a two-hour stage show (with a cast of between fifty and sixty performers) presented nightly at 7:30 p.m. and 11:30 p.m., with 864 seats located in portions of the former Ohio Theater's auditorium and balcony. The Mayfair booked many of the 1930s' most popular entertainers: Tommy Dorsey, Sophie Tucker, Ted Lewis, Xavier Cugat, Noble Sissle, Isham Jones and Faith Bacon. New Year's Eve revelers in 1936 paid a six-dollar cover charge to enjoy the music of Red Nichols and his Five Pennies.

Safety Director Eliot Ness and Cleveland Police officers periodically raided the casino in search of illegal gambling. During one search for gaming rooms and equipment, the officer in charge told reporters, "If it's here, I'm going to take it out. If it isn't, I'll go out." The raids never uncovered any evidence of unlawful activity.

The supper club experienced financial difficulty throughout its two-year history. In fact, rumors of the casino's demise began even before its grand opening. Tangible signs of monetary problems appeared when the Mayfair closed (except for the cocktail lounge) during the summer of 1936. In December 1936, the nightclub declared bankruptcy with reported liabilities of $321,548 and assets of $112,223 (including $2,000 in cash). The New York French Casino chain expressed interest in purchasing the club, but the sale never materialized. The casino reopened on December 25, 1936, under the direction of Durries "Duke" Crane from Detroit. His innovations included converting the lobby into a sidewalk café.

As financial problems continued to inundate the supper club, the Internal Revenue Service placed a $1,729 tax lien on the property. On November 25, 1937, plagued with liabilities of $177,927 and assets of only $84,657, the Mayfair Casino closed permanently. After the return of furnishings to their original suppliers, the only remaining asset of the once lavish supper club, an unused liquor supply, sold at a public auction for about $3,500.

For ten weeks in 1940, an exhibit in the Ohio Theater lobby displayed human oddities from New York World's Fair. The expedition's publicity promised armless wonders, midgets, giants, fat people, sword swallowers, a man with two mouths, another man with lamb's wool hair and a girl with alligator skin; all this and more cost a mere twenty-five cents. During the first months of the United States' entry into World War II, a coast guard recruiting center used the shuttered theater lobby. Otherwise, the theater and lobby remained closed until 1943, when Loew's converted the old Mayfair Casino into a movie house. No serious damage had occurred to the original theater décor because the nightclub remodeling had utilized false walls, floors and ceilings. The Ohio Theater, now embarking on its third life, joined the neighboring Playhouse Square theaters as a beautiful 1920s-style movie palace.

The Ohio's movie theater phase started strongly with a nine-week first-run engagement of *For Whom the Bell Tolls*. But for the remainder of the decade, the theater's lackluster bookings consisted primarily of films moved from the State or Stillman Theaters, first-run B movies or double-feature reissues. In the late 1940s, except for a ten-week run of Laurence Olivier's *Hamlet*, the Ohio developed into a showplace for monster hits; the top attraction of 1948 consisted of the double-feature reissues of *Son of Frankenstein* and *Bride of Frankenstein*. The following year, reissues of *Frankenstein Meets the Wolf Man* and *Dracula's Daughter* composed the year's best box-office week.

In the first half the 1950s, the Ohio's only first-run bright spots consisted of Marlon Brando in *Julius Caesar* (a five-week run) and *Guys and Dolls* (which held for thirteen weeks). By the mid-1950s, Hollywood had implemented a strategy to help combat the effects of television: the release of big-budget, long-run, road-show presentations reminiscent of the 1920s, when

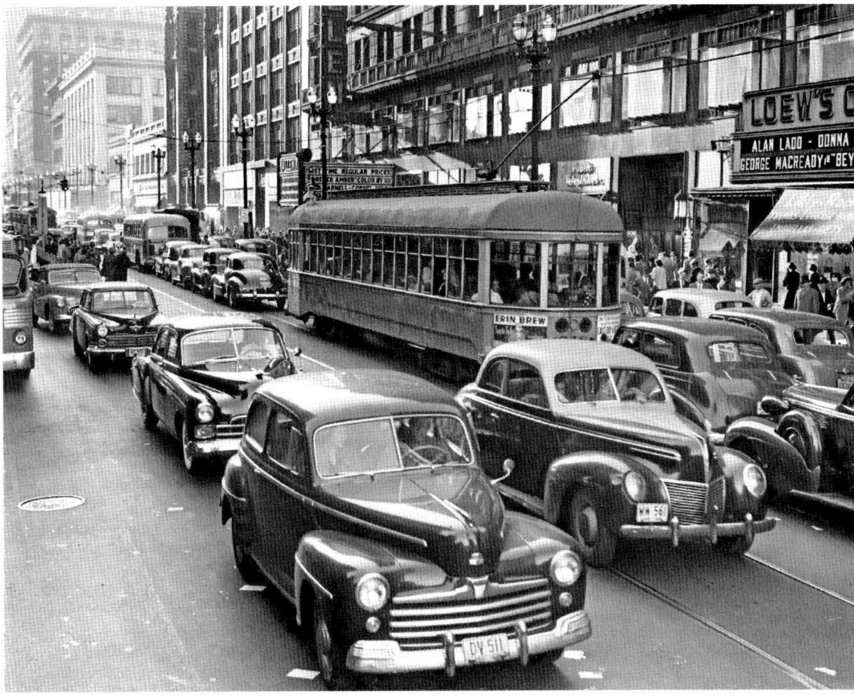

Pictured in 1948, the Ohio Theater presented *Beyond Glory*, a film starring Alan Ladd, Donna Reed and George Macready. To the west, *Forever Amber* attracted large crowds to the Allen Theater. *Courtesy of Cleveland Public Library, Photograph Collection.*

filmmakers used the same tactic to contend with the escalation of radio. The Ohio's smaller size made it a clear choice to showcase prestige films, just as it had done in the jazz age.

In 1956, a twenty-nine-week engagement of *The Ten Commandments* launched the Ohio's second road-show era. When it debuted in Cleveland, the Cecil B. DeMille epic had been shown only at the Criterion Theater in New York, and that run had started just a week earlier.

Next, the Ohio exhibited for forty-two weeks the wide-screen, 70mm film version of *Around the World in Eighty Days*, followed by a forty-seven-week run of *South Pacific* and a forty-eight-week engagement of *Ben-Hur*. Twelve more road-show presentations followed in the 1960s: *Exodus* (thirteen weeks), *King of Kings* (thirteen weeks), *West Side Story* (nineteen weeks), *Mutiny on the Bounty* (sixteen weeks), *Cleopatra* (twenty-six weeks), *The Fall of the Roman Empire* (ten weeks), *The Sound of Music* (ninety-one weeks), *The Bible* (thirty weeks), *The Happiest Millionaire* (six weeks), *Doctor Dolittle* (sixteen weeks), *Gone with the Wind* (fourteen weeks) and *Star* (seven weeks).

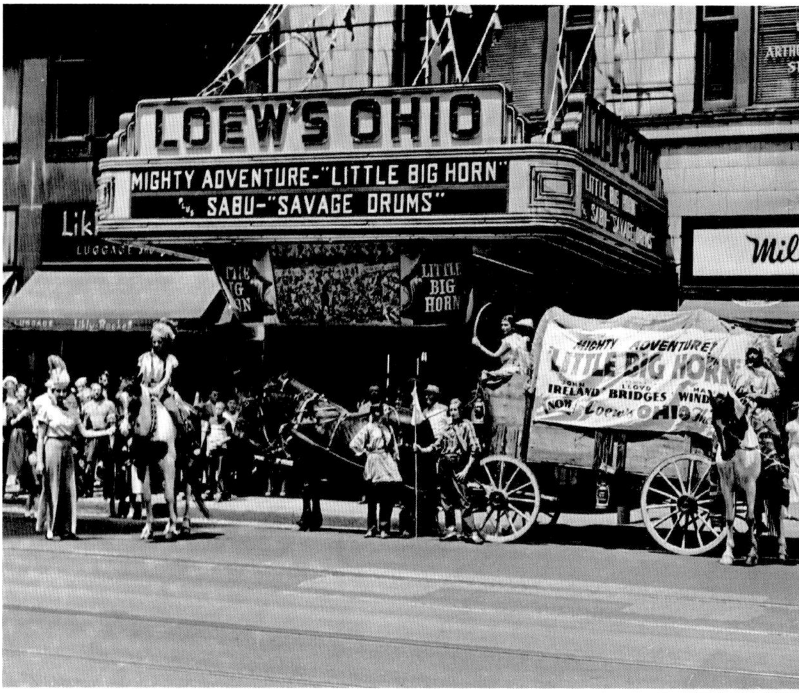
LOEW'S OHIO
MIGHTY ADVENTURE-"LITTLE BIG HORN"
SABU-"SAVAGE DRUMS"
LITTLE BIG HORN
MIGHTY ADVENTURE!
LITTLE BIG HORN
IRELAND BRIDGES
NOW Loew's OHIO

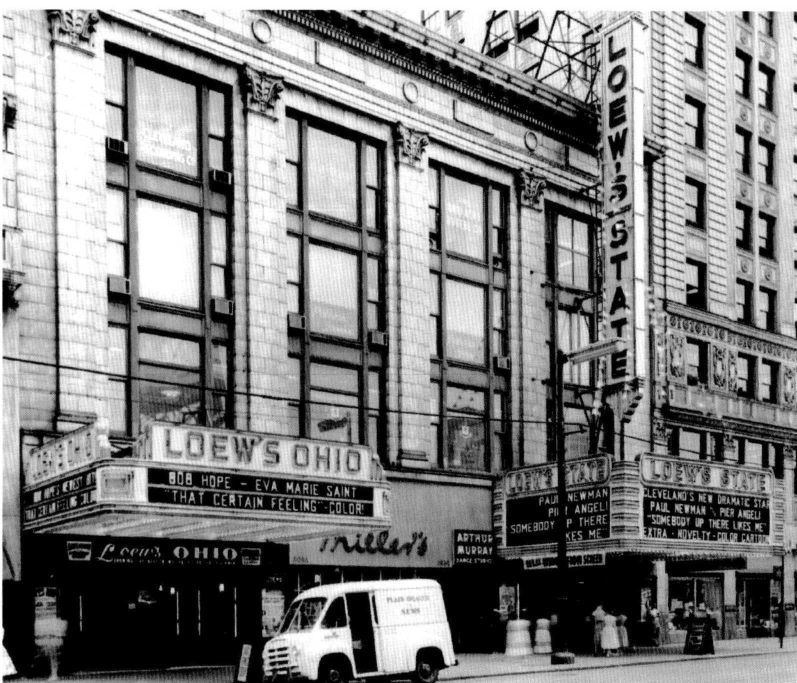
LOEW'S OHIO
BOB HOPE - EVA MARIE SAINT
"THAT CERTAIN FEELING"-COLOR!
LOEW'S STATE
Loew's OHIO
Miller's
ARTHUR MURRAY
LOEW'S STATE
CLEVELAND'S NEW DRAMATIC STAR
PAUL NEWMAN PIER ANGELI
"SOMEBODY UP THERE LIKES ME"
EXTRA - NOVELTY - COLOR CARTOON

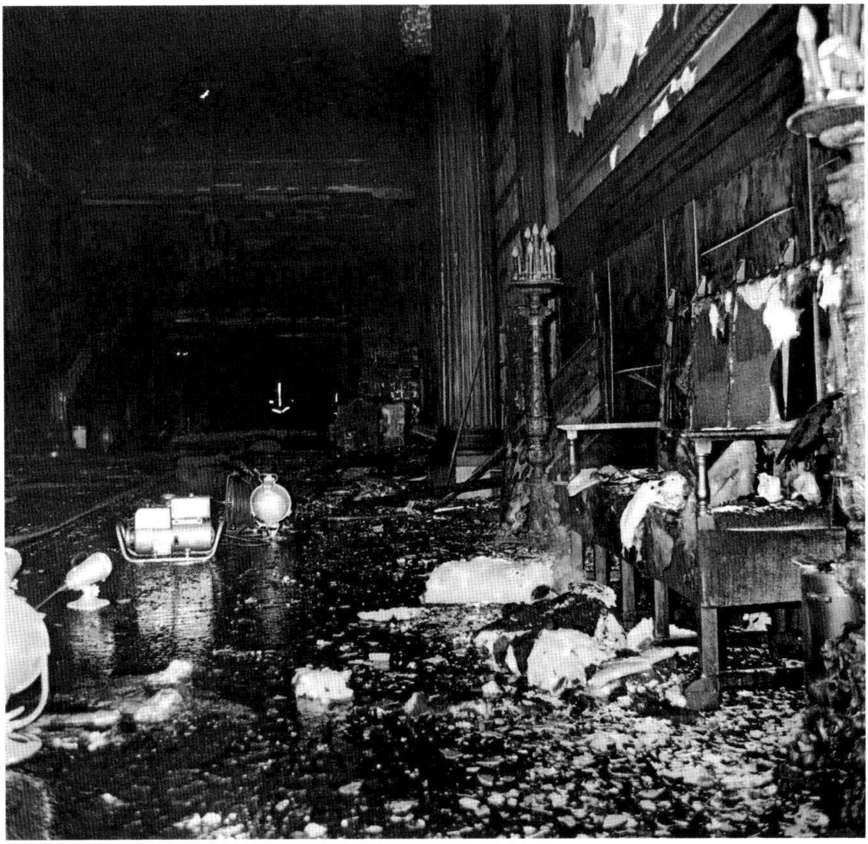

In 1964, a devastating fire destroyed a major part of the Ohio Theater. *Courtesy of Cleveland Public Library, Photograph Collection.*

Opposite, top: In July 1951, actors portrayed cavalrymen and Native Americans, accompanied by horses and a covered wagon, to promote the film *Little Big Horn*. *Courtesy of Special Collections, Michael Schwartz Library, Cleveland State University.*

Opposite, bottom: In July 1956, the State and Ohio Theaters still attracted good crowds to popular movies. *Courtesy of Special Collections, Michael Schwartz Library, Cleveland State University.*

On July 5, 1964, about one week following the completion of an extensive theater renovation, an overheated motor in the lobby concession stand caused a devastating fire that destroyed the beautiful lobby murals, mezzanine ceiling, carpeting and chandeliers. After pondering the fate of the Ohio, Loew's decided to repair the theater rather than close it. In reality, this renovation merely hid the fire damage behind false ceilings and new drywall spray painted bright red.

Julie Andrews as *Mary Poppins* created a sensation when the revamped Ohio Theater reopened on December 25, 1964. Ushers used walkie-talkies to control the enormous crowds and unearth empty seats for standing-room patrons. The thirteen-week run could have been profitably extended, but an even bigger blockbuster sat waiting in the wings. Immediately following *Mary Poppins*, Julie Andrews returned as the star of *The Sound of Music*. The film continued for an amazing ninety-one-week engagement.

On May 3, 1968, 20th Century Fox selected the Ohio to present the initial preview of the studio's forthcoming Christmas attraction, Julie Andrews in *Star*. Based on the life of entertainer Gertrude Lawrence, the studio expected another long-run triumph from the big-budgeted movie. But current bookings, shared with neighborhood theaters, averaged less than $3,000 per week while long-run, reserved-seat movies became short in supply. The Ohio needed to uncover a few profitable movies to remain in business until *Star* arrived at Christmas. A reedited, wide-screen version of *Gone with the Wind* helped fill part of the void. The Civil War epic had already played a first-run, reserved-seat engagement for thirty-four weeks at the neighborhood Shaker Theater; the film then moved to the Ohio Theater for an additional fourteen weeks. By the time the Ohio began its portion of the forty-eight-week run, the Shaker Theater had nearly exhausted the potential market for the film classic. Yet the poorly attended engagement, along with B movies and a pair of erotic films, did achieve the objective of keeping the Ohio in operation.

Needing a miracle to survive, the short-term fate of the Ohio rested with the success of *Star*. Sadly, the Julie Andrews magic had vanished. On February 9, 1969, the Ohio closed following a disastrous run of *Star*; the State Theater shut down the same day. The two boarded-up showplaces joined the Allen, which had ceased operation in 1968.

In the 1970s, the Ohio lay in near ruins—a victim of fire, vandalism, neglect and apathy. Although the theater stood abandoned, vandals used the still-operating water supply to turn on balcony fire hoses that created extensive water damage to the ceiling and wood. Teetering on the threshold of destruction, the Ohio persevered to become the first of the Playhouse Square theaters to be extensively renovated.

For more than ten years, an extraordinary civic effort kept the Ohio Theater one step ahead of the ominous wrecking ball. Then the Great Lakes Shakespeare Festival, a suburban performing arts organization, committed to relocating to the downtown theater. A $4 million, nine-month renovation culminated in the Ohio's reopening on July 9, 1982.

Intricate plasterwork on the ceilings and walls, damaged almost beyond repair, received a careful restoration. A green and ivory color scheme duplicated the original theater colors. The renovation work unexpectedly uncovered the Ohio's first wooden stage, complete with trapdoors. Yet much of the renovation constituted repair work rather than true restoration. The theater's great lobby bore little resemblance to its original grandeur. Mirrored walls replaced the ruined lobby murals, and the former ivory staircases could not be faithfully reconstructed.

The Great Lakes Shakespeare Festival's rousing first season at the Ohio, now a one-thousand-seat playhouse, debuted with *As You Like It*, the same Shakespeare classic that had opened the organization's very first season back in 1962. In twenty years, the top price had escalated from $2.00 to $12.75.

The festival obtained the rights to present an eight-and-a-half-hour adaptation of Charles Dickens's *The Life and Adventures of Nicholas Nickleby*, the first staging of the massive production outside London and New York. Forty-six actors performed three hundred roles in the show's ninety-six scenes. With a budget of $500,000, *Nicholas Nickleby* reigned as the most costly play ever staged in Cleveland, surpassing the Cleveland Ballet's expenditure of $425,000 to launch its version of the *Nutcracker*. A sell-out at nearly every performance, the Dickens classic attracted four thousand visitors from outside northeast Ohio, some from as far as Europe. The resounding success ended the debate concerning whether Clevelanders would travel downtown to enjoy first-rate entertainment.

In 1986, the now renamed Great Lakes Festival assembled an all-star cast (Jean Stapleton, Polly Holliday, William Hickey, Abe Vigoda and Tony Roberts) to produce a world-premiere revival of *Arsenic and Old Lace*. Following its run at the Ohio Theater, the show moved to New York for a successful run. In 1989, the festival launched a production of *A Christmas Carol* that continues to thrive to the present day.

In 2008, the company (now known as the Great Lakes Theater) relocated to a custom-built facility in Playhouse Square's Hanna Theater. During its twenty-six-year residence at the Ohio Theater, festival performers, in addition to the *Arsenic and Old Lace* cast, included Hal Holbrook, Lynn Redgrave, Olympia Dukakis, Cloris Leachman, Avery Brooks, Ruby Dee, Tony Randall, Claire Bloom and Robert Foxworthy.

The Ohio Theater functioned as the second home of the former Akron-based Ohio Ballet. Through the decades, the theater hosted touring dance companies, a children's series, big-band and jazz performances, chamber music groups and early concerts by the Cleveland Pops Orchestra.

Entertainers performing at the Ohio included Whoopi Goldberg, Jackie Mason, Norah Jones, Natalie Merchant, Bryan Adams and Booney Jones.

Since its 1982 reopening, the theater has hosted several important movie events. In 1984, the Ohio exhibited the 15.5-hour film *Berlin Alexanderplatz*. Directed and written by Rainer Werner Fassbinder, the portrayal of life in Germany between the world wars originally aired as a German television miniseries. Nine hundred people gathered between noon and 9:00 p.m. on a Saturday and Sunday to view the film and spend a total of 3 additional hours on breaks, including pauses for weekend dinners.

The Ohio hosted the world premieres of five films: *Violets Are Blue*, *Sweet Liberty*, *Light of Day*, *Superman IV* and *Major League*. Cleveland's International Film Festival staged the premieres of the first two movies; the second included an in-person visit by Alan Alda.

On February 2, 1987, Michael J. Fox and Joan Jett chatted with audience members, some of whom had paid a top price of $225 to see the first showing of *Light of Day*, a film set in and partially filmed in Cleveland. A half-year later, three hundred moviegoers paid $250 each to dine at the Stouffer Public Square Hotel restaurant and then view the world premiere of *Superman IV* in orchestra seats. Another set of patrons purchased $50 balcony tickets that also entitled them to cocktails and hors d'oeuvres in the lobby of the Ohio or State Theater. *Major League*, a fictionalized comedy about the Cleveland Indians, debuted on April 4, 1989. Corbin Bernsen (who played third baseman Roger Dorn) and a gathering of real Cleveland Indians attended the premiere, but baseball legend Bob Feller upstaged the entire group when he showed up for the film's premiere.

The Ohio Theater continues as a vital part of Playhouse Square's wide variety of entertainment offerings by presenting vocal, dance and music concerts, ballets, operas, plays, musicals, lectures and the Great Lakes Theater's annual production of *A Christmas Carol*.

Chapter 15

THE HANNA THEATER

The 1,421-seat Hanna Theater debuted in 1921, less than two months after the opening of the competing Ohio Theater. Designed in an Italian Renaissance and Pompeian style, the theater's décor featured green and gold carpets, dark green seats, frescoed walls, Louis XVI furniture, a fireplace and a coffered ceiling decorated with gilded plaster medallions, each containing classical figures such as Cupid, Psyche and Pegasus. Unlike the grand lobbies of Euclid Avenue's movie and vaudeville palaces, the Hanna's small, no-frills utilitarian lobby (just exceeding twenty feet in each direction) resembled New York City's legitimate theaters, constrained in space because of their placements on crowded side streets.

An early 1920s economic downturn plagued both the Hanna and Ohio Theaters as they attempted to obtain touring shows. Controlled by the Shubert organization, the Hanna augmented Shubert's musicals and operettas with performances by grand opera, Shakespearean and minstrel troupes. As the economy improved, the Hanna hosted stage legends Alfred Lunt and Lynn Fontanne, Helen Hayes and Ethel and John Barrymore along with first-rate performers including Humphrey Bogart, Al Jolson, Eddie Cantor, Ed Wynn, the Marx Brothers, Mae West, Fanny Brice and Jeanne Eagles. Magician Howard Thurston required eight train cars to transport the props needed to perform his mystifying illusions during his numerous Hanna appearances. In 1925, Harry Houdini performed sleight-of-hand tricks, escaped from chains, swallowed needles and exposed bogus psychics.

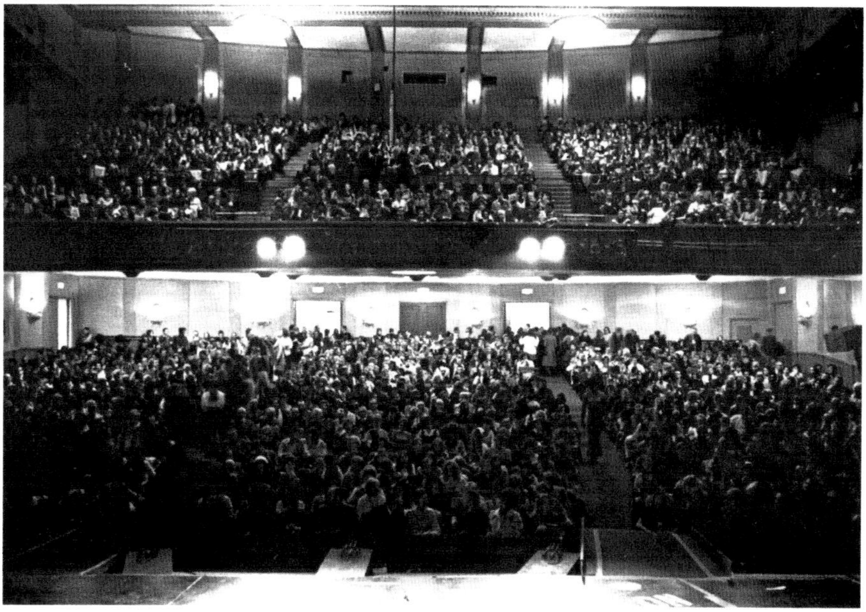

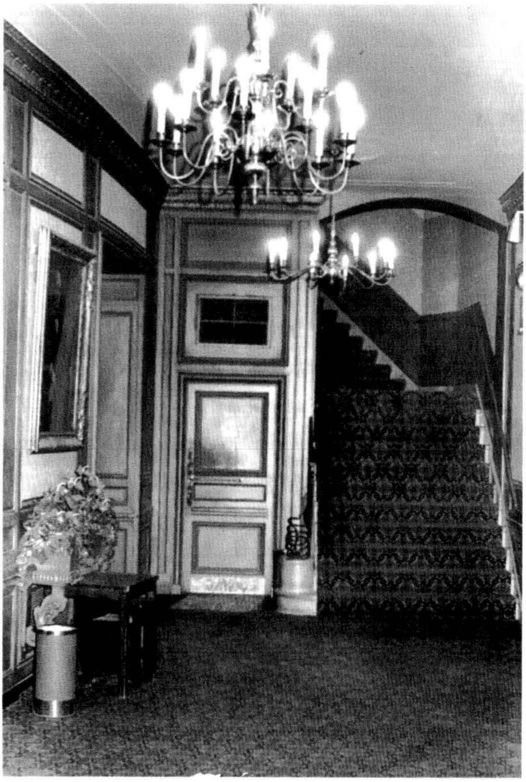

Above: Since the Hanna's debut in 1921, capacity crowds have greeted many productions. *Courtesy of Special Collections, Michael Schwartz Library, Cleveland State University.*

Left: Although very attractive, the Hanna's lobby does not rival the grandeur of the neighboring old movie palaces. *Courtesy of Special Collections, Michael Schwartz Library, Cleveland State University.*

Debuting at the Hanna in 1922, Eva La Gallienne's eight performances at the theater spanned more than fifty-four years. Katharine Cornell set the record for appearing in the most shows, twenty-two different plays from 1926 into 1958. In 1925, a summer stock presentation of *White Cargo* (a story of white slavery in America) completed a nine-week run and then moved to the Metropolitan Theater for five more weeks. Less than a year following the Hanna's debut, the theater hosted its first road-show movie, a four-week run of D.W. Griffith's *Orphans of the Storm*. In 1926, the World War I epic *The Big Parade* completed an eight-week, reserved-seat engagement.

In a disastrous 1933–34 season, the Hanna presented only nine weeks of live entertainment. In response to the Depression, the Shubert circuit substantially reduced the top price of dramatic productions from three to two dollars, but the organization soon collapsed. The Hanna developed a repertory company and added movies to fill the void created by the shortage of touring presentations. But even in the depths of the Depression, Orson

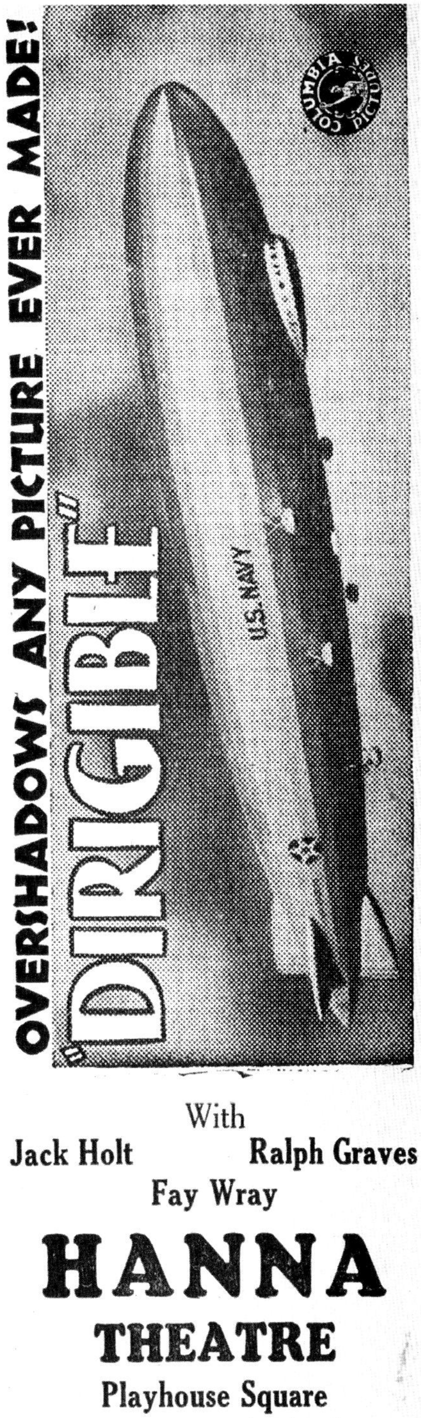

In 1931, the Cleveland Public Library created a bookmark to promote the film *Dirigible*. *Courtesy of Cleveland Public Library Archives.*

Welles and Katherine Cornell drew crowds to view their interpretation of *Romeo and Juliet* and the Hanna booked plays starring Katharine Hepburn, Judith Anderson, Jose Ferrer, Hume Cronyn, Cornella Otis Skinner and Gertrude Lawrence.

In the first two years of the 1930s, the Hanna exhibited three road-show movies: *All Quiet on the Western Front*, *Trader Horn* and *Dirigible.* In 1933, when a three-week strike by musicians, stagehands and moving picture operators closed traditional movie theaters, the Hanna filled the void by presenting mainstream movies combined with vaudeville acts or the locally popular Emerson Gill orchestra. Later that year, the Hanna booked two unusual films: *Mädchen in Uniform*, a classic German film, and *Forgotten Men*, a movie featuring real-life veterans discussing their experiences during World War I. The Hanna presented five road-show movies during the remainder of the 1930s: Cecil B. DeMille's *The Crusaders*, *A Midsummer Night's Dream*, Norma Shearer and Leslie Howard's version of *Romeo and Juliet*, *The Good Earth* and *Lost Horizon.* A six-week engagement of *The Birth of a Baby*, a serious educational film, traced the life of a child from the mother's first visit to her doctor until a short time after the child's birth.

In 1940, the Hanna staged the world premiere of *Zone of Quiet.* Written by a Cleveland doctor, the play concerned the tribulations of working in a hospital. A few days prior to the opening, the surprised cast at a rehearsal observed two policemen frisking one of the cast members. A passerby had reported the actor to the police after witnessing him twirling a revolver (actually a stage prop) as he relaxed outside the theater during a break. Cleveland-born Martin Fuss, cast in the play, would return to downtown Cleveland to present world premieres of several of his major Hollywood movies; by then he used his adopted name, Ross Hunter. Also in 1940, Montgomery Clift acted in *There Shall Be No Night* only one month after celebrating his twentieth birthday.

Milton Krantz, the newly appointed Hanna manager in 1941, continued in the position for the next forty-two years. Patrons of the Hanna witnessed many noteworthy events that year. Al Jolson made his final Hanna appearance. Stage and film actor Charles Butterworth starred in the world premiere of *Father's Day*; following the performance, the Hanna hosted a coast-to-coast radio broadcast in which critics commented on the show. On the Hanna screen, a three-week, reserved-seat showing of *Ku Kan* presented an account of the Japanese-Chinese War from the viewpoint of China. Newspaper advertising declared, "It's your duty to see the havoc wrought by Jap bombs on peace-loving people." The film began its run the week following Japan's attack on Pearl Harbor. But the March 18 debut of *Fantasia* surpassed the excitement of any of these events.

Cleveland joined eleven other cities in presenting the innovative film that combined Disney animation with a classical music score in stereophonic sound. Technical experts from the Disney Studio and sound engineers from RCA arrived several weeks prior to *Fantasia*'s first showing to install new projection and sound equipment. Following its red-carpet premiere, accompanied by klieg lights and radio commentators, more than 100,000 people viewed the film during a nine-week, reserved-seat engagement.

Oklahoma! debuted at the Hanna in 1943 just seven months after its Broadway unveiling. Although attracting capacity crowds, the Hanna incurred considerable extra expense by returning 95 percent of the mail-order ticket requests for the sold-out performances. Two years later, *Carmen Jones* established a new box-office record. During the 1940s, twenty-six-year old Jackie Gleason, Mary Martin, Jean Stapleton and Ernest Borgnine made their first Hanna appearances. In 1947, Charlton Heston, Sidney Poitier, Carl Reiner and Bob Fosse, all twenty-five years old or younger at the time, appeared on the Hanna stage.

Following World War II, Hanna audiences revived an old Victorian custom: complaining about ladies' hats obscuring the view of the stage. A letter to the *Plain Dealer*, written by an irritated male theatergoer after a 1946 performance of *On the Town*, described the hat worn by a lady in front of him as "a combination of a scoop shovel, like we used to get coal out of a freight car, and a stove pipe hat of the Abe Lincoln type." Two years later, in another letter, a male described an obtrusive female hat as "a tall hat with feathers about a yard up in the air."

In 1948, to accommodate the enormous ticket demand for Mary Martin in *Annie Get Your Gun*, the Hanna moved the production to the larger downtown Music Hall. This practice, continuing into the 1980s, deprived the Hanna of the initial showings of many great musicals.

Films presented in the 1940s included *That They May Live* (a French propaganda film created to keep France out of World War II), *No Greater Love* (a Russian film portraying the evils of the war) and *The Ravaged Earth* (a United States documentary dealing with atrocities committed by the Japanese military). The Hanna also generated a two-week run by combining *Ecstasy*, the stale Hedy Lamarr film that had already played multiple-week engagements at numerous theaters, with *One Thrilling Night*, a mediocre B movie.

In 1951, the Hanna increased its capacity from 1,435 to 1,515 seats. Hampered by higher touring costs, the theater presented only ten weeks of live entertainment. The following year, a sensational two-week run of *Guys and Dolls*, assisted by prices soaring up to $6.15 per ticket, established new box-office records. In 1953, Shaker Heights native Paul Newman, yet to be cast in a movie, appeared as a supporting player in the pre-Broadway engagement of *Picnic*. That same year, the unknown twenty-three-year-old Steve McQueen acted in *Time Out for Ginger*.

In the 1950s, several famous actors made their initial Hanna appearances: Henry Fonda, Rosalind Russell, Deborah Kerr and Lauren Bacall. Compensating for a lack of product throughout the decade, the Hanna also welcomed special appearances by Jimmy Durante, Victor Borge, Jose Greco, Mike Nichols and Elaine May, Blackstone the Magician, Tom Lehrer, Shelly Berman and Hank Williams.

The Hanna's film selections for the decade began with a four-week road-show version of the 1951 British import *Tales of Hoffman*. In 1954, the theater installed a new and larger movie screen to more successfully exhibit Italian and British imports and mainstream American films. As the decade ended, the Hanna hosted a three-week silent film festival.

In 1956, actress Augusta French, a cast member of *The Boy Friend*, window shopped along Euclid Avenue and Huron Road. An assailant carrying a knife dragged her into a nearby alley. Threatening to kill her, he punched her on the head and face, broke several of her teeth and cut her arm. The mugger fled when her screams for help attracted attention, although she lost her purse containing $112. Downtown acts of violence escalated in the 1960s. When a parking garage attached to the Hanna opened in 1969, newspaper advertising advised patrons that they no longer needed to risk assault or robbery when they attended the theater.

In the 1960s, as the downtown movie palaces faded, theatergoers unable to view the latest Broadway shows in the safety of their own suburbs braved the real and perceived dangers of downtown to break Hanna box-office records eight times during the engagements of *The Pleasure of His Company*, *The Music Man* (two weeks with the most expensive tickets soaring to seven dollars), *The Sound of Music* (three weeks), *How to Succeed in Business Without Really Trying* and *Funny Girl*. Other shows reaching near-capacity business included Sid Caesar in *Little Me*, Ginger Rogers in *Hello Dolly* and Art Carney in *Lovers*. In 1970, while urban planners debated whether suburbanites would ever again patronize downtown theaters, the Hanna's 4,733 season subscribers composed the nation's largest single-week subscription base for touring shows.

In 1971, capacity crowds filled the Hanna for two tours representing opposite ends of the musical spectrum. June Allyson headlined a nostalgic

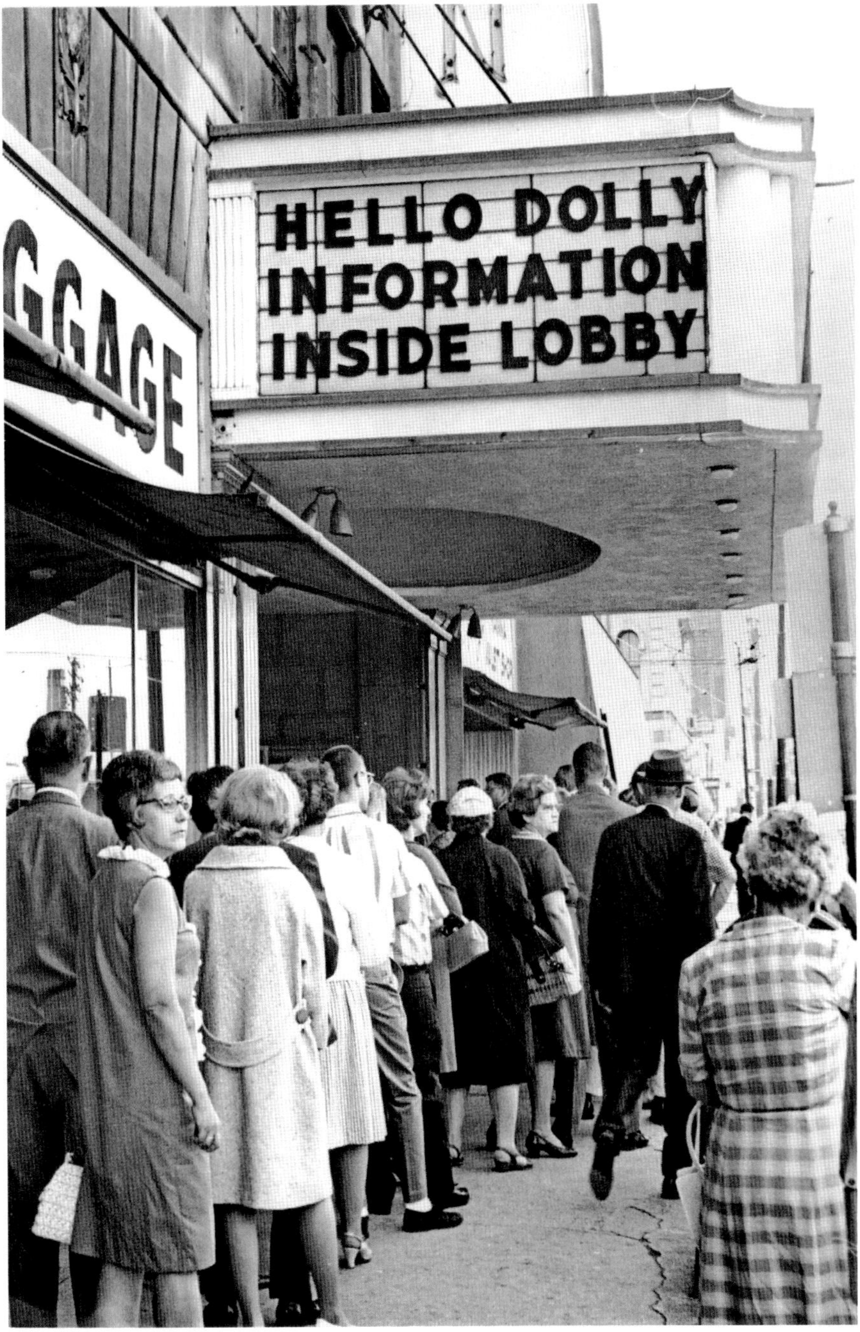

Even as the Playhouse Square movie theaters declined, long lines formed to purchase tickets for Hanna Theater productions. *Courtesy of Special Collections, Michael Schwartz Library, Cleveland State University.*

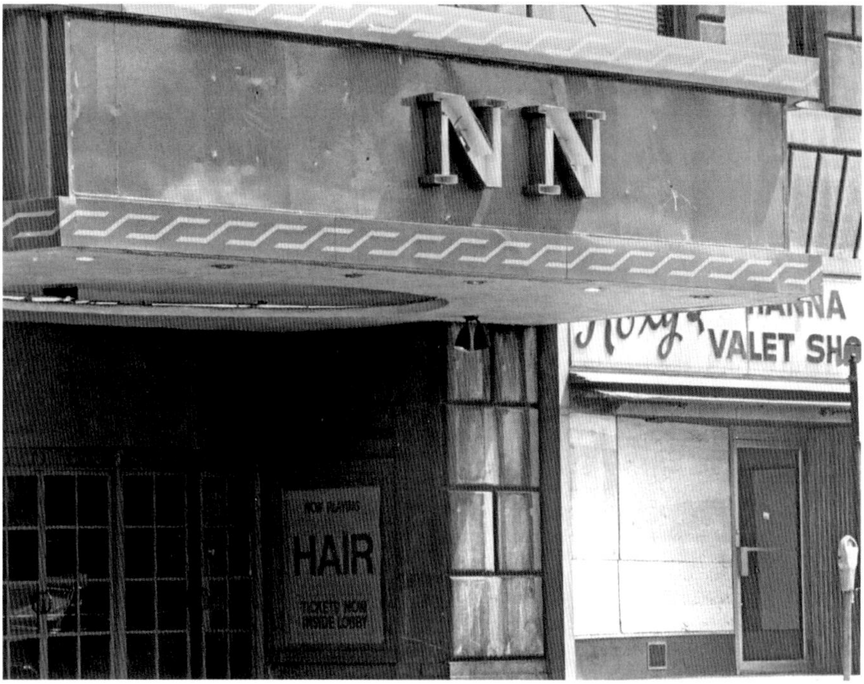

During the controversial engagement of *Hair*, a bomb hurled at the Hanna damaged the theater's marquee. *Courtesy of Special Collections, Michael Schwartz Library, Cleveland State University.*

revival of the 1925 hit *No, No, Nanette*, while the contemporary rock musical *Hair* created considerable controversy. The theater hired six extra ticket sellers to handle the record-breaking mail-order requests for *Hair* tickets. Although Cleveland's Vice Squad labeled the show vulgar and tasteless, the officers concluded that *Hair* did not violate any standards or laws regarding indecency. A few days after the musical's opening, a Hanna employee discovered three sticks of dynamite hidden in front of the theater. A day or two later, the audience and cast evacuated the Hanna because of a bomb threat. Telephone warnings of explosions continued; the theater even received a postcard alerting the management of a future bombing.

During the seven-week engagement of *Hair*, a fire in the Pick Carter Hotel killed four members of the show's company; in each case, a young mother and her infant daughter had died. After the tragedy, a bomb hurled at the Hanna bounced off the marquee and exploded on the sidewalk, shattering more than forty-two windows in the Hanna building.

In 1974, the Hanna hosted the world premiere of Yul Brynner in *Odyssey*, a play that, after much redoing, would still fail in New York. Two years

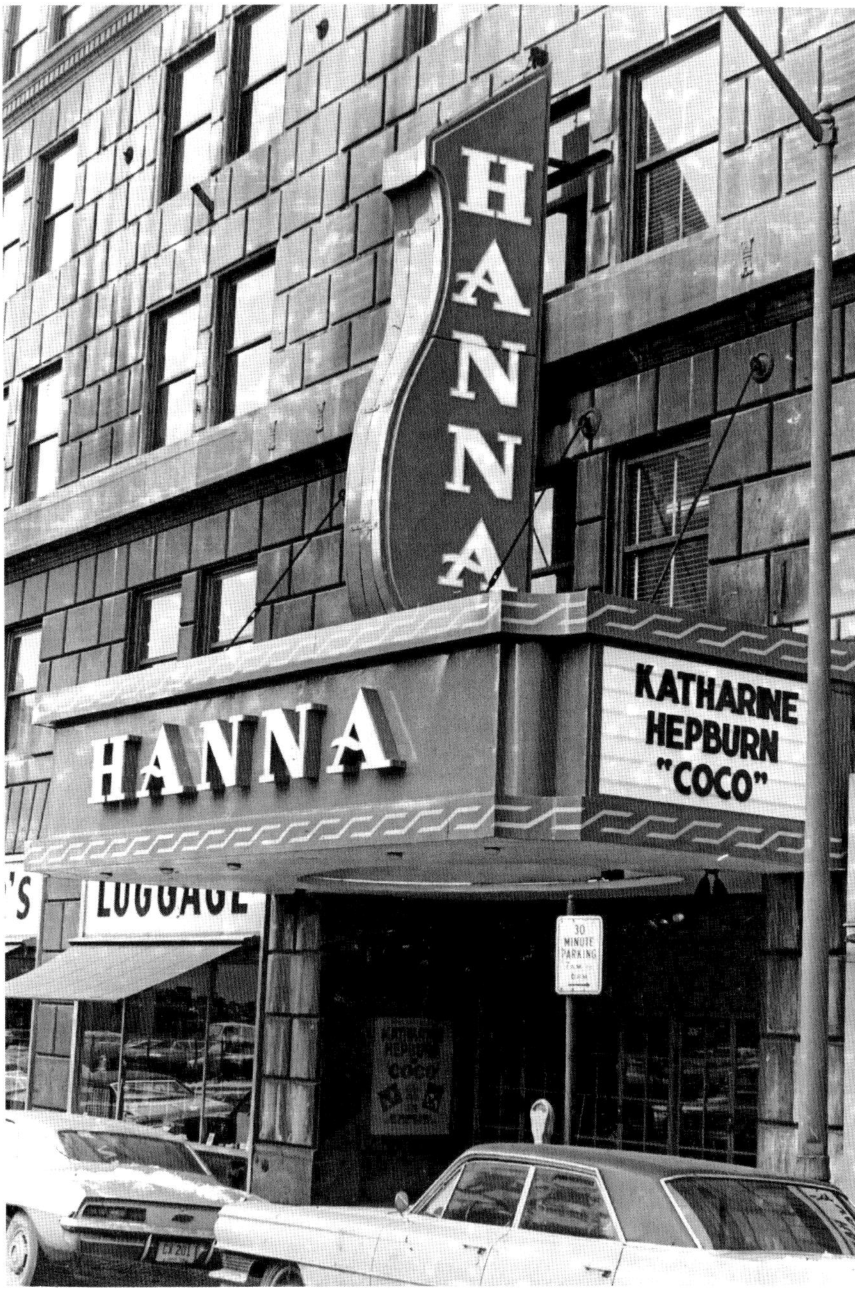

Although prominently advertised on the Hanna marquee, the larger Music Hall staged Katharine Hepburn's 1971 appearance in *Coco*. *Courtesy of Special Collections, Michael Schwartz Library, Cleveland State University.*

later, as a stunt to publicize the sluggishly attended engagement of *Grease*, promoters launched one thousand balloons from Public Square, each one containing a free ticket to the show. A wind quickly propelled most of the balloons northward over Lake Erie, never to be seen again.

The Cleveland Ballet and the Cleveland Opera, destined to become two of the city's foremost performing arts organizations, debuted at the Hanna in 1976 and 1979, respectively. Both groups performed at the Hanna into the early 1980s, helping the theater fill a growing number of otherwise dark weeks.

The Hanna's box-office record fell a dozen times in the 1970s, during the engagements of *Hair* (two weeks), *No, No, Nanette* (two weeks), *Bubbling Brown Sugar*, the Houston Grand Opera's production of *Porgy and Bess*, *A Chorus Line* (four weeks) and *The Wiz* (two weeks). Beginning at ten dollars, the Hanna's top price had reached sixteen dollars by the end of the decade.

The 1981 engagement of Neil Simon's *I Ought to Be in Pictures* unexpectedly began very poorly. A gunman entered the theater the day before opening night, pointed a pistol at two employees and proclaimed, "I want all your money. Give it to me now or I'll blow your head off." He escaped with $7,000. In 1982, Lana Turner, making her only appearance at the Hanna, generated little excitement starring in *Murder among Friends*.

In the 1980s, even return engagements generated new box-office records. Receipts for a return of *A Chorus Line* soared as patrons paid up to eighteen dollars per ticket. Three weeks of *Annie*'s second Cleveland appearance each set a new box-office mark as top-priced tickets rose to twenty-two dollars.

The next period in the Hanna's history constituted a plot worthy of the best dramas ever presented on the theater's stage. The Cleveland Ballet, outgrowing both the Hanna's stage and seating capacity, moved to the larger Music Hall. The Cleveland Opera relocated to the State Theater when it reopened in 1984, and Broadway shows soon followed the same course. In the process, the Hanna lost virtually all of its booking power. Persisting rumors about the Hanna's future ranged from permanent closure to a conversion into a movie house or a purchase by the Playhouse Square Foundation.

In 1984, William Roudebush, a former Cleveland Playhouse director, organized a company to book and develop shows for the now mostly abandoned Hanna Theater. After only three months, Roudebush characterized his idea as "economically unfeasible" and folded his company. The next year, city councilman Dennis Kucinich attempted to persuade Shirley MacLaine (his friend and the godmother of one of his children) to star in a show at the Hanna, but the event never took place. A "Hanna

Alive" group struggled to obtain funding to reopen the theater, but instead, the organization itself died.

In 1986, veteran movie theater operator Morrie Zyrl booked films into the Hanna, including *Shoah* (a nine-and-a-half-hour documentary concerning Holocaust survivors) and a five-week festival of Japanese films directed by Akira Kurosawa. For the next two years, a collection of mostly second-tier rock stars performed on the Hanna stage.

In 1989, members of the recently disbanded Cleveland Playhouse resident company combined with former Playhouse costume, prop and set designers to form the nucleus of the Cleveland Actors Theater Company. The group staged four plays at the Hanna in five months before abandoning its project.

In the first seven years of the 1990s, the Hanna sat vacant except for a very brief period of use by Hilarities Comedy Club. In 1992, the Another Door Theater Company, a professional dinner theater organization, considered converting the Hanna into a 350-seat dinner theater. A forty-dollar ticket would have covered parking, dinner, the show and after-dinner dancing on the Hanna stage, but the dinner theater never materialized. In 1997, Ray Shepardson returned to Cleveland, converting the Hanna into a cabaret theater. The experiment failed within one year.

Finally, in 1999, the Playhouse Square Foundation purchased the Hanna. Unlike other Playhouse Square theaters, the foundation didn't really save the Hanna from a wrecking ball. The former owners never threatened to demolish the Hanna, but the multitude of past failures severely muddled any concrete future plans. Playhouse Square needed time to consider its options, so rather than embarking on an immediate renovation, the foundation instead invited Clevelanders to attend the wedding ceremony and reception of Tony Nunzio and Tina Vitale, both held at the Hanna Theater.

Most Cleveland theatergoers had never witnessed anything quite like *Tony 'n Tina's Wedding*. Rather than sitting in seats while actors recite a formal script, the audience played the parts of the wedding guests. In this "interactive theater" experience, the twenty-five-member cast used a general plot outline composed of about twenty different subplots that unfolded during the evening. Wedding guests (the audience) could simply watch the fun while enjoying a meatball and spaghetti dinner, a Champagne toast and a slice of wedding cake and dancing to the accompaniment of a four-piece band. But as guests interacted with members of the Nunzio and Vitale families and friends, they more fully appreciated the conflicting plots and strange events occurring during the evening. Since the cast relied on their improvisational skills, no two evenings ever played out exactly the same way.

Although wedding guests attending the second preview of *Tony 'n Tina's Wedding* expected many quandaries to unfold during the evening, no one anticipated the dilemma developing outside the Hanna. A few hours earlier, almost in front of the theater, a subcontractor installing fiber-optic cable had punctured an unmarked water main with his backhoe. Water, rising nearly fifty feet in the air, created knee-deep wading through the streets as it poured into shops and building basements. Businesses on the block all closed—except for the wedding. Guests plodded through mud-covered sidewalks to reach the theater while wondering what would come next in this rather unusual evening.

The show opened on August 29, 2000, and continued through December 2, 2002; Tony and Tina participated in 801 wedding ceremonies and receptions. In real life, Lisa Ray (cast as Tina) actually married Andy Weiland (cast as Tony's brother).

Following several more long-run shows, Playhouse Square finalized its plans for the Hanna's future use. In 2008, the Great Lakes Theater relocated from the Ohio Theater to adopt the Hanna as its new home. The Cleveland Jazz Orchestra also uses the Hanna as its home base.

An extensive remodeling of the Hanna created a new high-tech venue with much greater intimacy between the audience and actors. A reduction in capacity to 550 seats guarantees that no patron will be situated more than twelve rows from the stage. A modern thrust stage extends into the audience on three sides and can be lowered to create a traditional proscenium stage with a full orchestra pit. Audience members can choose traditional theater seating or view a production from private boxes, lounge-style seats or tall chairs near the bar area.

Originally conceived by Dan Hanna, an industrialist and newspaper publisher, as a memorial to his father, Mark (who owned the Euclid Avenue Opera House), the Hanna Theater has successfully adapted through the decades to competitive threats, economic downturns, financial difficulties and changes in patrons' tastes.

Chapter 16

THE ALLEN THEATER

On April 1, 1921, the newest lights shining in Playhouse Square belonged to the 3,003-seat Allen Theater, located in the eight-story Bulkley Building. The theater's 133-foot lobby, highlighted by bronze doors and gilded mirrors, led to a 33-foot domed rotunda encircled by sixteen black walnut Corinthian columns accented in blue and gold. A fountain and suspended chandelier added to the rotunda's beauty. Both the rotunda and foyer received their architectural inspiration from the sixteenth-century Villa Madonna, a prominent home located about eighteen miles outside Rome.

While still in their teens, brothers Jules and Jay J. Allen (both born in Pennsylvania) purchased a Canadian movie theater, eventually expanding their operation to encompass fifty theaters. The brothers entered the United States market by constructing the Cleveland movie house, a decision that quickly turned into a financial failure. Lacking the necessary contacts and expertise to effectively battle America's movie theater chains, the Allen brothers mostly booked movies unwanted by their American competitors. Loew's purchased the Allen within one year of its opening but did not advertise it as a Loew's theater until 1928.

As a Loew's theater, the Allen's bookings in the 1920s comprised C.B. DeMille's early motion pictures and films starring Lon Chaney, Clara Bow, Joan Crawford, Greta Garbo and Gloria Swanson. But competition forced Loew's to include live entertainment along with films. In addition to vaudeville performers and film stars, the Allen booked many first-rate

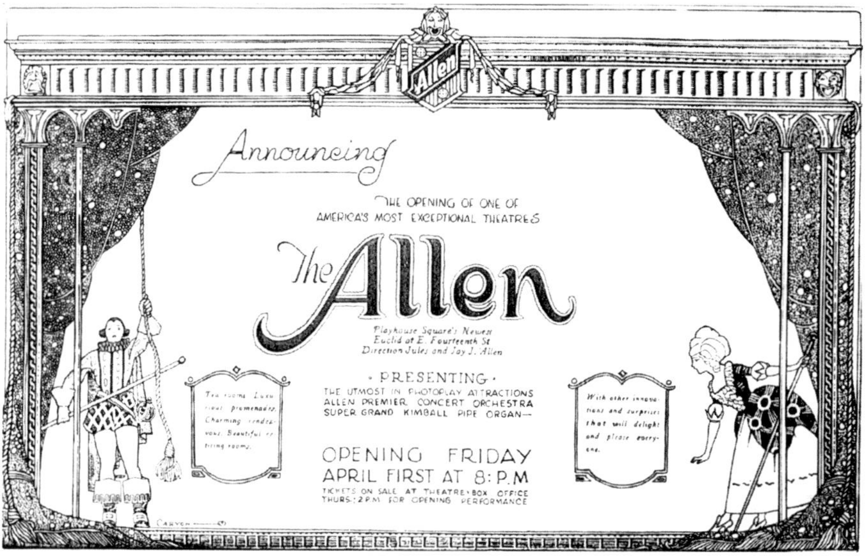

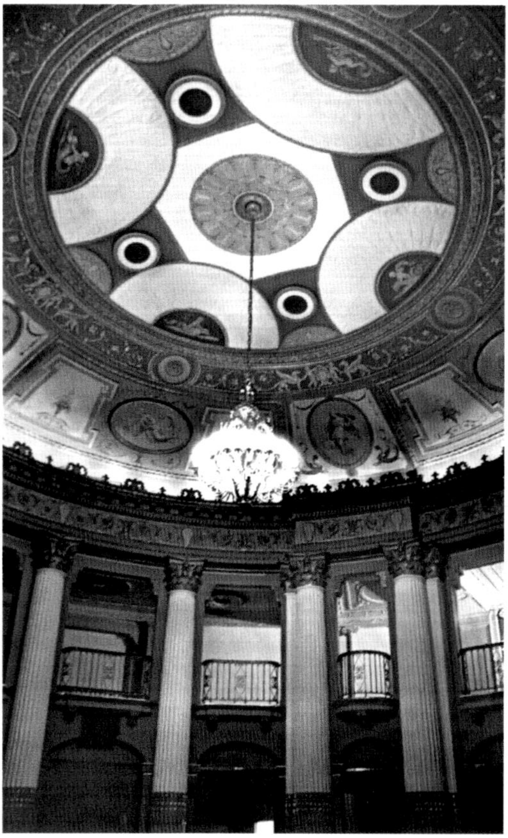

Above: Although the Allen owners delivered on their promise of creating "one of America's exceptional theatres," the playhouse turned into an immediate financial burden. *Courtesy of Cleveland Public Library, Photograph Collection.*

Left: A thirty-three-foot domed rotunda, surrounded by sixteen Corinthian columns, continues as the centerpiece of the Allen's architecture. *Courtesy of Special Collections, Michael Schwartz Library, Cleveland State University.*

orchestras. In 1926, a full-size stage replaced an original diminutive platform, built for movies, which had extended just a few feet.

Philip Spitalny, conducting the Allen's thirty-five-piece orchestra to accompany silent movies, developed into the theater's most popular entertainer. As jazz music mushroomed in popularity, Spitalny shortened his first name, entertaining audiences as Phil Spitalny and His Jazz Maniacs. The Allen soon eliminated both movies and vaudeville during Spitalny's trendy "Jazz Week" concerts, booked about eight to ten weeks apart. Concert highlights included "Chinese Jazz Week," "Spanish Jazz Week" and "Charleston Week," the latter highlighted by audience participation dance contests. Spitalny's "Russian Jazz Week" presented satirical songs such as "The Russian Rag" and "The Hotsky-Totsky Blues." Audiences even joined in the fun by playing kazoos. When sound movies eliminated the need for theater orchestras, Spitalny organized an "all-girl" orchestra and embarked on a long career encompassing theaters, nightclubs, concert halls, radio and television.

In 1928, Fox newsreels, the Allen's first experiment with sound movies, featured the voices of Mussolini expressing dire warning about impending political traumas and the Prince of Wales discussing and demonstrating the latest trendy dance steps. In 1932, the theater ended its run as a Loew's playhouse to reopen as an independent theater. Struggling during the Depression, the Allen added Sunday night Cleveland Orchestra concerts and girlie shows such as Count Berni Vici's *Spices of 1934* revue, highlighted by "The Fountain of Sex" and "Nudity in Gold." In the lobby, handwriting expert Pam Garvin revealed the virtues and shortcomings of audience members' personalities. A former vaudeville tap dancer, Garvin earned substantially more money by moving from theater stages to their lobbies. Miss Helen Royer, her assistant, had previously toiled as a professional boxer known as "the girl Jack Dempsey."

In 1934, RKO purchased the Allen; the chain also owned Cleveland's huge Hippodrome Theater and much smaller downtown Lake Theater. RKO implemented a triple-theater "move-over" policy whereby films debuting at the Hippodrome would move to the Allen and then extended their runs even longer at the Lake. Move-overs, B movies and reissues became the Allen's standard set of bookings. Only on rare occasions did the theater play a major motion picture as a first-run booking; these notable exceptions included a six-week run of *The Pride of the Yankees* and five-week runs of *The Razor's Edge* and *The Egg and I*.

In the 1950s, while box-office receipts declined at other movie theaters due to television's daunting competition, the Allen experienced its most successful decade by exhibiting first-run Warner Brothers films and longer-run blockbuster movies from Columbia Pictures: *The Bridge on the River Kwai*, *The Caine Mutiny*, *Giant*, *Sayonara*, *Mister Roberts*, *A Star Is Born*, *Battle Cry*, *Anatomy of a Murder*, *A Streetcar Named Desire*, *The Searchers* and others.

In 1951, *David and Bathsheba* established a new one-week house record with receipts of $32,000 at a top price of $1.19. Two years later, 69,843 people paid a total of $40,000 to witness *Bwana Devil*, the first modern film in 3-D. Set in 1848, the story of a man-eating lion that had stopped construction of a new railroad in an African jungle carried the advertising catchphrase "a lion in your lap, a lover in your arms." Later in 1953, *House of Wax*, another 3-D offering, came close to establishing a new box-office mark with a $39,000 week.

The 3-D craze lasted less than two years. The process required two projectors simultaneously showing a pair of synchronized film images. Theaters used oversized film reels containing about one hour of viewing time. When the hour elapsed, an irritating intermission allowed for rewinding the film and mounting two more reels onto the projectors. The flimsy, uncomfortable glasses, required to coordinate the pair of film images, annoyed audiences. Inferior color matching among the dual images often created poorly focused movies that reportedly caused severe eyestrain, headaches and nausea. The movie industry responded by claiming portions of the public already suffered from undetected eye problems that the 3-D process helpfully uncovered.

In late 1953, *How to Marry a Millionaire*, the Allen's first CinemaScope motion picture, generated $42,000 in receipts and another record-breaking week. Later in the decade, Liberace and his brother George appeared in person to publicize their film debuts in *Sincerely Yours*, and John Wayne and Ward Bond promoted the opening of *The Searchers*. In 1956, the Allen staged the world premieres of two films, *There's Always Tomorrow* and *Autumn Leaves*.

On December 12, 1959, Howard Higley, manager of the Allen since 1933, sustained a bullet in his right hip during a holdup in which three robbers fled with $104. Higley spent seventy days recuperating in a hospital. Although the criminals carefully hid their identity by wearing masks, police easily identified the trio following their bragging to friends, in a Cedar Avenue delicatessen, about robbing a theater and shooting the manager.

Forty years after Phil Garbo had created the original Allen Theater decorative scheme, he repeated the assignment during an extensive 1961 renovation. The theater's series of lobbies sparkled brightly following a complete redecoration in a Renaissance motif highlighted in gold and softened by azure and coral. Midnight blue and gold carpeting complemented auditorium decorations that included a gold stage curtain and drapes. During the renovation, the Allen installed a new fifty-foot movie screen, new projection and sound equipment and state-of-the-art heating and air conditioning.

The 1950s momentum continued into the first half of the 1960s with another collection of long-run hits: *The Music Man* (eight weeks); *The Cardinal* (seven weeks); a reissue of *The Ten Commandments* (seven weeks); six-week runs for *To Kill a Mockingbird*, *Gypsy*, *Come September*, *That Touch of Mink* and *The Thrill of It All*; and five-week engagements of *Who Was that Lady?*, *Ocean's 11*, *Splendor in the Grass* and *Bye Bye Birdie*.

But in the mid-1960s, the Allen's box-office receipts plunged as the theater exhibited new films simultaneously with suburban theaters. As a temporary solution, the Allen booked three "prestige" long-run road-show films: *Those Magnificent Men in Their Flying Machines* (thirteen weeks), *The Great Race* (fourteen weeks) and the longest run in the theater's movie history, *The Sand Pebbles* (seventeen weeks). Other imaginative ideas included exhibition of a filmed version of Richard Burton's live performance in *Hamlet* and closed-circuit telecasts of boxing matches and an Indianapolis 500 race. When everything else failed, the Allen experimented with soft-porno films.

Near the Allen's closing as a movie showplace, the theater partitioned part of the auditorium into a ladies-only section to protect females from would-be molesters. In late 1967, potential patrons needed to call the theater to obtain the names and show times of the adults-only double bill composed of *Caressed* and *The Seducers*. Booking anything that might draw enough business to pay its bills, the Allen immediately followed the porno double feature with another reissue of *The Ten Commandments*. The Allen mercifully closed on May 9, 1968. The owners decided shutting down the Allen and paying the rent for the final eighteen months of their lease would be less expensive than suffering even greater losses by remaining in operation.

Unlike its soon-to-be boarded-up Euclid Avenue neighbors, the Allen almost immediately reinvented itself as a venue for live rock entertainment. The many acts booked included James Brown, Jackie Wilson, Jefferson Airplane, the Doors, the Moody Blues and the Grateful Dead.

In 1971, the Playhouse Square Association leased the Allen for its first big non-rock attraction, a concert by the Budapest Symphony Orchestra. Yet the Allen's reputation as a rock venue still persisted. When a potential patron telephoned a television station to obtain more information about the orchestra, the station operator told her it must be some sort of rock group.

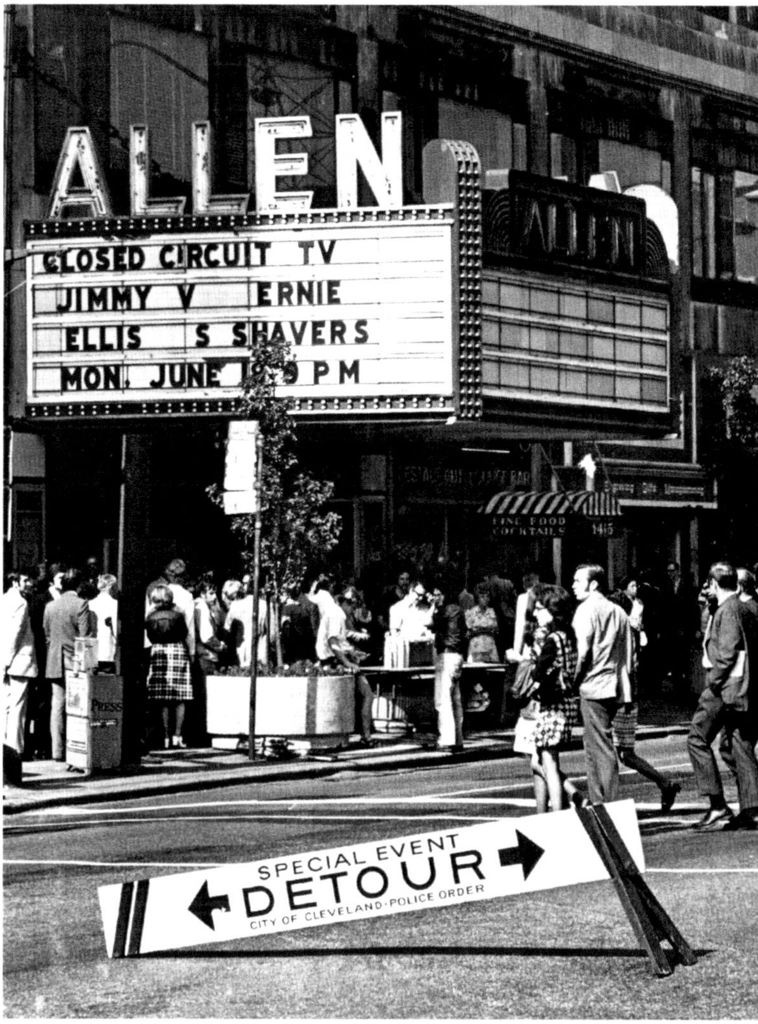

In 1973, the crowd converging on the Allen Theater paid ten dollars to witness a telecast of an Ernie Shavers v. Jimmy Ellis boxing match. The spectators departed early, as Shavers knocked out Ellis in the first round. *Courtesy of Cleveland Public Library, Photograph Collection.*

The successful event inspired the association to focus on the Allen when staging additional concerts and events.

Meanwhile, Playhouse Square activist Ray Shepardson lived on money obtained from popcorn sales and funds raised by selling his furniture; a bank nearly repossessed his automobile as he struggled to find uses for the old downtown theaters. In this period, Shepardson envisioned the Allen's conversion into a two- or three-screen movie theater. In 1972, the Playhouse Square Association booked, on the same day, spiritual leader Bishop Fulton J. Sheen for an afternoon event and political activist Angela Davis for an evening homily. Complaints from the building's tenants regarding the later presentation led to Playhouse Square being evicted from the Allen. Shepardson then turned to the State Theater lobby to present the legendary cabaret show *Jacques Brel Is Alive and Well and Living in Paris*.

Under a different management, the Allen hosted diverse bookings, including activist Ralph Nader; political figures George McGovern, Sargent Shriver and Bella Abzug; the rock opera *Jesus Christ Superstar*; the Czechoslovakian film *Adrift*; a Hungarian film; and four closed-circuit Muhammad Ali boxing matches. Comedians George Carlin, Redd Foxx, Lily Tomlin and Richard Pryor performed at the Allen, along with jazz artists Dave Brubeck and Miles Davis. But the period is most remembered for the numerous rock performers playing on the Allen stage: Bruce Springsteen, Linda Ronstadt, Aerosmith, Pink Floyd, Genesis, Journey, Darryl Hall and John Oates, Eric Clapton, the Bee Gees, the Eagles, the Doors, the Doobie Brothers and many others.

In 1976, Ray Shepardson confirmed he had no plans to use the theater from which he had been banished: "We have our hands full enough with the State, Ohio and Palace." But two other entertainment establishments quickly filled the void.

In early 1977, the Old Allen restaurant debuted in the theater's lobby and rotunda. Filet mignon, prime rib and strip steak dinners commanded $8.95. In less than two years, the eatery declared bankruptcy, but Yesterday's Restaurant opened a few months later, followed by The Lobby in 1984 and 1985.

Also in 1977, the auditorium underwent a $200,000 conversion into a "Laserium." Sitting in reclining chairs underneath a seventy-foot bubble dome, audiences enjoyed music and coordinated designs created by four laser beams that formed geometric configurations on the dome's ceiling. Shown in sixteen to twenty cities throughout the country, the Laser show attracted about sixteen thousand people per month in Cleveland during its initial performances. The Laserium novelty continued at the Allen for twenty months before the show closed. Although sixteen years would pass before the theater staged another entertainment event, the Allen entered an exhilarating period where avoiding a wrecking ball constituted its primary priority.

In 1982, the Cleveland Foundation purchased the Bulkley Building with the intention of selling the Allen Theater to the Playhouse Square Foundation. But in 1987, an investor group headed by William N. West purchased the

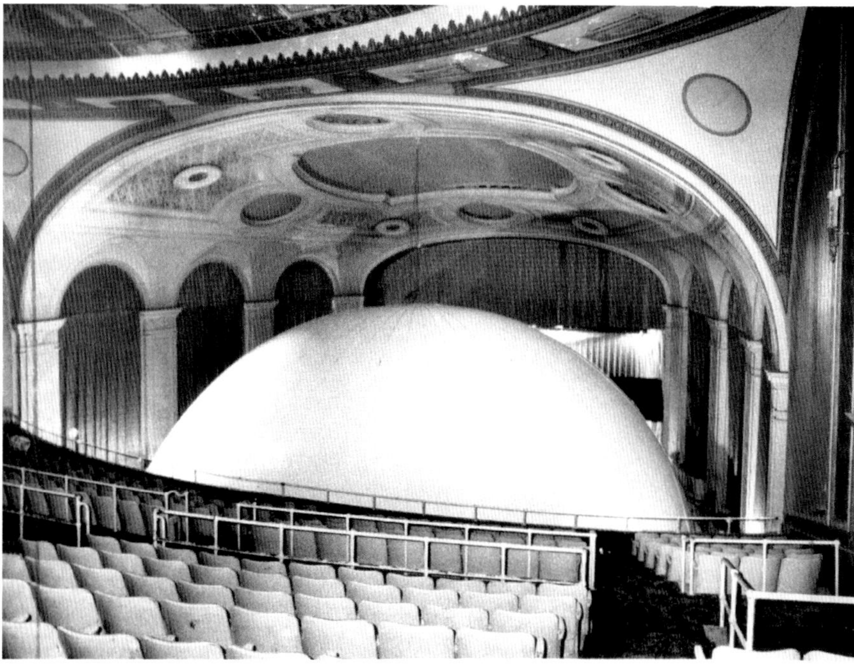

For twenty months beginning on March 6, 1977, audiences enjoyed laser shows in a seventy-foot dome situated in the Allen's former stage area. *Courtesy of Special Collections, Michael Schwartz Library, Cleveland State University.*

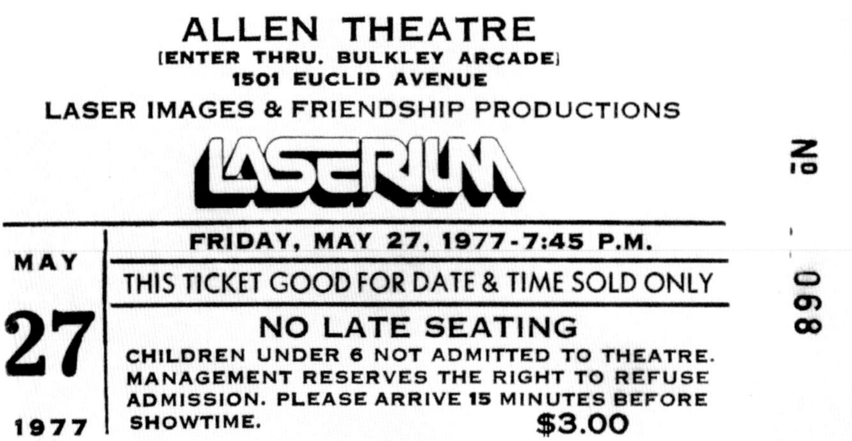

In 1977, three dollars purchased an innovative evening of laser designs set to classical and rock music. *Courtesy of the author.*

Bulkley Building and Allen Theater by outbidding Playhouse Square. The new owners planned to demolish the Allen to create space for a restaurant and specialty shops. A group of concerned citizens formed ATRC (Allen Theater Redevelopment Coalition) to identify uses and tenants to save the theater. As a makeshift measure, the Cleveland Landmarks Commission imposed a one-year ban on the theater's demolition. During that period, West dismissed a plan by Ray Shepardson as "not meriting serious consideration" and a proposal by the Playhouse Square Foundation as "totally unacceptable."

To call attention to the theater's looming peril, ATRC staged an Allen Theater birthday party that it promoted as possibly the final such party. Wearing party hats and blowing noise makers, members of the group handed out cupcakes to Euclid Avenue onlookers.

Although the Cleveland Landmarks Commission protection ended in 1989, the Allen's inclusion as part of a newly created landmark district delayed demolition for another year. A panel of experts, meeting in the renovated Ohio Theater, conducted a three-hour discussion regarding the Allen's rescue from demolition. Meanwhile, the ATRC obtained twenty thousand names on petitions demanding that the theater be preserved. A bulldozer closed in on the Allen, guided not by the developer but rather by

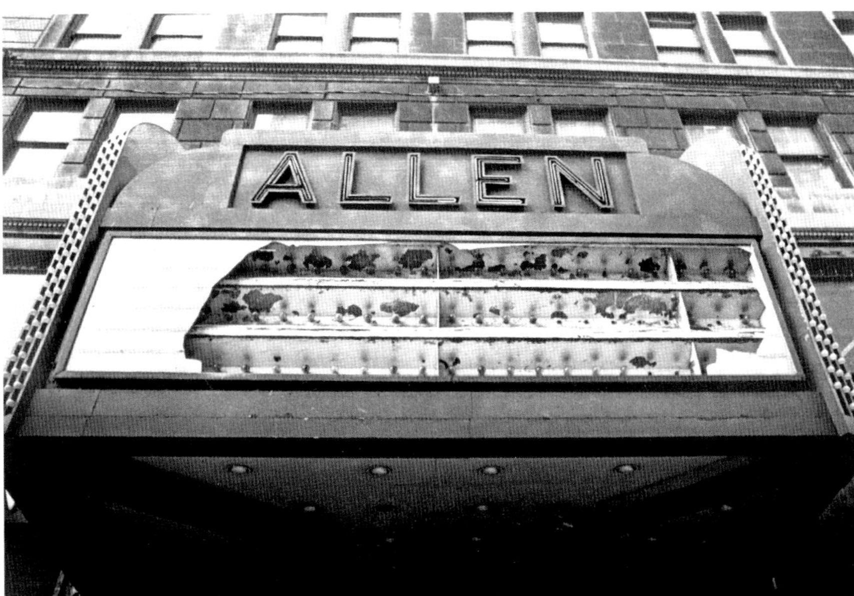

The Allen's dilapidated marquee symbolized the decline of Cleveland's movie houses. *Courtesy of Special Collections, Michael Schwartz Library, Cleveland State University.*

a group of protesters desiring to raise awareness of the theater's immediate danger. Ray Shepardson—now a national expert on theater restoration with successfully completed projects in Detroit, Chicago, St. Louis, Los Angeles, Seattle, Louisville, Minneapolis and San Antonio—attended a rally held on Euclid Avenue to save the Allen.

In 1992, support for the Allen's restoration collapsed. The Playhouse Square Foundation admitted the theater's reopening would create unwanted excess capacity. Although preservationists insisted the Allen could be reused, no developer had generated an economically viable plan to use the theater. The Planning Commission reluctantly approved the theater's demise while the Cleveland Foundation agreed to donate $400,000 to landscape part of the site following the Allen's demolition. Concurrently, the Restoration Society lost its four-year battle to save the Allen.

The only conceivable hope for the Allen seemed to be an unlikely loss of interest by the developer, notwithstanding his five years of concerted effort to destroy the theater. But in 1993, as a wrecking ball began the repugnant task of pounding the theater's walls, West and the Playhouse Square Foundation reached an agreement to rescue the theater.

A sharp business decline, accompanied by a severe real estate bust, prevented West from implementing his plans for the Allen site. Needing cash to help pay the Bulkey Building's mortgage, West consented to lease the Allen to Playhouse Square, which considered dividing the Allen into at least three spaces, perhaps for use as a cabaret, party center and magic club.

From late 1994 into the spring of 1997, Playhouse Square contemplated viable uses for the Allen, planned the theater's restoration and obtained the necessary funding. At the same time, audiences returned to enjoy two long-running shows: *Forever Plaid* and *Shear Madness*. Even in 1994, Playhouse Square seriously considered creating a movie theater in the Allen's balcony. Three years later, Playhouse Square announced that rather than subdividing the Allen, the theater would be transformed into a 2,500-seat showplace to accommodate long-run Broadway shows and other entertainment events. Construction of a modern stage house accompanied the theater renovation.

In 1998, the Allen reopened with a two-week engagement of the London stage hit *Jolson*. A three-week run of *The Producers* established a new Cleveland box-office record with receipts of $3,820,411. Following two eight-week runs at the State Theater, *Phantom of the Opera* returned for three engagements at the Allen, the first for seven weeks and the next two for four weeks each. The Allen booked returns of other megahits (*Miss Saigon*, *Les Miserables* and

Cats) for much shorter engagements and newer Broadway shows including *Ragtime*, *Titanic*, *Footloose* and Mickey Rooney in *The Wizard of Oz*.

In 1999, the Cleveland Orchestra performed at the Allen for nearly nine months during the renovation of its permanent Severance Hall facility. The Allen hosted periodic performances by the Cleveland Pops Orchestra, the Ohio Ballet, the International Folk Festival, the Singing Angels, the Pennsylvania Ballet's version of *The Nutcracker* and children's and teen's theater series. Popular performers appearing at the Allen included Tony Bennett, Kenny G, Michael Buble, Michael Feinstein, Engelbert Humperdinck and the Righteous Brothers.

Unfortunately, the Allen never achieved its objective of consistently hosting long-run Broadway shows; realistically, it probably never could have. The theater's reopening matched a sharp decline in the availability of new mega-Broadway touring productions. In addition, the long-run Broadway shows hosted by cities such as Chicago or Los Angeles are usually individually produced productions rather than stops on a tour. Ten years of operation demonstrated that the naysayers of the previous three decades may have been correct—Playhouse Square did not need a third large venue.

On August 23, 2010, the Allen closed again, but this time with the hope for a much brighter and practical future. An extensive remodeling created a trio of versatile performing spaces to serve as a new home for the Cleveland Playhouse. The main auditorium suffered a drastic downsizing from 2,504 seats to slightly fewer than 500. The addition of two completely new and even smaller theatrical venues added another 500 seats. A "Second Stage" theater became a state-of-the-art facility capable of changing its shape to accommodate performances requiring a maximum of 350 seats. A 150-seat "Laboratory Theater" is used by both the Cleveland Playhouse and Cleveland State University for smaller productions, workshops, play readings and student projects. Ultimately, the Allen did become partitioned, a fate that Ray Shepardson had anticipated forty years earlier.

Chapter 17

THE PALACE THEATER

Vaudeville historian Joe Laurie Jr. said it perfectly: "The Albee in Brooklyn, the Palace in Cleveland and the Memorial in Boston—they were the cathedrals." Powerful vaudeville czar Edward F. Albee called Cleveland's Palace "the crowning achievement of my life." *Variety* enthusiastically reported that the theater put Cleveland "at the top of the theatrical universe." The *Saturday Evening Post* commented, "The Palace Theater in Cleveland, which opened with much ceremony in the fall of 1922, is conceded to be one of the finest theaters in the United States, if not the world." Broadway columnist Ben F. Hotzman editorialized, "We have our Palace Theater on Broadway. But truth and a discerning eye for beauty compels us to subscribe to the statement that the Cleveland edition is the biggest headliner the B.F. Keith circuit has ever served up to the theatergoing public."

Construction of the 3,680-seat Palace began on January 22, 1921. A variety of problems, including labor difficulties, delayed the opening until November 6, 1922. Even after being substantially completed, local unions prevented performances for two weeks while they debated which union had jurisdiction to install metal frames around the glass in the theater.

The opening proved to be worth the wait. The walls, pillars and floors are constructed of white marble imported from Carrara, Italy. Many of the original sparkling crystal chandeliers from Czechoslovakia, 154 in total, are still located throughout the theater. Outer doors and interior box offices are made of bronze. A large battleship-gray carpet containing 9,000,272 knots, each individually tied by hand in Maffersdorf, Czechoslovakia, once graced

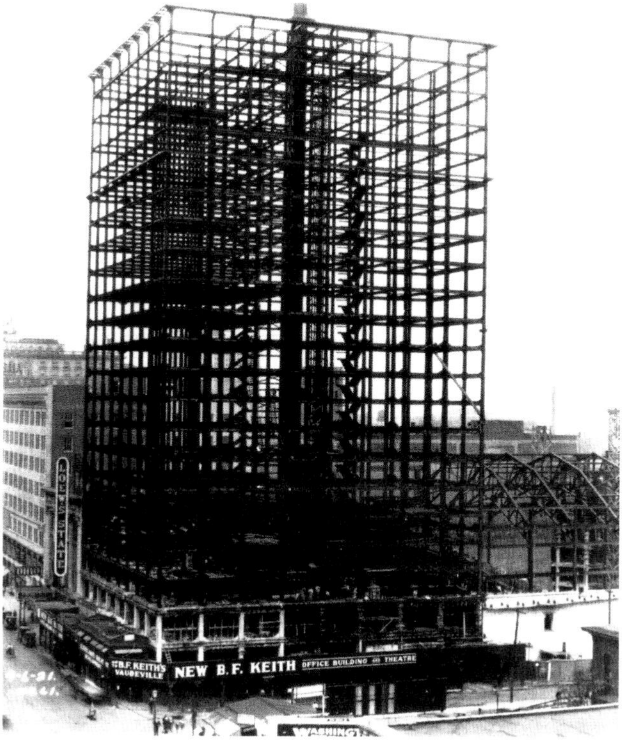

Left: Under construction in September 1921, the twenty-two-story Keith Building's most conspicuous tenant would be the magnificent Palace Theater. *Courtesy of Cleveland Public Library, Photograph Collection.*

Below: The Palace's grand lobby featured five replicas of chandeliers from the Palace of Versailles, an impressive art collection, marble staircases and a huge Czechoslovakian rug. *Courtesy of Cleveland Public Library, Photograph Collection.*

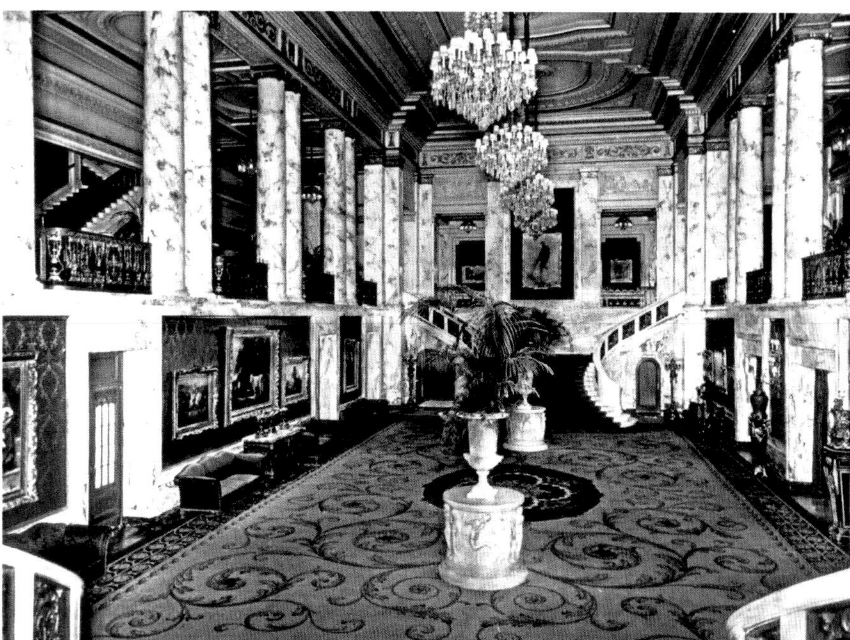

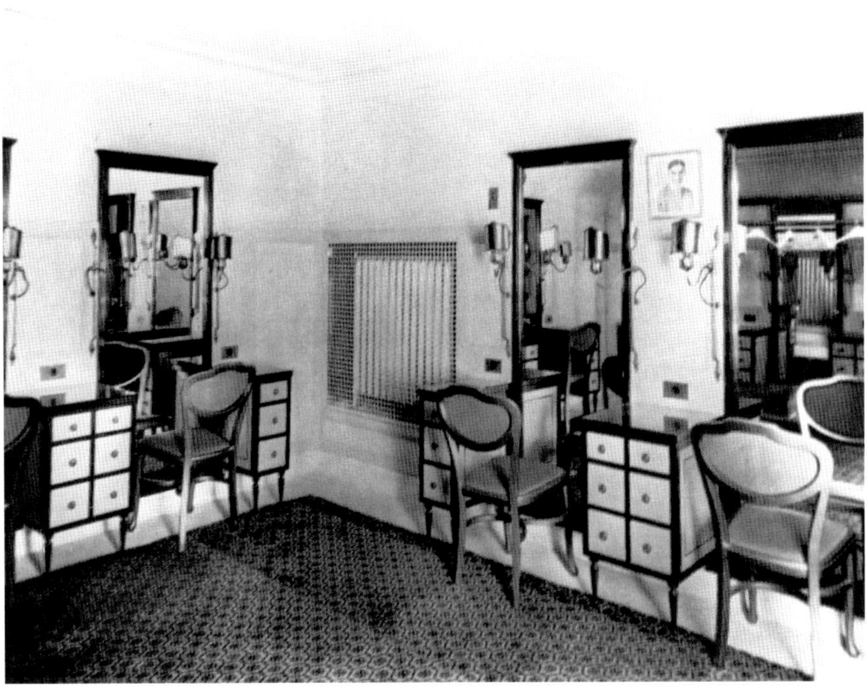

The Palace's twenty-two dressing rooms ranked among the finest on the Keith circuit. Some performers requested to live in the dressing rooms rather than in local hotels. *Courtesy of Special Collections, Michael Schwartz Library, Cleveland State University.*

the grand lobby. The theater's original major colors, ivory and gold, blended with mulberry brocade wall coverings. Twin curving marble staircases with intricate bronze inserts still lead to the mezzanine and balcony. The first landing contained two magnificent silver and bronze cachepots from Paris. Inspiration for the upstairs furniture came from Louis XIV, Louis XV and Louis XVI period pieces.

The original stage, relatively large for its time, measured fifty-nine feet wide, thirty-five feet high and ninety feet deep. Two seven-story towers remain standing to the east and west of the auditorium. Entering the west tower's stage door in the 1920s, performers encountered a space resembling an elegant hotel lobby, complete with a wood-burning fireplace. Dressing rooms incorporated marble baths and showers. Amenities available to performers consisted of a beauty parlor, barbershop, tailor shop, laundry room, billiard room, miniature golf course and hospital accommodations staffed by a registered nurse. The theater even provided admirable housing for performing animals highlighted by a specially designed basement area containing washing and grooming facilities.

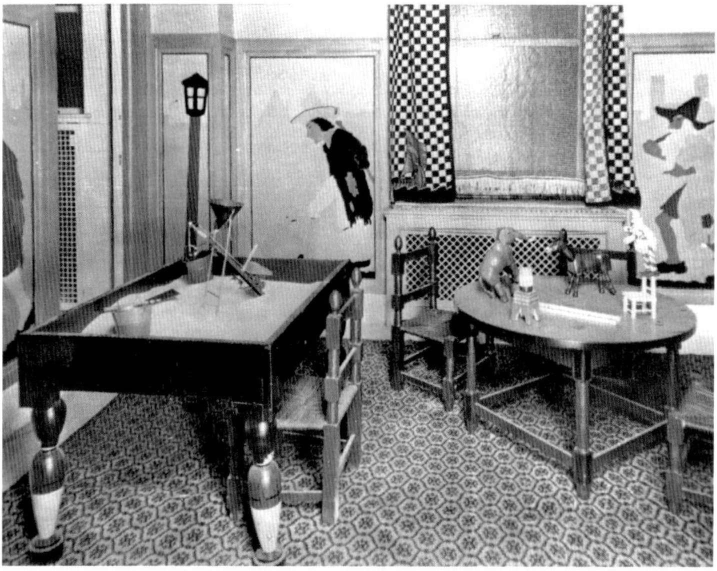

Located in the east tower, the Palace nursery provided accommodations for the performers' children. *Courtesy of Special Collections, Michael Schwartz Library, Cleveland State University.*

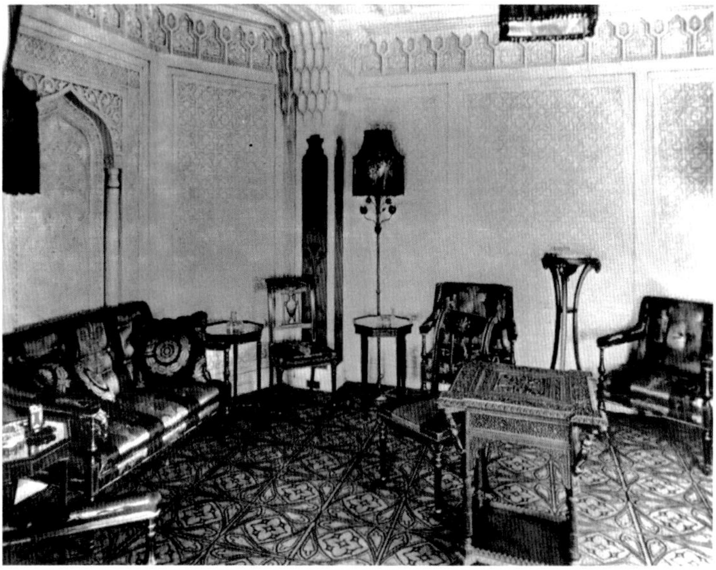

The Palace accommodated jazz-age flappers with a proper place to smoke. A Hindu motif covered the walls of the Egyptian Smoking Room. Furniture consisted of Egyptian designs and wrought-iron lamps incorporating gold embroidery and red silk shades. *Courtesy of Special Collections, Michael Schwartz Library, Cleveland State University.*

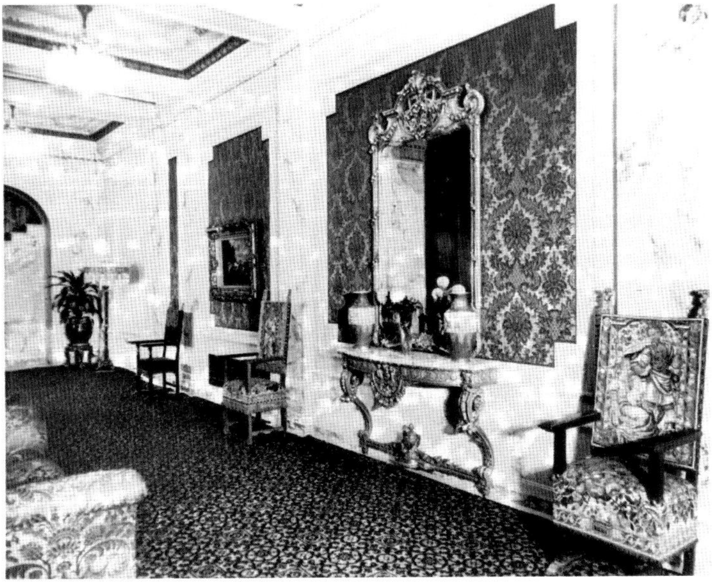

The beautifully appointed east mezzanine is shown as it appeared in 1922. *Courtesy of Special Collections, Michael Schwartz Library, Cleveland State University.*

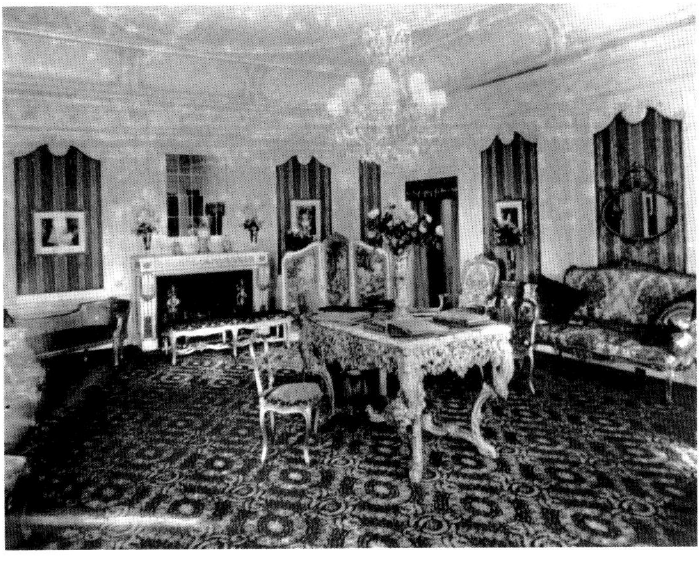

A selection of beautiful furniture, obtained by the Keith organization on its worldwide searches to acquire antiques, decorated the ladies' mezzanine lounge. *Courtesy of Special Collections, Michael Schwartz Library, Cleveland State University.*

Usherettes, dressed in elegant black velvet, greeted the first-night patrons. Three special trains brought celebrities and prominent New York City high society members to the grand opening; representatives of the Astor and Ringling families underscored the society list.

Following a few obligatory speeches, the house lights dimmed. After the Palace orchestra played "The Star-Spangled Banner," the curtain officially opened for the first time. A female acrobat emerged from a large phonograph horn prop, executing a few athletic tricks, including balancing on her partner's head. Pantomime artist Willie Schenkton then took the stage to become the very first billed Palace entertainer. Elsie Janis, an internationally famous actress, singer, dancer and mimic, headlined the opening week.

A typical big-time vaudeville program consisted of about eight performances. Acrobats, animals, ice and roller skaters, cyclists or other acts that did not require talking composed the "dumb act" that usually opened the show since their performances would not be ruined by the stir and noise of latecomers. Performers who sang or talked considered placement in the first position very insulting. A few of vaudeville's "dumb acts" achieved stardom by adding humorous banter to their routines; juggler W.C. Fields and rope trickster Will Rogers are examples.

Singers or dancers often occupied the second position. During the applause following the "dumb act," dancers signaled their desired tempo to the orchestra leader by beating their feet on the stage. The sound resembled a horse pounding its hoof, and dancers to this day are still called hoofers. A comedy sketch or one-act play followed in the next spot. Plays ranged from old melodramas with unknown casts to new works featuring top Broadway stars including Ethel Barrymore and Helen Hayes. Novelty acts typified the next positions. The entertainer performing directly before the intermission needed to resonate with the audience. Rising new performers or popular but declining stars often filled this slot. Stagehands used the intermission to set up for acts requiring large sets or an expanded number of performers, such as a chorus. The headline act appeared next. One or two acts followed the top billing; their purpose largely consisted of clearing out the theater in an orderly fashion. Initial performances consumed about three minutes each. Stage time, increasing with each position on the bill, peaked at roughly twenty minutes for the featured performer.

When vaudeville added movies and expanded to three-a-day continuous performances, the closing spot usually featured a boring short film or an annoying live act. Management used the finale to encourage the audience to leave the theater before the beginning of the next show.

Cartoons and newsreels would soon achieve the same result in motion picture theaters.

A new Palace show started each Monday with two complete performances daily, one at noon and the other at 8:00 p.m. Additional weekend shows began at 11:00 p.m. Matinees cost $0.30, while prices for evening performances, depending on the seating location, ranged from $0.30 to $1.65.

The B.F. Keith organization developed standards that elevated vaudeville to new levels of respectability. Vulgarity, absolutely prohibited at all times, included using the words "devil," "spit" and "cockroach." The word "radio" also appeared on the banned list; the Keith company considered this new competitor especially vulgar.

Enjoying Palace entertainment developed into a weekly ritual for many Clevelanders. Families from as far as fifty miles away visited the Palace on Sunday afternoons. High school students cut Friday classes to view matinees. Saturday evening at the Palace served as a standard date for many couples. Even the Monday matinees had a special following. Stagehands from Keith's East 105th Street Vaudeville Theater attended the first Monday Palace performance to familiarize themselves with the routines. When a 105th Street performer used the same material, the stagehands offered rather convincing recommendations to revise the act.

Palace employees carefully observed audience members to prevent bogus insurance claims against the theater. One woman eating sticky candy dropped a piece on her expensive coat. To place the blame on the theater, her husband rubbed the candy on her seat. An observant usher, viewing the entire incident in detail, negated the couple's claim for a new coat. Another woman threatened a lawsuit against the Palace after deliberately falling down a step and twisting her ankle. A theater matron had witnessed the premeditated phony accident and ended the lawsuit discussion.

In 1923, the Dr. Lee DeForest Phono-Film show, a collection of talking pictures, correctly anticipated the future direction of movies. But at the time, talking films created little interest among vaudeville viewers. In fact, as early as 1912, audiences had booed earlier versions of talkies off Keith stages. Movie patrons remained unimpressed with sound until Al Jolson changed their minds. Following the 1928 release of *The Jazz Singer*, a prediction by Joe Schenck, president of United Artists, may not have seemed as implausible as it does today. Schenck believed talkies constituted "a passing novelty that is doomed to fade from vogue in about six months."

By 1925, the Keith organization could no longer ignore the popularity of movies and decline of vaudeville. John Ford's film *The Iron Horse* introduced a "vaudefilm" format combining movies with a reduced number of vaudeville acts. Continuous showings from noon to 11:00 p.m. replaced the previous two-a-day format; entertainers now performed three shows each day, with a fourth show added on Sunday.

In the mid-1920s, vaudeville star Nora Bayes earned $5,000 for a week's work entertaining at the Palace; opera singer Johanna Gadski collected $3,250. Newcomers Burns and Allen ($500), Jack Benny ($350) and Bing Crosby ($150) anchored the other end of the pay scale.

Events in 1928 proved to be among the most significant in the Palace Theater's history. Radio Corporation of America (RCA) understood the tremendous potential of sound motion pictures but required an elaborate business strategy to successfully enter a market dominated by Western Electric. The plan involved developing the required technology, purchasing a motion picture company to produce the films and buying theaters to exhibit the finished product.

Vaudeville playhouse owners, anticipating the imminent demise of the genre, demonstrated little reluctance to sell their theaters. RCA purchased the B.F. Keith and Orpheum chains; the transaction involved the sale of 535 theaters, including the Cleveland Palace. RCA also acquired Joseph P. Kennedy's motion picture companies. These transactions formed the nucleus of the new Radio-Keith-Orpheum (RKO) Company.

The most powerful vaudeville organization in the world built the Palace Theater. Only six years later, the showplace became part of a new corporation chartered to produce and distribute sound movies. Advertisements announcing the formation of RKO promised, "This is a new era in vaudeville." But RKO quickly demonstrated its intentions by firing vaudeville czar Edward Albee; he died two years later.

Similar to most theaters, the Palace suffered through the Depression. But by 1938, Mae West had established a new house record with $35,000 in ticket sales at a top admission price of seventy-five cents. Lines formed at 8:30 a.m. for the initial 11:00 show, and a standing-room-only audience greeted West's first performance.

The emerging big-band era made a visit to the Palace even more exciting. In 1939, Kay Kyser's band broke the Palace's box-office record. At the other extreme, the theater unsuccessfully attempted to exhibit movies without live entertainment; only twelve people attended one showing of the film failure *Career*. At times, live entertainers even failed; Benny Goodman met with indifference despite the publicity of a coast-to-coast radio broadcast. *Variety* explained that in Cleveland, "The kids are the only ones who go for that jitterbug stuff."

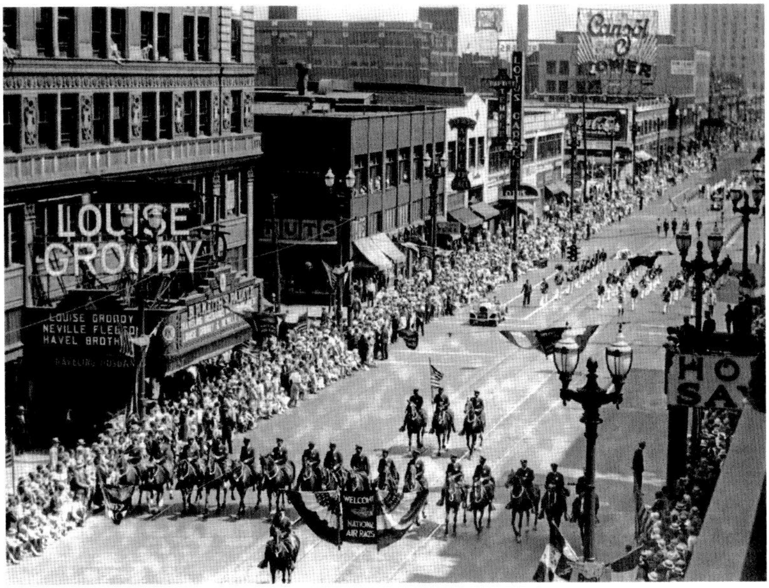

Broadway star Louise Groody entertained at the Palace while a parade down Euclid Avenue celebrated the beginning of the 1931 National Air Races. *Courtesy of Special Collections, Michael Schwartz Library, Cleveland State University.*

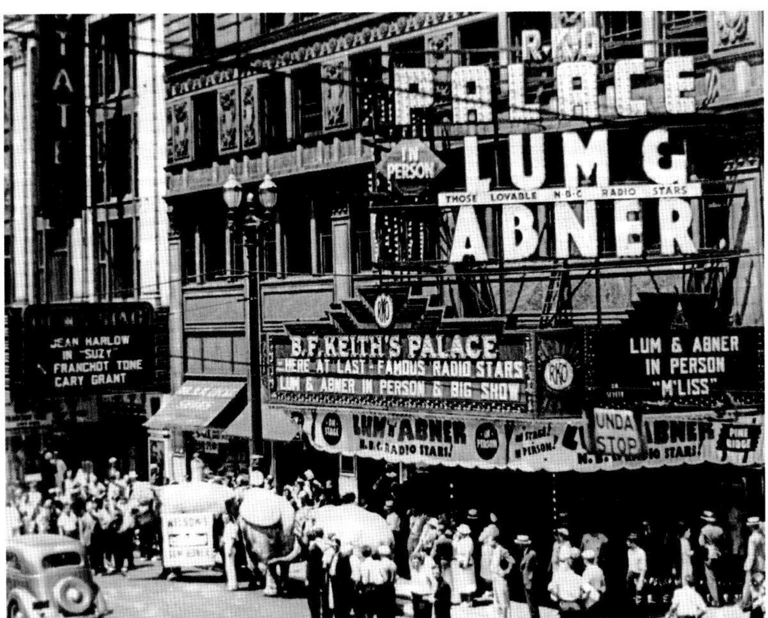

In 1936, Adele Nelson's Dancing Elephants troupe, a warm-up act for radio comics Lum and Abner, generated publicity by its presence in front of the Palace. *Courtesy of the Lum and Abner Society.*

In 1944, Tommy Dorsey set a new box-office record. A few months later, three consecutive weeks (headlined by Betty Hutton, Lena Horne and the motion picture *Wilson*) all exceeded $50,000. But the combination of live performances and movies created a very negative experience that year. A group of rowdy teenagers disrupted Jan Savitt's big-band show by shrieking and moaning in mock ecstasy as Phil Regan sang "Night and Day." The bored youths had come to see *Son of Dracula* on the movie screen. *Cleveland Press* columnist Stanley Anderson viewed their behavior as "the outward manifestation of the disease which makes for juvenile delinquency."

Catherine Gloria Balota, a fourteen-year-old usherette at the Palace in 1939, proved that sometimes dreams really do come true. Wanting desperately to enter show business, Catherine performed at the Cleveland Stage Door Canteen and Chin's Chinese Restaurant at 106th Street and Euclid Avenue while attending West Tech High School. In 1946, she debuted on the Palace stage as part of the Spike Jones troupe. Her comic parodies of "My Man" and "My Heart Sings" fit perfectly into the general mayhem created by Jones. Using the name Kaye Ballard, she achieved fame on Broadway and in the movies and television. She returned to Playhouse Square in 2003, starring in *Nunsense* at the Ohio Theater. The 1946 Jones entourage featured two other former Clevelanders: Mickey Katz (the father of Joel Grey) and Dr. Horatio Q. Birdbath, who provided bird and animal imitations.

In 1948, Jack Benny established a new house record with $70,000 in receipts at a $1.10 top price. That same year, millionaire Howard Hughes purchased controlling interest in RKO; his reign created an era of chaos. Hughes later sold the theater chain while the film studio collapsed.

Scheduled for June 13, 1951, the first closed-circuit boxing telecast paired Joe Louis against Lee Savold. The Palace, along with theaters in Washington, D.C., Baltimore, Albany and Chicago, purchased the rights to the transmittal. Although committed to the experiment, Palace management expressed little enthusiasm for the planned date. The fight, added to the regular attraction, did nothing to boost attendance because every ticket to a live performance by legendary Josephine Baker had already been sold. Fortuitously, rain poured on the New York Polo Grounds the night of the fight; the rescheduled date did not conflict with Josephine Baker.

The fight attracted a capacity audience. A projector magnified an image from a seven-inch television onto a three-hundred-square-foot (twenty feet by fifteen feet) screen lowered in front of the movie screen. The transmission, although not as sharp as a film, did not create any technical problems. The

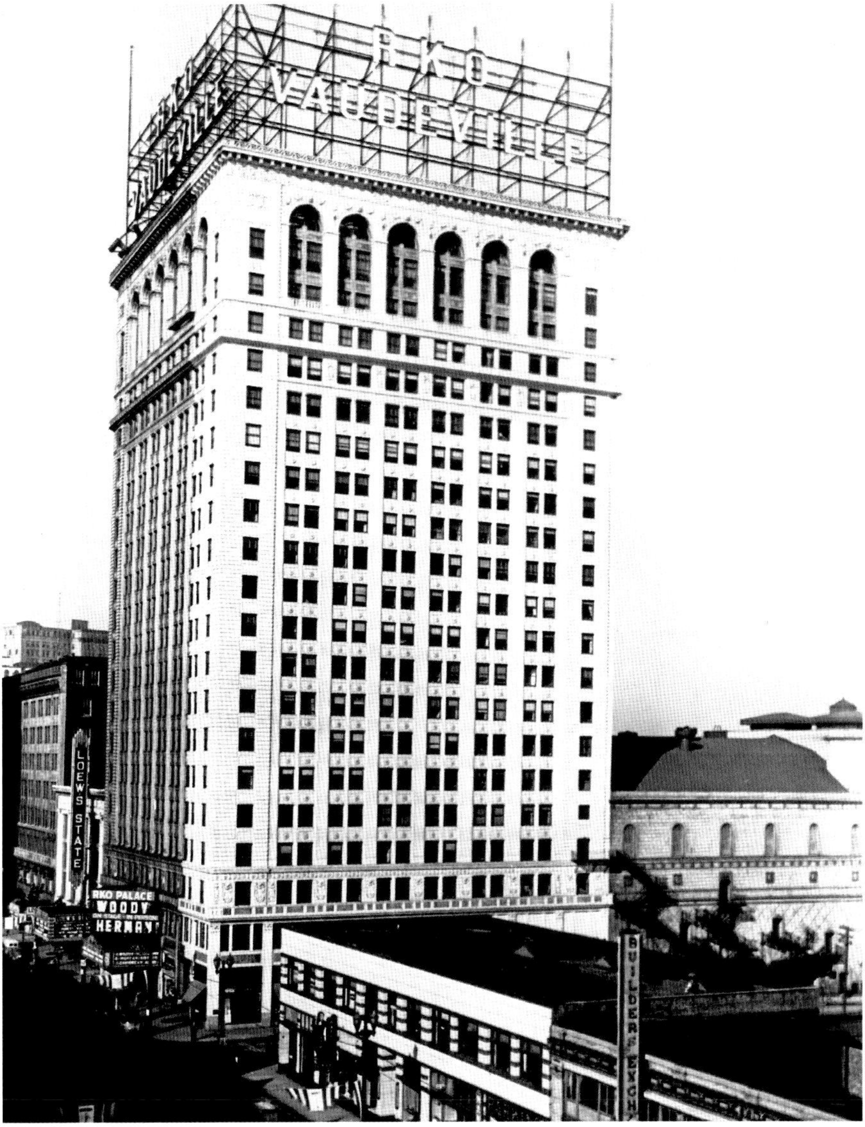

In 1945, Woody Herman remained popular even as the big-band era faded. Once advertised as the world's largest electrical sign, the obsolete "RKO Vaudeville" (top) verbiage still remained in ten-foot letters. *Courtesy of Cleveland Public Library, Photograph Collection.*

admission price, which included the movie *The Prowler*, increased fifteen cents from the usual eighty-cent charge. Telecasts of important boxing matches remained a profitable venture for downtown movie theaters until their closing in the late 1960s.

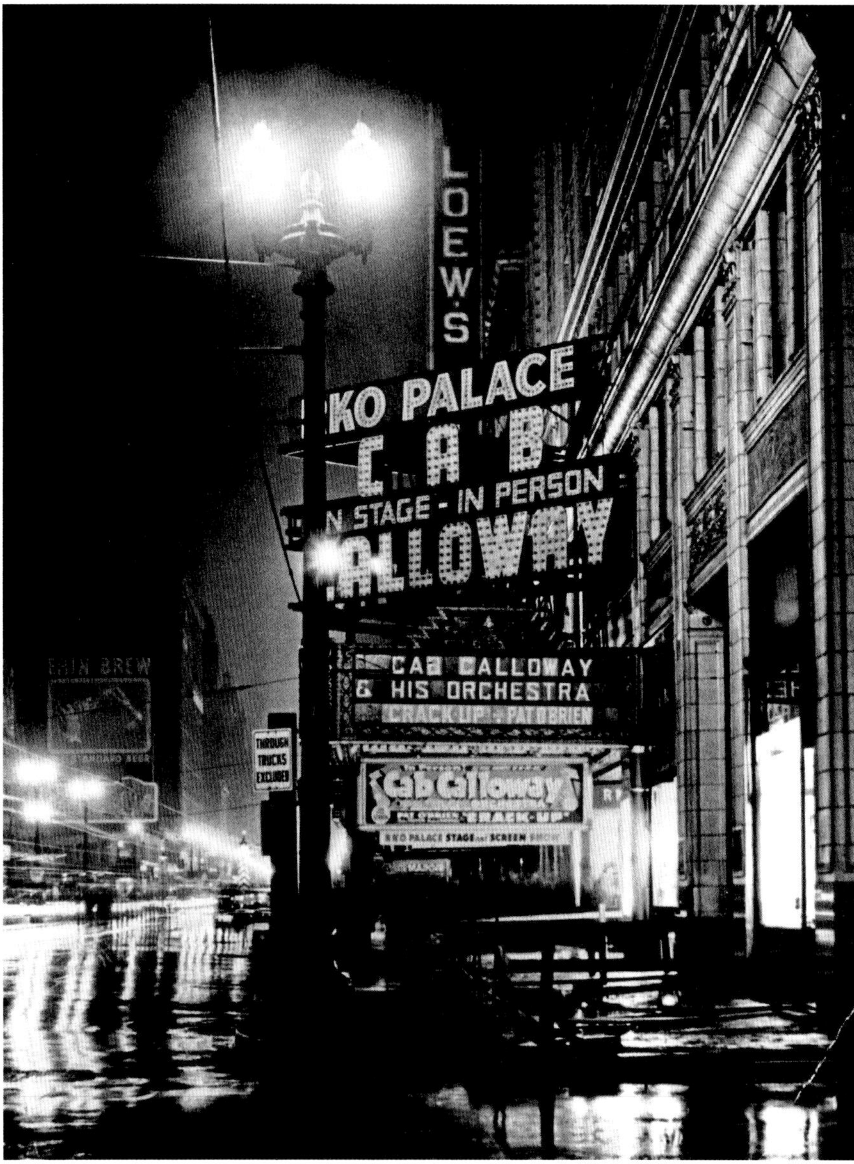

Cab Calloway entertained Palace patrons on a rainy November evening in 1946. *Courtesy of Cleveland Public Library, Photograph Collection.*

In 1954, the Palace hosted the world premiere of Ross Hunter's *Magnificent Obsession*. Jane Wyman, Barbara Rush and Agnes Moorehead visited the theater on the gala opening night. Also that year, Peggy Lee's thirty-one-city tour played mostly in auditoriums, sports arenas

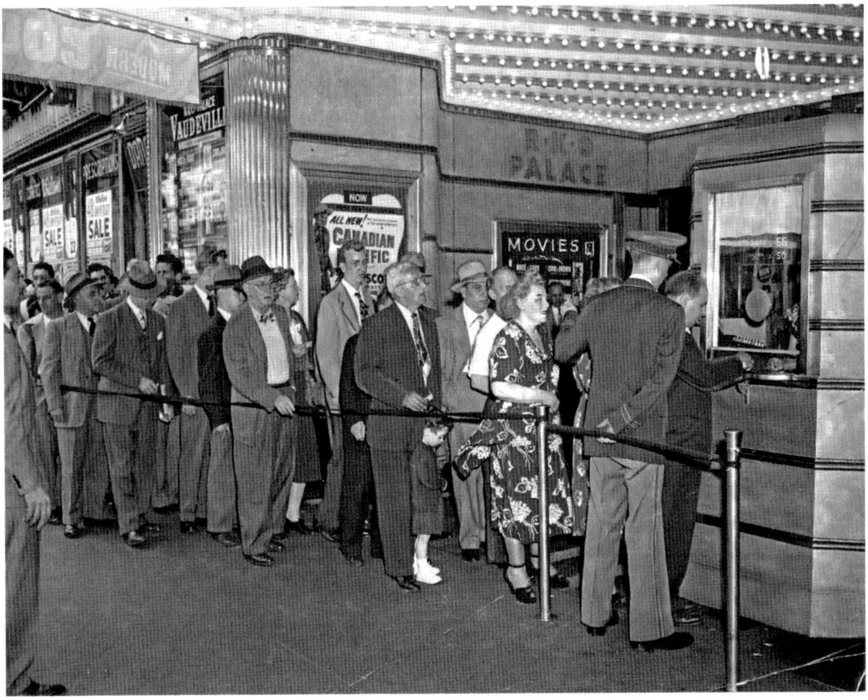

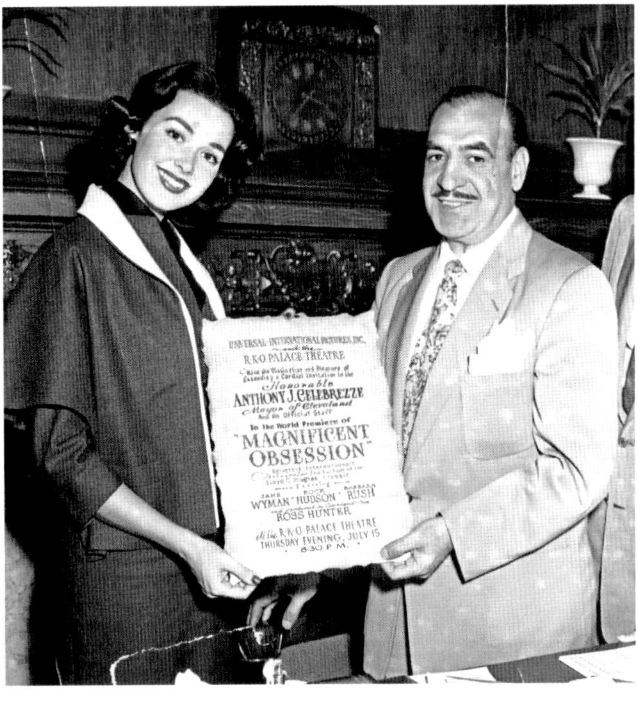

Above: A nostalgic 1949 vaudeville show generated a large Palace crowd. *Courtesy of Cleveland Public Library, Photograph Collection.*

Right: Actress Barbara Rush and Cleveland mayor Anthony Celebrezze display an invitation to the world premiere of *Magnificent Obsession*. *Courtesy of Special Collections, Michael Schwartz Library, Cleveland State University*.

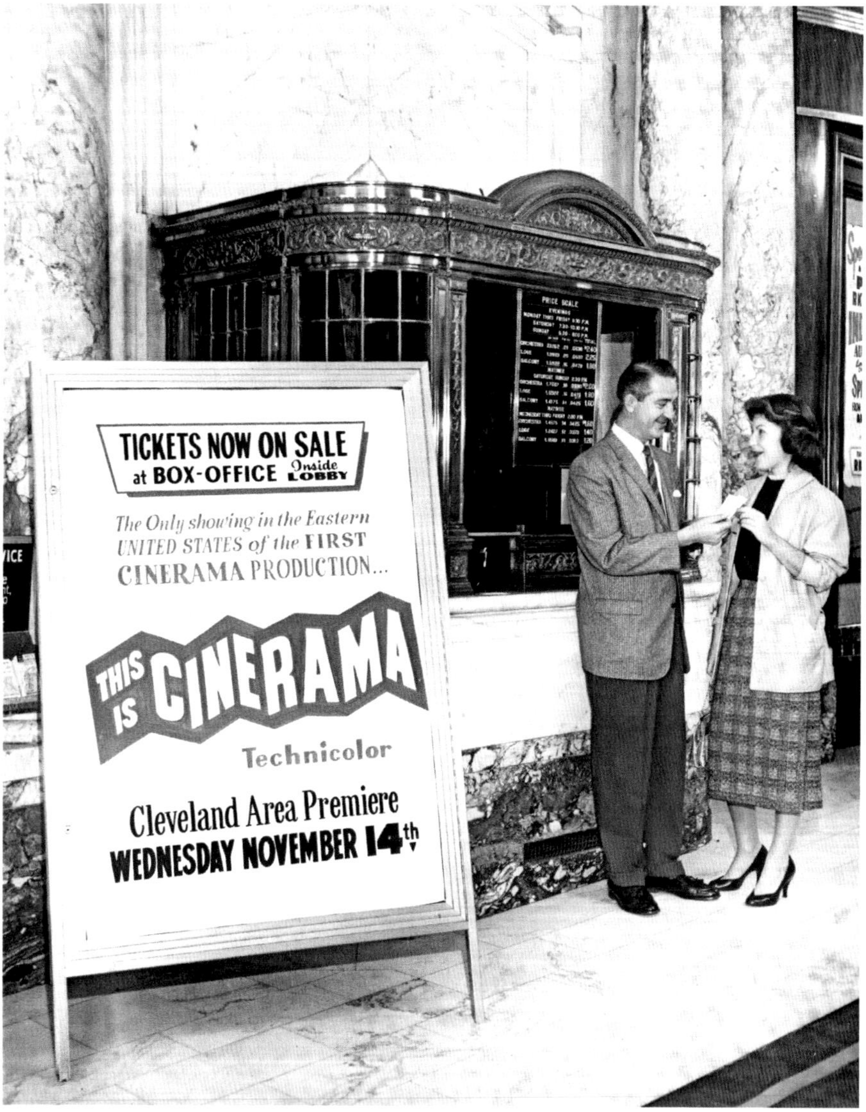

Palace manager Max Mink personally presented *This Is Cinerama* tickets to Marlene Lurie, the first person to purchase seats for the initial triple-projector film. *Courtesy of Special Collections, Michael Schwartz Library, Cleveland State University.*

and dance halls. She commented to the Palace audience: "I wish [show business] would return to theaters as comfortable as the Palace. This is the first theater we played in and it's heavenly compared to the barn-like auditoriums we've seen so far."

Despite a major world premiere and praise from performers, the Palace, relying on RKO for its films, existed in disaster mode. The theater turned to Universal-International and 20th Century Fox but mostly booked mediocre films unwanted by the Hippodrome. Needing something dramatic to instill it with new vitality, the Palace obtained the wide-screen Cinerama movies at just the right time.

Cinerama employed a unique three-lens camera, each lens capturing one-third of the total screen image. Three projectors blended the trio of films onto an incredibly large seventy-five-foot-long by twenty-six-foot-high curved screen covering an arc of 146 degrees, approximately the arc interpreted by the human eye. A louvered screen, composed of 1,100 overlapping strips of vertical perforated tape, prevented light from reflecting across the screen. A stereophonic sound system used seven separate sound tracks with speakers located at the front, sides and rear of the theater.

Clevelanders had waited more than four years for the opening of *This Is Cinerama*. Following its New York success in 1952, Cinerama began road-show engagements in other cities; the smaller Ohio Theater seemed the logical choice for Cleveland. But long runs of *The Ten Commandments* and *Around the World in Eighty Days*, along with the already booked *South Pacific*, severely delayed the Ohio's availability. The Cinerama management considered renovating the dilapidated Carter Theater on East 9th Street, remodeling the downtown Euclid Avenue Baptist Church, using either of two movie houses at East 105th Street and Euclid Avenue or acquiring a suburban theater. The Palace finally secured the Cinerama rights for Cleveland. Even with the long delay, Cleveland became only the twenty-seventh city in the world to exhibit Cinerama.

This Is Cinerama opened at the Palace on November 14, 1956, with prices ranging from $1.25 to $2.40. The initial five Cinerama films consisted of travelogues without stars or plots. A prologue, presented on a conventional-sized movie screen, helped accentuate the dramatic effect when a giant image unfolded on a rapidly expanding screen. The first Cinerama film began with a roller coaster starting its climb, pausing for an instant and then plunging into a spectacular descent. The Cinerama cameras, mounted on the front seat of the roller coaster, created an extremely realistic effect. The film played for thirty-two weeks, the longest movie run in the history of the theater. The Palace exhibited Cinerama movies continuously from November 14, 1956, through September 19, 1959, accumulating $2.2 million at the box office. Later, *The Best of Cinerama*, in its world-premiere engagement, presented highlights from the initial five travelogues.

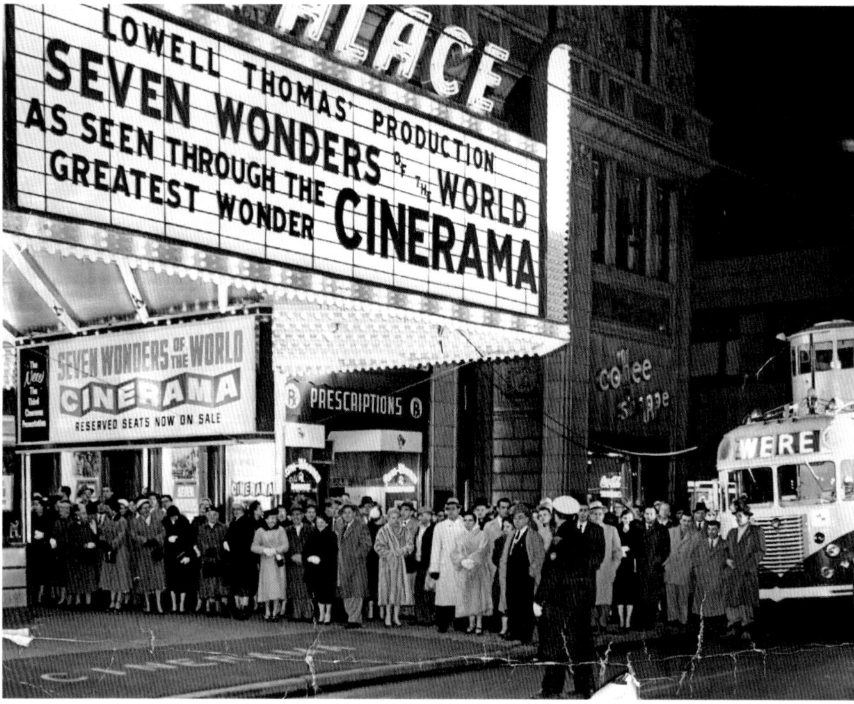

In 1958, a crowd gathered for the Palace premiere of *Seven Wonders of the World*, the third Cinerama film. *Courtesy of Cleveland Public Library, Photograph Collection.*

In 1962, Cinerama returned with a format incorporating well-known actors in films supporting actual plots. The Palace exhibited *The Wonderful World of the Brothers Grimm*; *How the West Was Won*; *It's a Mad, Mad, Mad, Mad World*; and *Circus World* in Cinerama. Still lacking a source for mainstream movies, the Palace booked nine other road-show films: *Porgy and Bess*, *Can-Can*, *The Agony and the Ecstasy*, *Spartacus*, *Judgment at Nuremberg*, *El Cid*, *The Blue Max*, *Is Paris Burning?* and *Krakatoa, East of Java*.

By the late 1960s, many exclusive road-show films had migrated to the suburbs while downtown theaters shared conventional first-run films with neighborhood theaters. In 1968, the Palace had degenerated into a pathetic, decaying shadow of its former glory. The theater's most remarkable accomplishment consisted of remaining open every day that year; never again could the theater make that claim. In 1969, although the Paul Newman and Joanne Woodward film *Winning* produced an incredibly awful $1,800 first week, the movie remained for a second week that yielded an even worse $1,600.

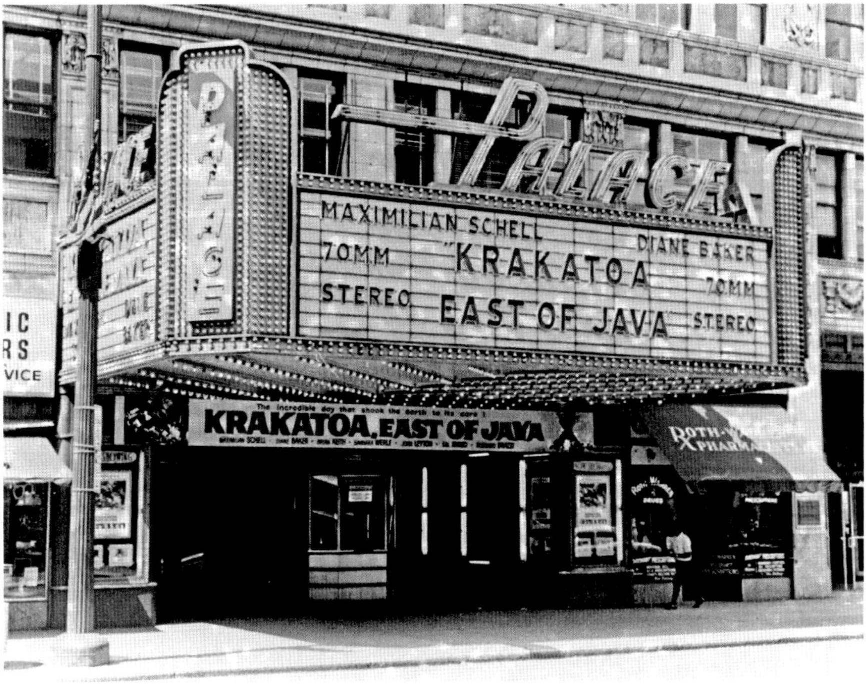

The Palace finally conceded defeat in the battle against first-run neighborhood theaters. For its finale, the theater obtained *Krakatoa, East of Java*. *Courtesy of Special Collections, Michael Schwartz Library, Cleveland State University.*

The Palace obtained an exclusive first-run booking of *Krakatoa, East of Java*, but the management announced the theater would close following the engagement. Some Clevelanders may have desired a last nostalgic look at this once magnificent playhouse that virtually no one ever expected to open again. The reported $50,000 opening week may have been exaggerated. If reliable, the figure represented the largest weekly receipts for a straight motion picture booking in the theater's history. A failure in the air conditioning equipment accelerated an attendance decline. The Palace closed on July 20, 1969. The owners carefully boarded and secured the Palace to prevent vandalism in the event of a later reopening. But at that time, few people saw any long-term hope for the once beautiful theater.

In 1973, mimicking the success of the State Theater's lobby cabaret, a Cole Porter revue continued in the Palace's 360-seat lobby theater for more than six months. Beginning in 1977, performances ranging from one-night stands to long-run cabaret shows continued through 1986 when the Palace closed for an extensive restoration.

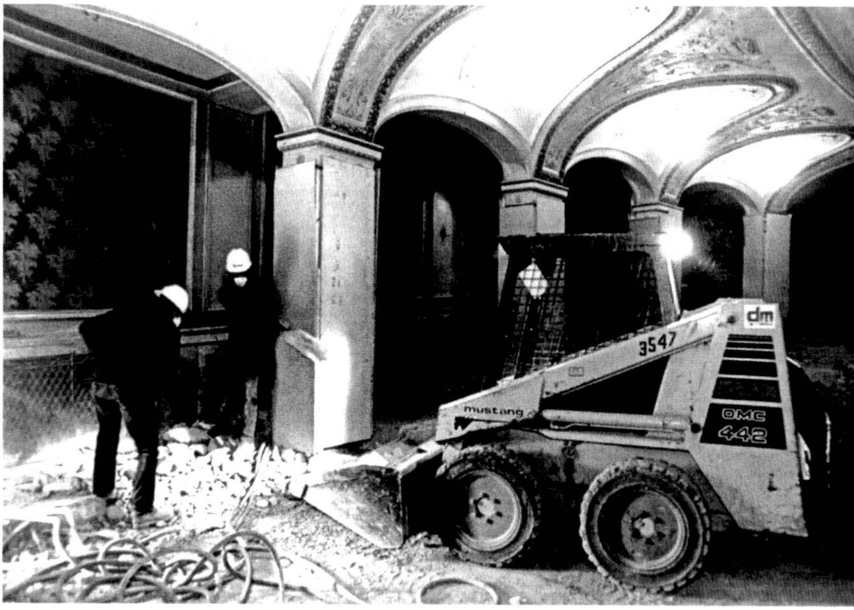

Eighteen years after the Palace closed, the theater's restoration is in progress. *Courtesy of the Playhouse Square Foundation.*

Skilled craftspeople refurbished 150 chandeliers, staircase railings and ornate plasterwork on the walls and ceiling. Artisans reconstructed stained glass in doors and exit signs and re-created the proscenium arch and side boxes destroyed by the Cinerama installation. The old nursery and billiard rooms created storage areas required by large touring shows. Modern electrical, heating and plumbing systems, along with state-of-the-art lighting and sound systems, enhanced the restoration. Larger seats and wider aisles caused a reduction in seating to about 2,900.

Beginning in 1988, the renovated Palace Theater presented Broadway shows; Las Vegas entertainers; music performances encompassing pop, R&B, country, jazz and gospel performers; dance troupes; magicians; and a children's series.

Performers from the 1930s and 1940s returned to the Palace following its reopening. Milton Berle, debuting at the Palace on February 7, 1931, returned for his final performance on October 6, 1994, a period exceeding sixty-three years. Tony Bennett, accompanied by Percy Faith and his thirty-eight-piece orchestra, first appeared in 1954 with ticket prices ranging from $1.10 to $3.30. Bennett's latest return, in 2014, stretched his Palace streak past the sixty-year mark.

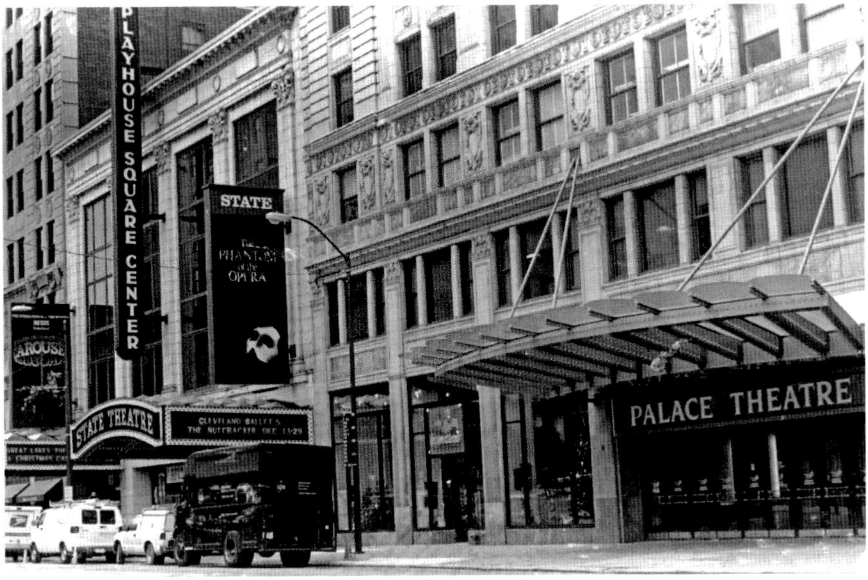

On December 7, 1996, crowds filled each of Playhouse Square's renovated Euclid Avenue theaters. *Courtesy of Diane Ghorbanzadeh.*

Red Skelton's performances spanned fifty-five years. Roddy McDowell, a special guest at the Palace premiere of the film *Wilson*, returned fifty-one years later to star in *Dial M for Murder*. Henny Youngman, part of a Tony Pastor/Perry Como show in 1943, returned in 1993. Mel Torme, a member of the Chico Marx Orchestra in 1942, made his final appearance in 1992. Sid Caesar's Palace shows, beginning with the 1944 wartime revue *Tars and Spars*, extended into 1994.

A few orchestras have remained popular even after the deaths of their famous leaders. The longest spans for orchestras at the Palace are Tommy Dorsey (sixty-seven years), Glenn Miller (sixty-six years), Cab Calloway (sixty-six years), Duke Ellington (fifty-four years) and Count Basie (fifty-one years). Two singing groups (the Ink Spots and the Drifters) have also passed the fifty-year mark, although their last performances contained none of the original members.

Performers have expressed their enthusiasm for the Palace restoration. Rita Moreno told a Palace audience, "This is where my soul lives, in the wonderful hallowed halls like the Palace Theater." Tony Bennett offered this advice: "If there are any city fathers out there, never tear this theater down. They don't make them like this anymore. They make them like file cabinets."

The Palace is one of five beautifully restored Playhouse Square theaters that are all modernized to accommodate requirements of twenty-first-century productions and audiences. Ironically, nearly every 1960s suburban and neighborhood movie theater contributing to the demise of the downtown showplaces has been closed, and most are demolished.

Chapter 18

THE CINEMA/LAKE/ ESQUIRE THEATER

The Cinema, the last of the Playhouse Square movie theaters to open and the first to shut down, debuted on October 14, 1928. Decorated in a blue and gold color scheme and launched as a one-thousand-seat, first-run theater, the showplace soon turned to second-run, double-feature bookings.

In 1930, the Cinema unwittingly participated in one of the biggest hoaxes in the history of the movies when it booked *Ingagi*, a film documenting a search for gorilla worshipers in Africa. Anticipating a long and lucrative run, the Cinema's management turned the theater entrance and lobby into a miniature jungle while agreeing to continue the exclusive first-run engagement as long as the film grossed more than $2,500 per week.

Produced by Congo Films, the movie purportedly documented the adventures of Sir Hubert Winstead, a noted scientist and explorer. An introductory voice-over asked audiences to forgive the bad photography and poor sound quality, both consequences of intense jungle heat. Suspicions regarding the movie's authenticity mounted when no scientist (or anyone else) could recall a famous traveler named Hubert Winstead. Doubts escalated even further as careful observers noted many of the film's African tribe members displayed prominent vaccination marks on their arms. The final straw arose when the movie's star gorilla sued Congo Films for his unpaid salary. Actually, a man in a monkey suit had portrayed the gorilla and brought about the grievance.

While continuing its run at the Cinema, national investigations discovered that the movie really comprised decades-old African

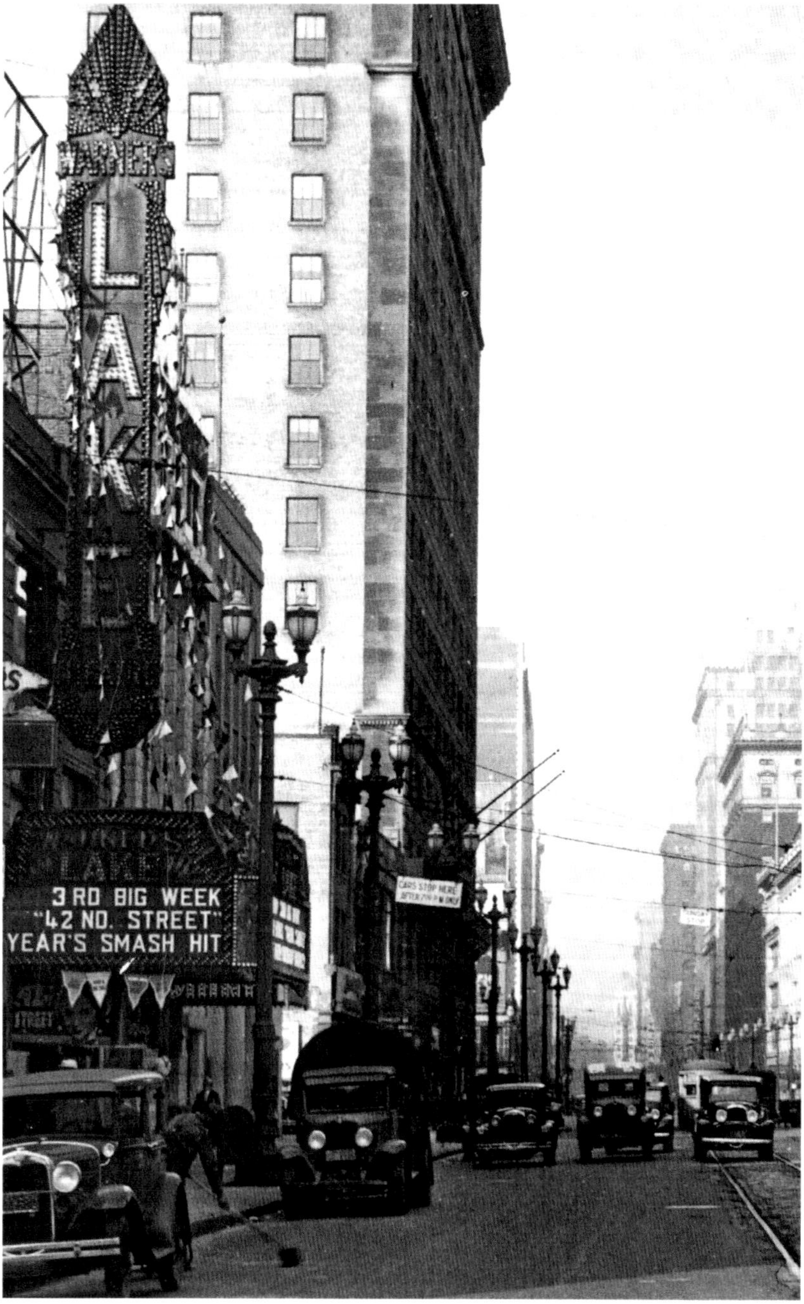

In 1933, the Lake Theater exhibited first-run Warner Brothers movies. *42nd Street* never played the advertised third week because of a labor strike. *Courtesy of Special Collections, Michael Schwartz Library, Cleveland State University.*

footage integrated with recently shot scenes at the Los Angeles Luna Park. White actors in blackface portrayed tribe members, Los Angeles schoolchildren stood in for pygmies and stuntmen wearing fur suits impersonated gorillas.

Although constituting a serious fraud, a judge ruled that a fake film could not invalidate a legitimate contract. As long as customers continued to purchase more than $2,500 per week in tickets, the court forced the Cinema to continue the film's embarrassing run. But business quickly collapsed following disclosure of the fraud, and the engagement ended after only three weeks.

In 1930, Warner Brothers purchased the theater. Following a complete renovation, manager Willott M. Warren noted the remodeling had "done away with everything save the walls." The renamed Lake Theater served as Warner Brothers' venue for first-run engagements of Edward G. Robinson in *Little Caesar*, James Cagney in *The Public Enemy* and Paul Muni in *I Am a Fugitive from a Chain Gang*.

In 1933, *42nd Street* debuted at the Lake with a huge publicity sendoff. The "42nd Street Special" arrived at the East 55th Street and Euclid Avenue train station with a carload of notables headed by Bette Davis, Jack Dempsey, Tom Mix and his horse King, Glenda Farrell, Leo Carrillo, Lyle Talbot, Preston Foster, Laura La Plante and twelve chorus girls who performed in the film. The celebrities joined a parade traveling down Payne and Superior Avenues to Public Square and then east on Euclid Avenue. Following lunch at the Hotel Statler, the stars journeyed to the huge Warner Brothers Uptown Theater, located at East 105th Street and St. Clair Avenue, to promote the film showing at the considerably smaller Lake Theater. A labor strike shortened the movie's run to only two weeks. Later that year, two other Warner Brothers musicals played longer runs: *Gold Diggers of 1933* (four weeks) and *Footlight Parade* (three weeks).

The Lake Theater's prominence lasted only a few years. In 1933, Warner Brothers leased the large Hippodrome, leaving the Lake with a collection of B movies, move-overs and reissues. Additionally suffering from the Depression, the theater opened only sporadically between 1934 and 1941. In the early 1940s, the Lake experimented with an intriguing foreign film policy by presenting double features combining movies from two different countries. The initial booking, the French film *The Virgin Bride* coupled with *School for Husbands*, a British movie, generated good business for five weeks. But the foreign film policy soon failed, and the Lake functioned mostly as a venue to extend the downtown runs of

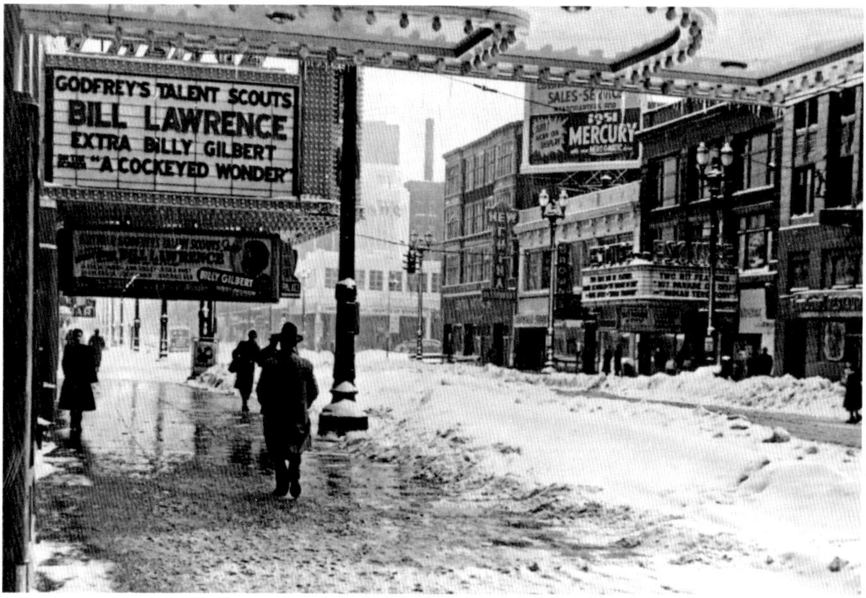

During a 1950 blizzard, the Esquire (across from the Palace) booked two B movies, *Hit Parade of 1951* and *Indian Territory*. *Courtesy of Cleveland Public Library, Literature Department.*

movies debuting at the Hippodrome. In 1948, Warner Brothers sold the Lake to a group of local owners.

The now 714-seat film house reopened as the Esquire Theater, originally displaying first-run films from the Republic studio. During its brief existence, the Esquire acquired a number of memorable bookings, including an eighteen-week first-run of *The Red Shoes*. The ballet film opened on Christmas Day in 1948 and returned in 1950 for a popular price showing that continued for eight weeks. Other long-run bookings included *Jolson Sings Again* (twelve weeks), *Lost Boundaries* (nine weeks), *Anna Lucasta* (five weeks) and *My Foolish Heart* (five weeks).

One of television's first casualties, the Esquire closed on May 28, 1951. The following year, the building ironically gained a second life as a television facility for WXEL (Channel 9) and its successor, WJW (Channel 8). The beautifully remodeled old theater included a television studio, rehearsal rooms, client visiting room and business offices. The site remained vacant for three years following the television station's move to another facility in 1975. From 1978 into 1980, the Center Repertory Theater used the studio to produce plays. In the mid-1980s, the demolition of the building created space for another ubiquitous downtown parking lot. During this period, a

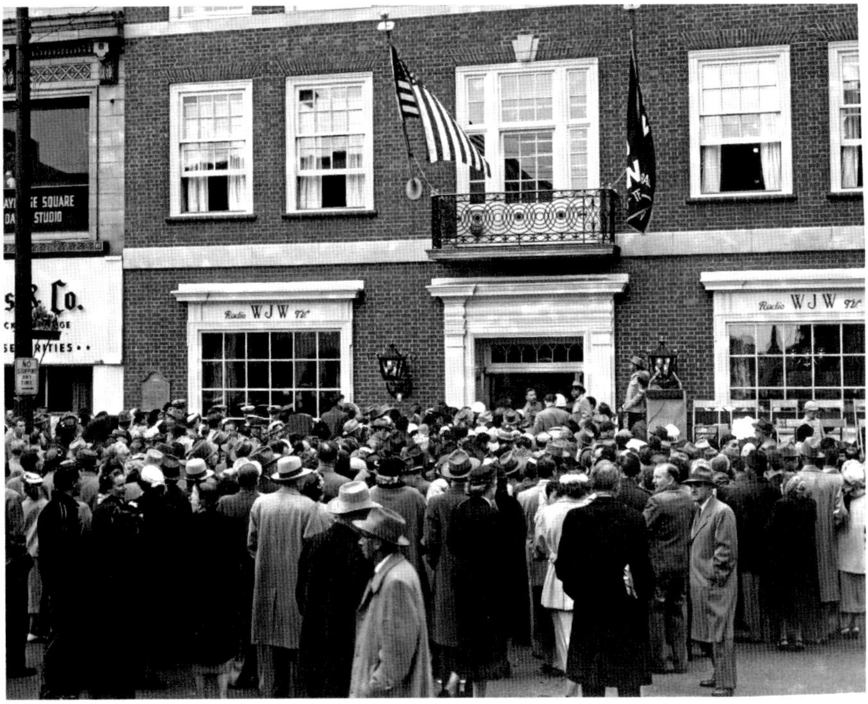

The Esquire Theater, converted into a television facility, is shown during the 1956 grand opening of WJW, Channel Eight. *Courtesy of Special Collections, Michael Schwartz Library, Cleveland State University.*

consultant hired by Cleveland suggested extending East Seventeenth Street from Euclid Avenue one block south to Prospect Avenue. Thirty-three years later, the city implemented this proposal, destroying the parking lot in the process.

Chapter 19

THE EMBASSY THEATER SITE

In 1887, a full-uniformed band marched from the Weddell House (a famous hotel located at the intersection of Superior Avenue and West Sixth Street) to the Columbia Theater to celebrate the playhouse's grand opening. Situated on the north side of Euclid Avenue between Public Square and East Ninth Street, the Columbia's amenities included a tunnel leading to restaurants on Vincent Street and a marble staircase connecting to a mahogany bar on Euclid Avenue. Described as "where the better class go," the theater promised "as fine a theater as any other opera house, only no opera house prices." Yet while general admission tickets sold for fifteen cents, reserved seats cost a much pricier fifty cents.

Columbia theatergoers faced an annoying dilemma when evening performances concluded after 11:00 p.m., the time the city turned off the streetlights. Patrons stumbled in darkness, often battling sidewalk and road construction, as they exited the playhouse. A police officer often stood on the corner of Euclid Avenue and East Sixth Street to guide befuddled audience members safely to the street.

Originally conceived as competition for the Euclid Avenue Opera House, the Columbia booked plays, vaudeville, minstrel shows and comic opera, often with interesting publicity tie-ins. During performances of the western-themed *On the Frontier*, every person purchasing a ticket received an authentic deed to a lot in Tulare, California.

In 1889, the renamed Star Theater specialized in presenting touring burlesque companies. Separated from male patrons by a heavy curtain, women viewed the performances from a side balcony. Several poles

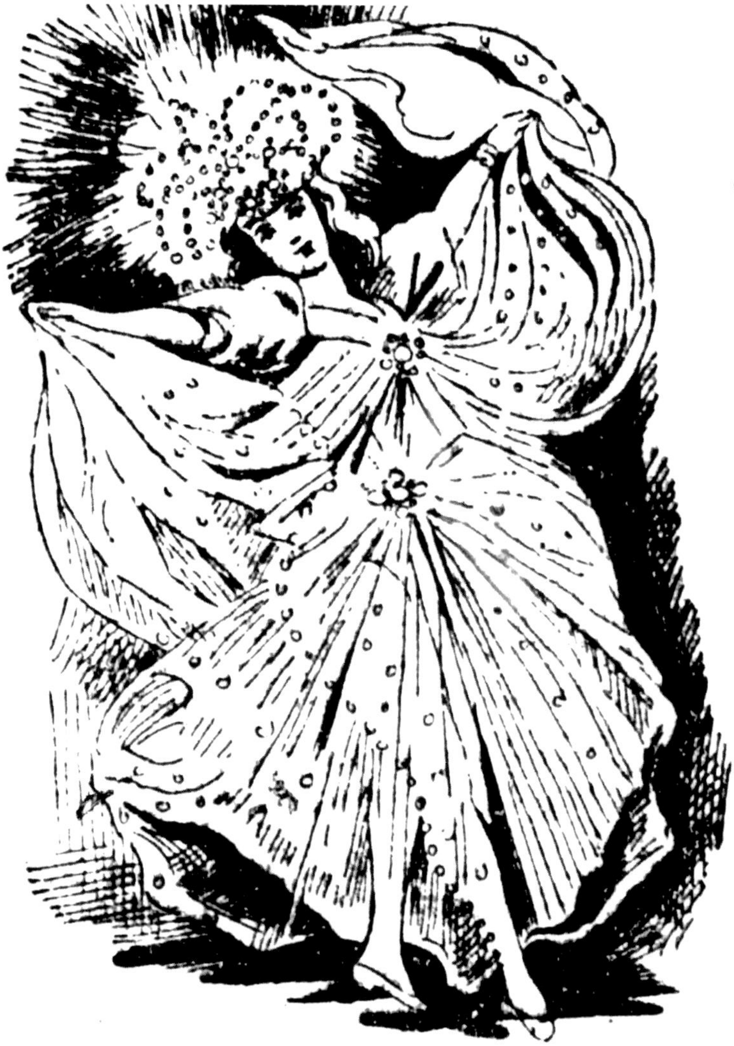

In the late nineteenth century, this Star Theater dancer illustrated the coexistence of burlesque and Victorian morality. *Courtesy of the* Plain Dealer.

obstructed views, causing audiences' heads to swing from side to side as can-can girls skipped across the stage. Men sitting in an exceptionally steep balcony almost seemed indecent when gazing down at the cleavage of scantily clad chorus girls. To circumvent blue laws, the Star staged sacred concerts on Sundays, inviting audience members and police inspectors to join in the singing of hymns. Almost immediately after the police departed, the hymns concluded and burlesque commenced.

In 1899, the Star introduced films as background "motion picture effects" for singers. The following year, the theater presented movies documenting the "best ten rounds" of the twenty-three-round heavyweight championship match in which James Jeffries defeated "Gentleman Jim" Corbett. In 1907, the Star complemented its burlesque bookings by installing a new motion picture machine known as the Girlagraph.

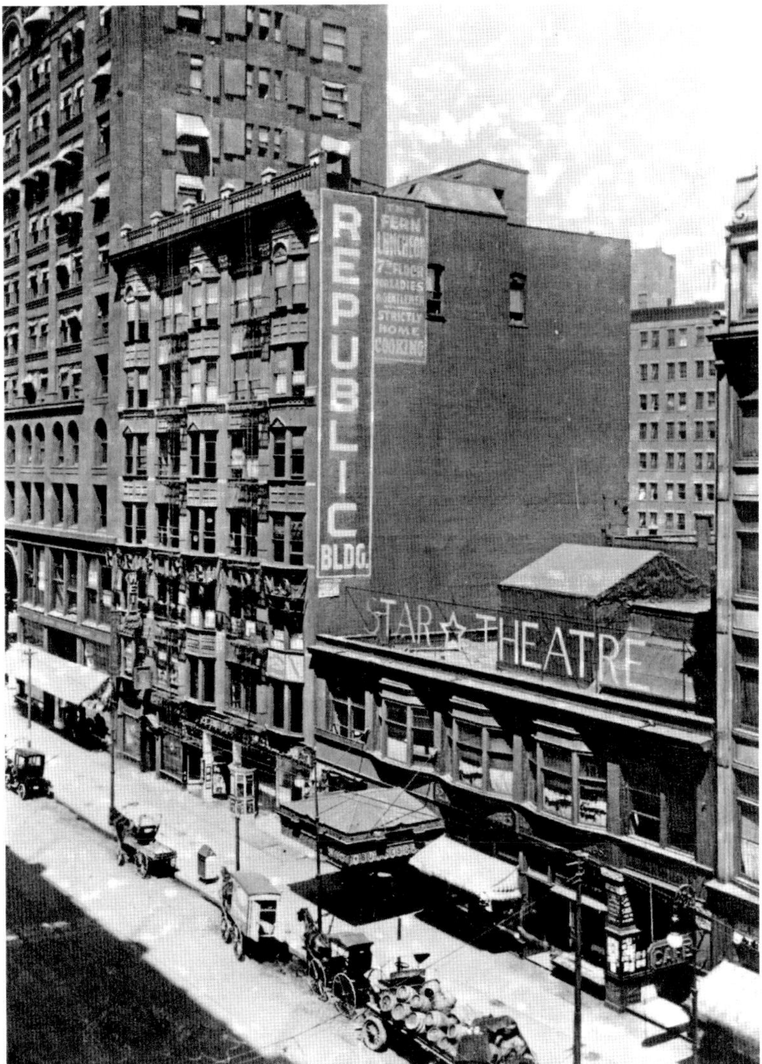

The Star Theater's site housed entertainment venues for slightly more than nine decades. *Courtesy of Cleveland Public Library, Photograph Collection.*

Peddling of peanuts, pop and candy ended in 1913 because management believed "it lowers the tone of the theater." In 1921, Bert Lahr performed on the Star stage; eighteen years later, he would achieve his greatest fame as the cowardly lion in a film version of *The Wizard of Oz*.

Renovated in 1925 as the 1,500-seat Loew's Cameo movie theater, the walls and ceilings, once covered with many coats of wallpaper, now displayed their original artistic plastering. In 1931, Loew's sold the theater

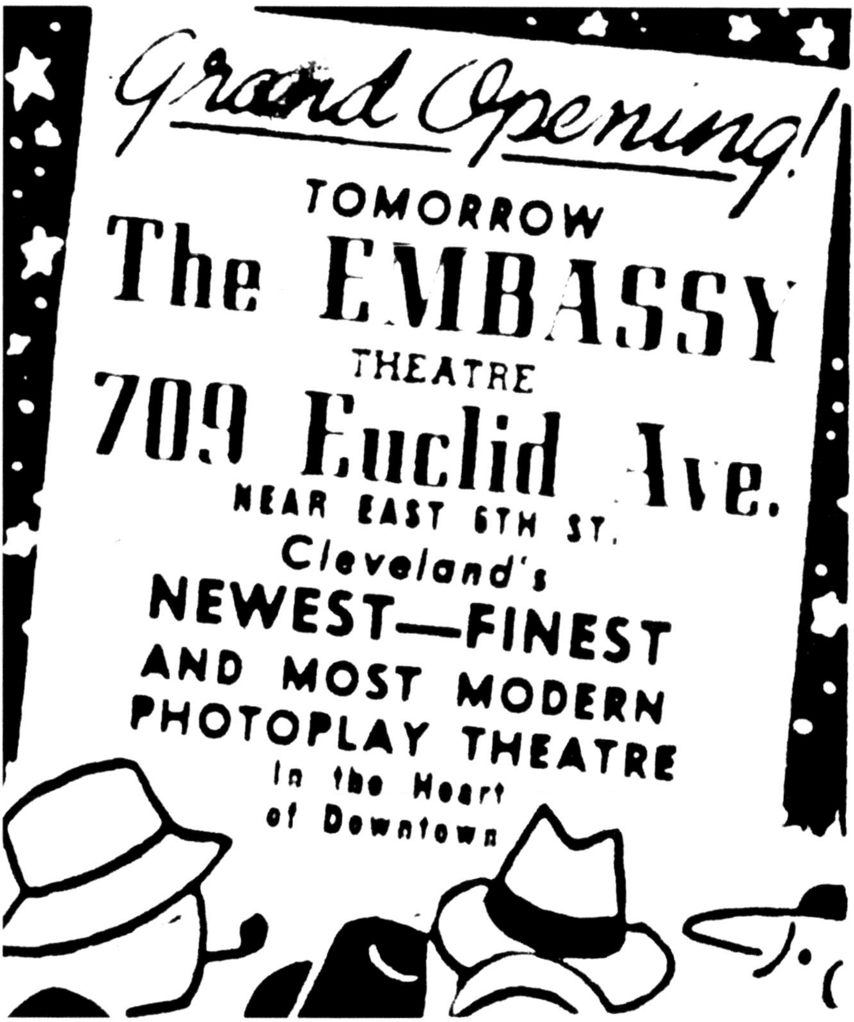

On October 13, 1938, the Embassy Theater celebrated its grand opening as the fourth showplace on this Euclid Avenue site. *Courtesy of the* Plain Dealer.

to a Cleveland group. Following an unsuccessful effort at exhibiting foreign movies, the Cameo briefly attempted reviving burlesque. Both Roxy owner George Young and legendary downtown publicity person Mitchell Dexter Plotkin recall seeing the recently formed comedy team of Bud Abbott and Lou Costello performing at the theater. The Cameo endured from late 1932 into 1938 by booking second-run double features.

In 1938, wrecking balls demolished the Cameo, except for east and west walls that would become part of the 1,200-seat Embassy, a new second-run movie theater debuting the same year. While an outside marquee flashed EMBASSY in green neon lights, customers entered a more subdued foyer decorated in gray and red. Warm shades of rose velour, with blue side lights, beautified the auditorium. The innovative theater offered special seats for the hearing impaired that included earphones.

Anticipating the Telenews Theater (which would begin operation a few years later just five blocks to the west), the Embassy originally showed only newsreels and short subjects between 11:30 a.m. and 1:00 p.m.

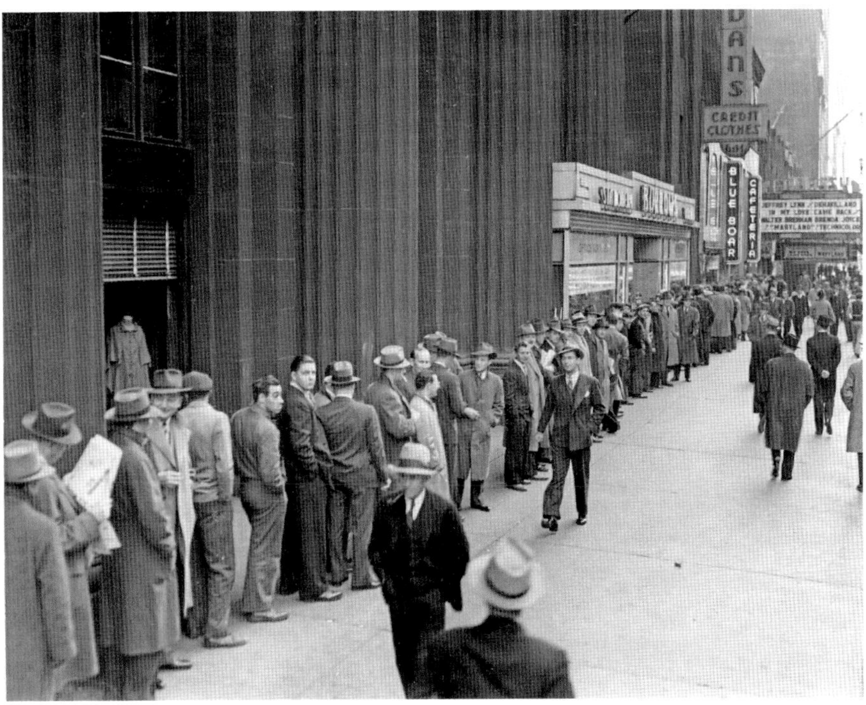

On October 16, 1940, males appearing to have formed a line at the Embassy Theater were actually registering for the draft at a downtown location near the theater. *Courtesy of Cleveland Public Library, Photograph Collection.*

For many years, the Embassy thrived on exhibiting second-run double-feature bookings. But in the 1950s, when the Ohio and Palace Theaters committed to long-run road-show film engagements, the Embassy successfully secured first-run films, including the Ohio premiere of Pat Boone and Shirley Jones in *April Love*. Beginning in 1969 when the Playhouse Square theaters closed and the Embassy shared first-run bookings with neighborhood film houses, the Embassy played *Bullitt* for eight weeks and *The Great White Hope* and *Diamonds Are Forever* for four weeks each.

In 1973, the Embassy turned to martial arts, black-oriented and horror films. The theater closed on November 27, 1977, for construction of the National City Bank (now PNC) Building. The Embassy's final attraction consisted of the double feature *Bloody Fist* and *Duel in the Tiger's Den*.

Chapter 20

THE TELENEWS/ TOWER THEATER

Before the emergence of television, movie theater newsreels provided the only readily available visual coverage of current news events. In 1941, Cleveland joined New York, Chicago and San Francisco in hosting a theater catering to the city's most news-hungry citizens.

Located on the north side of Euclid Avenue near Public Square, the 480-seat Telenews Theater presented one-hour film programs composed of newsreels, travelogues, educational films, short subjects, sports events, fashion trends and topics of local interest. The film editors crammed fifty to sixty subjects into the presentation. Repeated fourteen times each day for one week, new programs began on Friday evenings at 5:00 p.m.

Highlights of the opening-week selections consisted of a behind-the-scenes look inside the United States Naval Academy, a short film detailing views of Nazi Germany and describing how Hitler manufactured Germany's war machines, Lowell Thomas narrating a film short concerning French Indo-China and the Burma Road and a "Telenews Salute to Cleveland" that presented films of local news media operations, including the city's three newspapers and many local radio stations.

The twenty-five-cent admission also permitted patrons to enjoy a recreation room and lounge on the lower level, where they examined the latest magazines and newspapers while relaxing in reclining chairs. An art gallery displayed work created by members of the Cleveland Artists' Guild. The basement also incorporated a fully operational radio station, including space for a viewing audience.

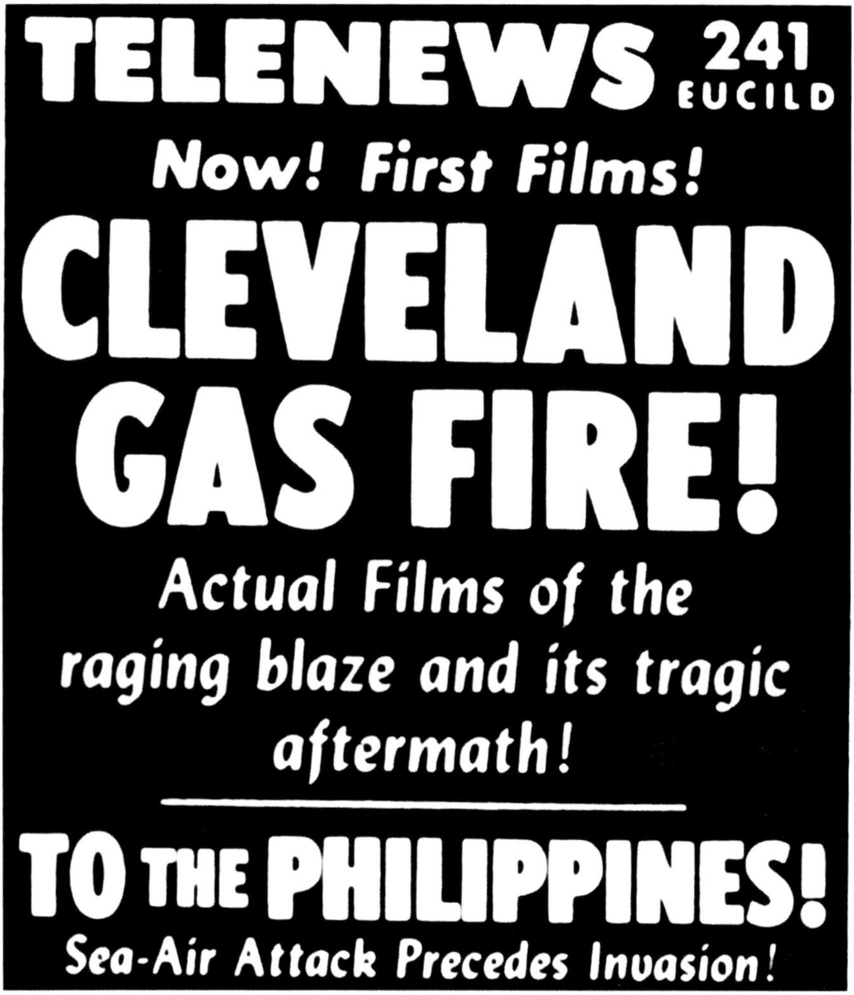

In late October 1944, the East Ohio Gas explosion reigned as the top headline at the Telenews Theater. *Courtesy of the* Plain Dealer.

Telenews thrived during the first half of the 1940s by exhibiting the latest film footage from Second World War fronts. After the war, the theater's numerous news subjects included rocket and atomic bomb tests, terrorist attacks in Jerusalem, the Alger Hiss trial, the Berlin air lift, Amazon headhunters, the World Series, Rita Hayworth's marriage to Aly Kahn, the death of Al Capone, an "adhesive" bra requiring no straps and a convention of nudists. In 1947, inadvertently contributing to its own demise, the theater displayed an actual working television in the downstairs lounge.

Television drastically reduced the public's interest in theater newsreels. In 1950, the Telenews management ended the news film format and explained its intriguing new strategy: "Our aim will be to show the unusual picture and our intention will be to show the best available in the field of unusual pictures." The renamed Coronet Theater booked a few British imports, a collection of documentaries, a filmed version of the opera *Il Trovatore* and a second-run engagement of Laurence Olivier's *Hamlet*. Attracting few customers, management ended the three-month experiment and reverted, for another year, to its former newsreel format, with Korean War films taking center stage.

In 1951, the Tower Theater replaced the newsreel house. Operated by the owners of the immense Hippodrome Theater, the tiny Tower booked films either not profitable enough to exhibit at the Hippodrome or whose downtown run could be successfully extended at the much smaller Tower. Most often, a film playing an initial week at the Hippodrome moved to the Tower for a second week. At the other extreme, the exceptionally popular four-week Hippodrome run of *The Snows of Kilimanjaro* played an additional two weeks at the Tower.

Although operating literally and figuratively in the shadow of the Hippodrome, the Tower enjoyed an occasional moment of its own fame. In 1953, the exclusive three-week first run of *A Queen Is Crowned* presented a film documentary of the coronation of Queen Elizabeth II with Laurence Olivier as narrator. Film stars John Ireland and Dorothy Malone paid visits to the Tower to promote their films and sign autographs.

On February 25, 1954, as downtown movie theater attendance declined, the Tower closed. Less than fifteen years old, the theater ended its life with an unintentional bang as a sixty-five-foot boom removing the shuttered theater's marquee snapped near its base. The heavy sign, weighing nearly a ton, crashed onto the sidewalk, symbolically designating the demise of the short-lived film playhouse.

Chapter 21

LATER DOWNTOWN CINEMAS

The media referred to Park Centre as a "miniature city." The first phase debuted in 1973, and the entire complex soon consumed all the land between East Twelfth and East Thirteenth Streets and Chester and Superior Avenues. A 300,000-square-foot, seventy-five-store retail plaza, situated between two apartment towers totaling one thousand units, promised to infuse downtown Cleveland with new life and vitality. The development incorporated twin first-run cinemas totaling five hundred seats, downtown Cleveland's first new movie theaters since 1941 (other than porno movie showplaces).

Unveiled just before Christmas 1974, one of the twin cinemas debuted showing *The Towering Inferno*, considered by some to be an odd selection for a multi-floor, twin-tower apartment complex. Yet the star-studded disaster film continued for sixteen weeks, the longest run in the cinemas' short history. Within one year, second runs and X-rated films (including the double feature *Teenage Bar Bunnies* and *Self-Service School Girls*) replaced the former first-run features. The theaters closed on February 28, 1978, barely more than three years after their much-heralded debut. In October, the cinemas reopened as bargain two-dollar, double-feature playhouses, but that experiment failed before the year ended.

Reviving the Judy Garland and Mickey Rooney tradition, proactive residents decided that, since movies failed at the theaters, they would put on their own shows. After removing the first six rows of Cinema II and installing a portable stage, the tenants formed the Park Centre Players, promoted as

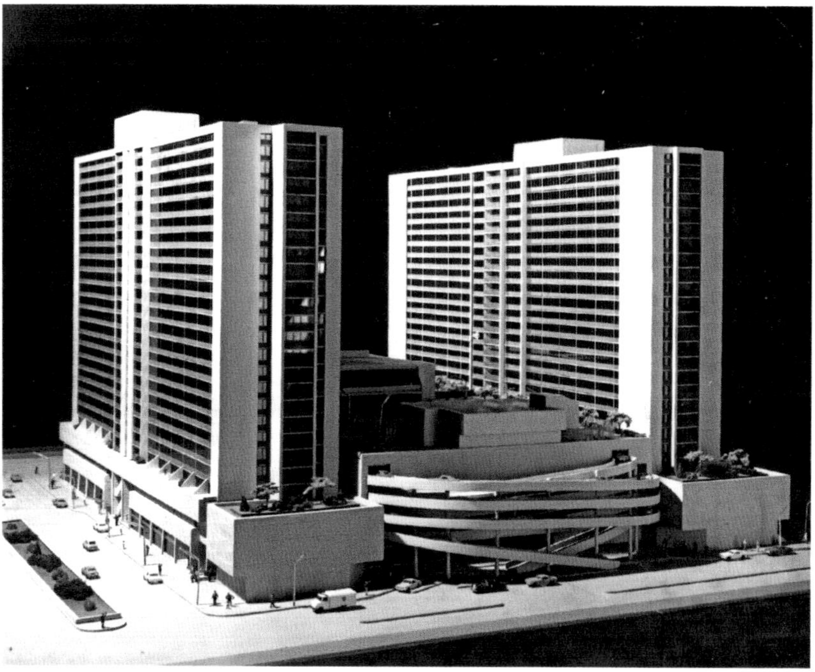

The large Park Centre complex (now known as Reserve Square) once housed twin first-run cinemas. *Courtesy of Cleveland Public Library, Photograph Collection.*

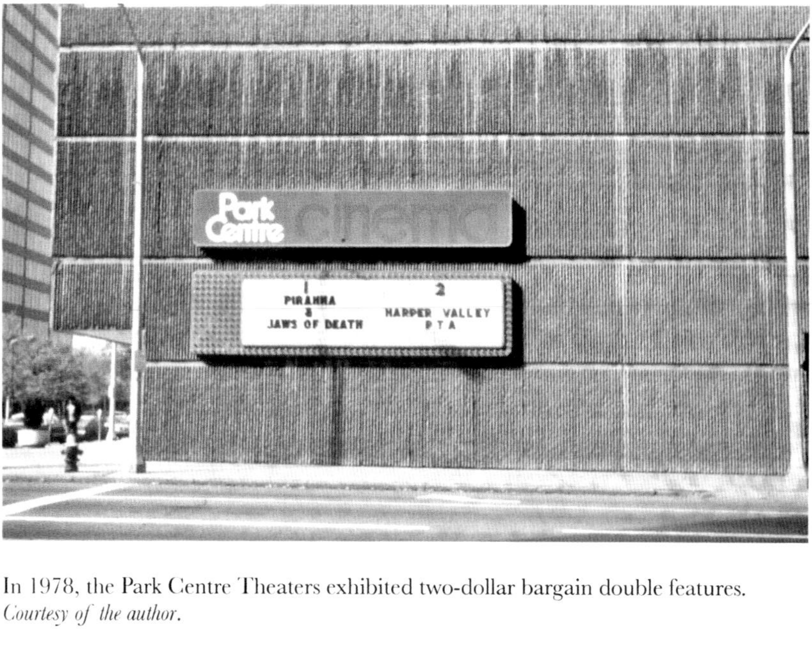

In 1978, the Park Centre Theaters exhibited two-dollar bargain double features. *Courtesy of the author.*

Cleveland's only downtown community theater. In addition to featuring the building's residents, the group conducted open auditions to cast productions including *A Streetcar Named Desire*, *Forty Carats*, *Our Town*, *The Lion in Winter* and *Witness for the Prosecution*. Cinema I served as a dressing room during the performances.

Concurrent with the acting venture, another tenant group founded a film society. During a three-year period, residents used Cinema I to screen scores of films ranging from Charlie Chaplin's 1914 comedy *Tillie's Punctured Romance* to the then recent made-for-television film *Deerslayer*. While a team of tenants sold tickets and buttered popcorn, resident David Horan operated both projectors, performing almost flawless reel changes while, on one occasion, also guiding a malfunctioning projector with a pencil to keep the reel moving. Both the players and film society continued into 1982, when a remodeling of the building eliminated the twin cinemas and ended the tenants' thespian and film endeavors.

Opened in 1990, an eleven-screen multiplex movie theater remains an anchor for the downtown Tower City Mall. The combined 2,800-seat cinemas usually operate similarly to their suburban counterparts. But each year in late March and early April, the Tower City theaters become especially distinct in hosting the Cleveland International Film Festival, one of the city's foremost cultural events that attracts more than 100,000 attendees annually.

In 1996, an Omnimax theater opened in conjunction with the new Great Lakes Science Museum. Although usually exhibiting science-themed films, the theater will also book an occasional mainstream Ominimax movie.

With the exception of a twenty-six-month period beginning in 1980, at least one active movie theater has existed in downtown Cleveland since 1896. Four restored theaters, each of which exhibited movies in the 1940s, 1950s and 1960s, are now combined with a fifth legitimate theater to form the nucleus of the Playhouse Square Foundation, one of the country's largest performing arts organizations. Downtown Cleveland residents and visitors view the latest films in a modern cinema format, watch Omnimax movies and stroll through beautifully restored 1920s-vintage theaters, all three options within walking distance of one another.

Appendix

THEATER LOCATIONS AND CURRENT SITE USAGE

Theater	Address	Current Site Usage
Allen	1407 Euclid Avenue	Allen Theater
Alvin	2352 Ontario Street	Tower City parking lot
American	716 Superior Avenue	Office building (Fifth-Third Bank)
Bijou Dream	410 Euclid Avenue	Corner Alley Bowling
Cameo	707 Euclid Avenue	Office building (PNC)
Carter	2071 East 9th Street	Office building (Cuyahoga County)
Cinema	1630 Euclid Avenue	Extension of East 17th Street
Columbia	707 Euclid Avenue	Office building (PNC)
Cornet	241 Euclid Avenue	Office building (former BP Building)
Embassy	707 Euclid Avenue	Office building (PNC)
Empire	788 Huron Road	AT&T Building
Empress	1867 East 9th Street	Office building (Ohio Savings)
Esquire	1630 Euclid Avenue	Extension of East 17th Street
Euclid	927 Euclid Avenue	Office building (currently under renovation)
Family	1882 East 9th Street	Office building (PNC)
Gaiety	1746 East 9th Street	Parking garage (Cuyahoga County Building)

Theater	Address	Current Site Usage
Grand	2173 East 9th Street	New York Spaghetti House (closed)
Hanna	2067 East 14th Street	Hanna Theater
Hippodrome	720 Euclid Avenue	Parking garage and surface parking lots
Lake	1630 Euclid Avenue	Extension of East 17th Street
Little Theater of the Movies	1867 East 9th Street	Office building (Ohio Savings)
Lower Mall	310 Superior Avenue	Office building (former BP Building)
Lyceum	Public Square	Office building (Old Illuminating Company)
Lyric	2173 East 9th Street	New York Spaghetti House (closed)
Mall	303 Euclid Avenue	Office building (former BP Building)
Miles	2071 East 9th Street	Office building (Cuyahoga County)
New Empire	2173 East 9th Street	New York Spaghetti House (closed)
Ohio	1511 Euclid Avenue	Ohio Theater
Orpheum	1882 East 9th Street	Office building (PNC)
Palace	1613 Euclid Avenue	Palace Theater
Princess	229 Euclid Avenue	Office building (former BP Building)
Priscilla	1867 East 9th Street	Office building (Ohio Savings)
Prospect	619 Prospect Avenue	Apartment building
Reel	2049 East 9th Street	Metropolitan Hotel
Roxy	1882 East 9th Street	Office building (PNC)
Saengerfest Hall	2466 East 55th Street	City park (former East Technical High School)
Standard	811 Prospect Avenue	Newly built theater (vacant and unnamed)
Star	707 Euclid Avenue	Office building (PNC)
State	1515 Euclid Avenue	State Theater
Stillman	1111 Euclid Avenue	Parking garage

Theater	Address	Current Site Usage
Strand	2123 East 9th Street	Parking garage
Telenews	241 Euclid Avenue	Office building (former BP Building)
Tower	241 Euclid Avenue	Office building (former BP Building)
Wonderland	1726 East 9th Street	Hampton Inn

BIBLIOGRAPHY

Bell, Archie. *A Little Journey to B.F. Keith Palace Cleveland*. Cleveland, OH: privately printed, 1922.

Hall, Ben M. *The Best Remaining Seats*. New York: Bramball House, 1988.

Laurie, Joe. *Vaudeville: From Honky-tonks to the Palace*. New York: Holt, 1953.

Mote, Patricia M. *Cleveland's Playhouse Square*. Charleston, SC: Arcadia Publishing, 2006.

Naylor, David. *Great American Movie Theaters*. Washington, D.C.: Preservation Press, 1987.

Schultz, Jean Emser, and Kathleen Kennedy. *Playhouse Square Cleveland: An Entertaining History*. Cleveland, OH: Playhouse Square Foundation, n.d.

Zietz, Karyl Lynn. *The National Trust Guide to Great Opera Houses in America*. New York: John Wiley & Sons, 1996.

INDEX

G

H

J

K

L

M

N

O

P

R

S

T

U

V

W

Z

ABOUT THE AUTHOR

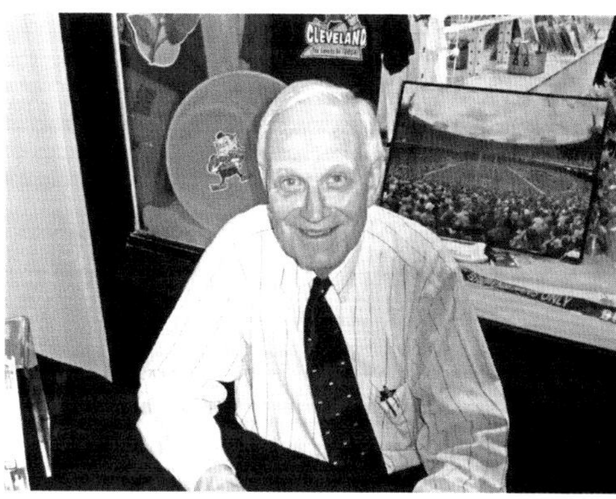

Since native Clevelander Alan Dutka's retirement from a business career, he has published five Cleveland history books: *Misfortune on Cleveland's Millionaires' Row*; *AsiaTown Cleveland: From Tong Wars to Dim Sum*; *Cleveland Calamities: A History of Storm, Fire and Pestilence*; *East Fourth Street: The Rise, Decline and Rebirth of an Urban Cleveland Street*; and *Cleveland's Short Vincent: The Theatrical Grill and Its Notorious Neighbors*. During his business career, he authored four marketing research books, including *Customer Satisfaction Research*, a primary selection of the Newbridge Executive Book Club that has been translated into Spanish and Japanese editions. Dutka is a popular speaker at historical societies, libraries and community centers. He has appeared on the *Feagler & Friends*, *Applause* and *Seven Minutes with Russ Mitchell* television programs, along with radio programs including *Dee Perry's Around Noon* and Jacqueline Gerber's morning program.